FEMINISM, VIOLENCE, AND REPRESENTATION IN MODERN ITALY

NEW ANTHROPOLOGIES OF EUROPE

Michael Herzfeld, Melissa L. Caldwell, and
Deborah Reed-Danahay, *editors*

FEMINISM, VIOLENCE, AND REPRESENTATION IN MODERN ITALY

"We Are Witnesses, Not Victims"

Giovanna Parmigiani

INDIANA UNIVERSITY PRESS

This book is a publication of

Indiana University Press
Office of Scholarly Publishing
Herman B Wells Library 350
1320 East 10th Street
Bloomington, Indiana 47405 USA

iupress.indiana.edu

© 2019 by Giovanna Parmigiani

Manufactured in the United States of America

Cataloging information is available from the Library of Congress.

ISBN 978-0-253-04337-5 (cloth)
ISBN 978-0-253-04338-2 (paperback)
ISBN 978-0-253-04340-5 (ebook)

1 2 3 4 5   24 23 22 21 20 19

This book is dedicated to my father,
Enrico Parmigiani, my mother, Maria Grazia Nicora, and
my grandmother, Aldina Maiorini, who only witnessed
the very early stages of this research:
you are missed immensely.

CONTENTS

ACKNOWLEDGMENTS

IN EMBARKING ON MY OWN "REPRESENTATIONAL CHALLENGE" BY writing this book, I feel deeply grateful. This research would not have been possible without the help of many persons who, in different ways, supported, challenged, provoked, encouraged, and cared for me and this creative enterprise.

I want to thank all the women who generously shared their lives and stories with me: first, the Macare—my beloved sisters and teachers—and the women of *Unione delle Donne in Italia* (Union of Women in Italy, or UDI). I thank you for your trust, for the many memorable moments spent together, for the warmth and generosity that you showed me since we met in 2011. I cherish your presence in my life and the many life lessons I learned by spending time with you. I hope that I do justice, in this book, to the beauty, complexity, passion, and political drive that animate your lives and that make you the exceptional human beings you are.

A special thanks to Pina Nuzzo, whose insights and political vision are always as elegant and lucid as her art. The ways in which your two passions—art and politics—intertwine in your life and political activism is always a source of inspiration for me. I am deeply grateful for your trust and for the intellectual and emotional labor you put into trying to find the right language for me to understand your artistic and political visions.

I thank DNA Donna, Laboratorio Donnae, Io Sono Bellissima, Cooperativa San Francesco, Flauto Magico, Femministe Nove, Evaluna, Donne Insieme, Agedo, LeA, UDI Modena, UDI Pesaro, Spazio Donna, Laboratorio Zarcar, Libreria Idrusa, Annacinzia Villani, Comune di Soleto, Comune di Sogliano Cavour, Comune di Presicce, Criamu, Panico Tamburi a Cornice, SoniBoni, Mascarimirì, Scuola di Counseling Espero, Le Costantine, Canali Creativi, and Giovanni from ANSA.

I am also particularly grateful to Enza, Loredana, Melania, Milena, Mac, Maria Antonietta, Marisa, Lidia, Lorenza, Claudia, Sabrina, Nadia, Lisa, Erica, Lara, Miriam, Maria Grazia, Francesca, Monica, Ilaria, Ingrid, Judith, Viola, Simonetta, Antonella, Cristina, Valentina, Rossella, Debora, Lori, Monica, Stefania, Caterina, Roberta, Federica, Letizia, Annalisa, Rita, Annarita, Rina, Caterina, Roberta, Brigitte, Ada, Silvia, Lucia, Giulia, Vania, Annarita, Saveria, Anna Maria, Roberta, Roberta, Moira, Leila, Oriana, Vita, Tina, Helen, Marina, Lucia, Mariarosaria, Beatrice, Sabina, Nicoletta, Cristina, Francesca,

Giuliana, Emanuela, Pilar, Ross, Raffaela, Ingrid, Ilaria, Anna Maria, Marianna, Maria Ada, and Elide. Thank you for your help, support, and friendship.

My gratitude goes also to Eunice, Steve, Eric, Jasmine, the Villas, the Belcastros, the Baroccis, Carolina, Salvatore, Rosamarina, Virginie, Claudio M., Elena, Fabio, Alina, Arjeta, Vincenzo, Rosa, Ulrike, Kelsi, Nonno Mario, the Galli family, the Monai family, the Zappa family, Annette, and Morgana.

A special thanks to Alessandra Bianco, whose help in obtaining the copyright of some of the images proved to be crucial, and to Pina Nuzzo, Enza Miceli, Maria Antonietta Nuzzo, and Lucia Sabato for their art, photos, and insights. I am grateful to Manuela Pellegrino, Nicoletta Nuzzo, Francesco Manni, Barbara Spinelli, Giovanni Pizza, Giovanna Zapperi, Alessandra Gribaldo, Loredana De Vitis, and Stefano Santachiara for sharing with me some of their research or materials.

I am especially grateful to the Anthropology Department at the University of Toronto and for the support of the Connaught Scholarship throughout my doctoral period.

A particular thanks to Andrea Muehlebach, Valentina Napolitano, Naisargi Dave, and Michael Lambek, whose stimulating and compelling insights were of key importance in my personal and academic growth: thank you for helping me think through my material and articulate my arguments with greater clarity. Thanks also to Natalia Krencil, for the invaluable help and support she provided in navigating the university bureaucracy. Thanks to Ivan Kalmar, Rita Astuti, Maurice Bloch, Fenella Cannell, Ugo Fabietti, and Aurora Donzelli for having supported me during the early stages of my postgraduate studies.

I am deeply grateful to Michal Herzfeld, whose engagement with my work was crucial: thank you for pushing me to elaborate further my arguments and writing style and to make my book, and my scholarship, a better one. Many thanks to Jennika Baines, Kate Schramm, and Indiana University Press for the support, encouragement, and dedication throughout the publication process. My gratitude also goes to the anonymous reviewers whose insights, suggestions, and passionate encouragement really made a difference in the final version of this book and in my authorship.

Aspects of this research appeared in the journal *Modern Italy*: I thank the editorial board and the anonymous reviewers for the insightful comments and suggestions.

I want to thank all the persons who, in different ways and occasions, have engaged with part of the text or arguments of the book: your insights, comments, challenges, and critical feedback have been of great importance to me and to this project. Thanks to Salvatore Giusto, Veronica Buffon, Letha Victor, Annalisa Butticci, Maria Efthymiou, Veena Das, Michael Jackson, Charles

Stewart, Stavroula Pypirou, Giovanni Pizza, Flavia Laviosa, Deborah A. Thompson, Lisa M. Stevenson, Gino di Mitri, John Kloppenborg, Marco Rizzi, Francis Cody, Megan Raschig, Laura McTighe, Emily Ng, Elisa Lanari, Aditi Surie von Czechowski, Sabina Perrino, Sabina Izzo, Gregory Kohler, Andrea Leone-Pizzighella, Zachary Androus, Alexandra Cotofana, Laurian Bowles, Manuela Pellegrino, Mariela Nuñez-Janes, Beth Uzwiak, Jessica Santos, Barbara Di Gennaro, Mauro Belcastro, Juliann Vitullo, Tania Rispoli, and the audiences of my papers.

A special thanks to both the Science, Religion, and Culture Program and the Center for the Study of World Religions at Harvard Divinity School—in particular to Ahmed Ragab and Charles Stang. The welcoming culture and the intellectual richness of these environments are, for me, an invaluable source of personal and scholarly growth.

Without my family, this research, this book, and, in many ways, my own well-being throughout the time frame covered by this manuscript would not have been possible.

A million thanks to my Salentine family and the *nonni* for the immense generosity, support, affection, hospitality, and patience you showed me in countless ways since we met. I feel deeply fortunate to have you in my life.

I am immensely grateful to my husband Giovanni and to my son Beniamino: without your practical and emotional support I could not have accomplished this. Giovanni: thank you for discussing with me, over and over again, the different lines of arguments of this book with great patience and insights. Thank you for navigating my emotional and practical journeys with *centratura* and flexibility: once again, this helped me immensely, especially during the difficult periods of my grief. Thank you, Beniamino, for bringing such a joy to my life: your sensitivity, intelligence, and good spirits make such a positive difference! I feel very proud to be your mom and want to thank you for having been so understanding, flexible, and generous, at your very young age, with me and my need to be away from home for extended periods of time. Home is where you two are.

FEMINISM, VIOLENCE, AND REPRESENTATION IN MODERN ITALY

INTRODUCTION

S EVEN HUNDRED AND SEVENTY-FOUR: THIS IS THE NUMBER of "femicides" (*femminicidi*, in Italian. Singular: *femminicidio*) that occurred in Italy between 2012 and 2017, as claimed by the Italian Ministry of Interior, which is an average of one woman killed (almost) every other day.[1]

Femminicidio, according to the Italian encyclopedia *Treccani*, refers to "the—direct or indirect, physical or moral—killing of women and of their social roles."[2] In Italian feminist circles, like the ones I joined for this research, femminicidio is indissolubly connected with "patriarchy." As a matter of fact, the women of *Unione delle Donne in Italia* (Union of Women in Italy, or UDI), who are at the core of this book, define femminicidio as "the killing of women for the fact of being women."

Interestingly, in spite of its numbers, until 2012 femminicidio was a mostly unknown word and concept in Italy. While *femminicidio* is not a neologism in Italian, differing in this way from its South American equivalent *femicidio*, it was nonetheless a word used only sparingly in nineteenth- and twentieth-century literature.[3] It began appearing in 2005, in particular because of the work of Barbara Spinelli. A lawyer and feminist activist, she published several contributions to the study of femminicidio and its legal value.[4] Although its use in 2011, at the beginning of my research, was not so widespread, it is currently widely employed in the media. The term has been included de facto in some of the most respected Italian dictionaries, it is acknowledged by the prestigious *Accademia della Crusca*, and it has become part of the everyday vocabulary of many Italians. Moreover, the word *femminicidio*, or *femicidio*, appeared in the title or was the topic of at least seventeen books published between 2012 and 2013 (and in many more later), in the name of some blogs (including the one by Barbara Spinelli), and as the subject of the theatrical piece (and book) *Ferite a Morte* (Wounded to Death), written and performed all over Italy by the actress Serena Dandini.[5] It was the topic of a reportage by the well-known TV journalist Riccardo Iacona (Iacona and Carreras 2012) and of one of his TV specials, the subject of a book by two distinguished Italian writers Lipperini and Murgia (2013), the object of a 2012 petition of the women's movement Se Non Ora Quando (SNOQ; see chap. 2), the concern of a number of articles and blogs on the internet and of a specific law (Law 119/2013) known as the Law on

Femminicidio (contested by Italian feminists), and eventually the subject of a specific Commission of Inquiry at the Italian Senate, established in April 2017.[6]

The emergence of this emergency, to quote Naisargi Dave's pun (2011, 656), is at the center of this book. The latter is the result of research conducted for twenty months overall, between 2011 and 2016, in the Salento area of Italy, doing participant observation among feminist activists. During this time, I had the chance to ethnographically witness the gradual legitimization of the emergency of femminicidio within Italian public opinion, from being an unknown word and phenomenon to making it to the front page of newspapers. At the same time, I could observe how violence against women and femminicidio—and not primarily sexual liberation and self-determination, as it happened during the 1970s and 1980s—fostered the emergence of a new "women's question" in Italy, and the creation of "women" as a new political subject. The latter, I argue in this book, can be described as a "community of sense" (Hinderliter et al. 2009; Parmigiani 2018) that gathered not around shared *ideas* on who a woman is or should be but on shared *feelings* and *affects* linked to being actual or potential objects of violence.

While it is my claim that the emergence of femminicidio and of a new women's question in Italy around violence against women were mutually dependent, my research in Salento (and beyond) showed also that there was not just one way to look at, experience, and represent these phenomena. On the one hand, in this book, by analyzing local and national discourses, I illustrate how the naturalization of the relationship between women and victims was a main trope in the Italian sociocultural context during the years 2011–2016. On the other hand, by presenting my ethnographic experience with my Salentine informants, I show how these women activists framed, experienced, and reacted to the widespread "women-as-victims" trope. By pursuing what I call an "affective politics of representation," they embarked on a representational and affective struggle that allowed them to become, be seen, and be represented as "witnesses, and not as victims" of violence and femminicidio—as one of their mottos, that of the *Staffetta* (see chap. 4), goes.

In this book, I analyze the ideological, existential, and representational struggle of my Salentine informants by focusing on their representational practices within a Rancièrian perspective, which links political activism and aesthetic (i.e., sensory and artistic) enterprises. Their politics was one of "becoming": rooted in aesthetic practices, moved by ethical commitments.[7] While the Salentine activists, entrenched in the *pensiero della differenza sessuale* (lit., "thought of sexual difference," see chaps. 1 and 2) and in Italy's distinctive political and social history, pursued their political goals in conversation with both national and local understandings of womanhood, I claim that their focus on being witnesses and not victims might contribute to international feminist debates on violence against women and victimhood.

In addition to Italian studies, feminist studies, and anthropology, I hope that this book can offer a contribution to current debates in visual studies, performance studies, cultural studies, and around "sensory politics."

Salento

Salento is part of the region Apulia, in the southeastern fringe of the Italian peninsula. It is, historically, a multicultural area: inhabited by Messapi, a pre-Roman population, it was conquered by the Romans. Later, and for centuries, it operated as a central junction in the relationships between Byzantium and "the Orient." It was conquered by the Normans, by the Svevis, and by France and Spain before being included in the territory of Italy after its unification in 1861. This land, for centuries referred to as *Terra d'Otranto* (Land of Otranto, a town in the province of Lecce), is surrounded by the Mediterranean Sea, and it is as close to the Balkans as to Apulia's neighboring Italian regions.[8]

In spite of the political past of Apulia—oriented toward center (*Democrazia Cristiana*) and right-wing governments—Nichi Vendola, a far-left politician, was elected as the governor of Apulia in 2005. He was later reelected for a second term in 2010 that ended in 2015, when Michele Emiliano, the center-left candidate, was elected. The presence of a far-left politician for ten consecutive years as the head of a region with more than four million residents is of particular relevance, especially in light of the Italian political situation of the past two decades. In a country that, overall, had been politically influenced by Italian billionaire and prime minister Silvio Berlusconi, by his politics, and by the center-right parties for twenty years (see chaps. 2 and 3), the fact that Apulia elected a far-left politician as its governor for two consecutive terms speaks to its uniqueness.[9] As a matter of fact, during his time as governor, Vendola started to represent, among Italian public opinion, the "anti-Berlusconi."[10]

One of my motivations for choosing Salento as a field for this research is linked, precisely, to its peculiar political climate. Right from the beginning of the first mandate, Vendola's policies gave priority to dealing with violence against women and women's politics with, for example, a "Program against Violence" and a "Plan for Social Policies," allocating financial resources to projects that emphasized the fight against violence against women as a political objective. The efforts of both of Vendola's administrations in relation to violence against women and femminicidio resulted in the 2014 enactment of an innovative regional law (Law 29, *Norme per la prevenzione e il contrasto della violenza di genere, il sostegno alle vittime, la promozione della libertà e dell'autodeterminazione delle donne* [Norms to prevent and counter gender-based violence, to support the victims, and to promote women's freedom and self-determination]). In addition to this important achievement, the Apulian territory witnessed the emergence of different local initiatives in support of women, also as a result of the passionate and unfailing activity of Apulia's *Consigliera di Parità* (Counsellor of Equality), Serenella Molendini.[11]

If the commitment of Vendola's administrations to women's causes was excellent in comparison to other national and regional initiatives, my choice of Salento was supported also by its activist past. As a matter of fact, women's activism is historically well established in Apulia. In spite of a certain degree of sexism and violence against women, the feminist movement has been present and active in this region since the 1950s.[12] Moreover, Salento is well-known for its *tabacchine* (women tobacco workers) who unionized at the beginning of the twentieth century and fought important battles for their working rights.[13] Notably, Salentinians tend to cite the 1935 revolt of Tricase, which occurred under Mussolini's rule: the women protestors, who were demonstrating against the decision to close the tobacco factory where they were employed, were shot by the police. The revolt ended with several injured people and five deaths. This latter event played a considerable role in the collective memory of the Salentinians I met, and especially of feminists, who tended to define themselves, their "presence in the world," and their belonging in a geographic history, in reference to examples of "protofeminism" in which the *tabacchine* had a special role.[14]

Another reference point worth mentioning in this protofeminist Salentine genealogy is that of the witches, or *macare* in the local dialect. It is not without significance that the feminist activists of the UDI with whom I worked decided to call themselves Macare. The adoption of this term, besides gesturing to the "queerness" (see chap. 6) of their being feminist women in the Salentine context, signaled a link with a particular local genealogy that was able to reinforce their sense of "presence in the world."

In sum, as my focus on violence against women and women's activism shows, Salento today is a "concentric juncture of times and spaces" (Pizza 2015, 179–180). Its prominent position within the ethnological and anthropological traditions—another reason supporting my field choice—makes Salento a "place of places," an "unstable social and political space that produces and reproduces further spaces of aggregation and contrasts" (Palumbo 2006, 46). In other words, echoing Palumbo's work, Salento today is an *iperluogo* (hyperplace).

"Making/Doing Tradition" in Salento: Pizzica, Tarantismo, and "Anthropological Tourism"

On June 29, 2015, at the Festival of St. Peter and St. Paul in Galatina, Salento, Italy, a man and two women with long, loose hair and bare feet, who were dressed in white gowns, arrived in a wooden cart pulled by horses. They stopped in front of the chapel of St. Paul, accompanied by a group of musicians and a woman dressed in black, and started reenacting the arrival of the *tarantate* for their yearly appointment with "the Saint" at the chapel of St. Paul. Bales of hay delimited a small area just in front of the door of the chapel, where the *macara* (singular of macare) who accompanied the two women and the man was setting the stage for the ritual by laying a large white cloth on the cobblestone pavement.[15] All of this, organized in collaboration with Club UNESCO of Galatina, happened in front of crowds of tourists and locals who, in an effort to record the event with their cameras and smartphones, were trying to find their way through the stands of souvenirs that packed the main square of Galatina.[16] While local musicians of the *Orchestrina Terapeutica* (Therapeutic Little Orchestra) played traditional *pizzica* tunes, these women and the young man interpreted the dance of liberation that some Salentine women had, until the 1990s, performed over centuries in order to be healed from a malaise believed to be connected to the bite of tarantula spiders.[17] These phenomena were notably described by de Martino in his *La Terra del Rimorso* in 1961, and video recorded by Mingozzi (1961).[18] The reenactment of the therapeutic ritual started in the front of the crowd and unfolded as a visual quotation of Mingozzi's documentary, appearing to my eyes as a form of remediation. Policewomen surveyed the area, preventing the spectators from crossing the circular border bounded by the bales of hay. After just a few minutes of enthusiastic dancing, the *tarantate*, the *tarantato*, and the musicians moved into the chapel, followed by cameramen. Someone closed the doors of the chapel: nothing visible was happening in front of our eyes, the eyes of the spectators. Only the repetitive, pulsing ternary sounds of the *tamburreddhi* (local tambourines) could be heard from the outside. The spectators of a spectacle that could not be "seen" remained there, waiting for something to happen, and for the ritual to unfold behind the closed doors of the chapel. Both in standard Italian and in the local dialect, locals offered various narratives and interpretations of *tarantismo* to curious and sometimes anthropologically informed tourists. Many of the latter asked extemporaneous questions to their fellow spectators, deemed to be authorities by virtue of being natives. Some of them talked about *tarantate* as a phenomenon that mostly affected women in the past and described them as sexually repressed; others considered them simply as persons bitten by a spider and explained the disappearance of *tarantismo* through the introduction of pesticides in agriculture that were lethal to spiders as well. One explained that an old acquaintance of hers who had been "bitten" by a tarantula spider that was yellow with red dots on its back had since not been able to tolerate the color yellow. Moreover, since then, the old acquaintance had found herself incapable of hurting spiders and destroying spider webs. If she ever did so accidentally, she always asked "her Saint Paul" to forgive her. Another Salentine woman joined the conversation, arguing that she had heard that tarantula spiders, far from declining in numbers were actually starting to repopulate the Badisco area, having been reintroduced by biologists. Some cited the name of Ernesto de Martino, often unwittingly attributing to the famous Italian ethnographer their own, more or less idiosyncratic, understandings of the phenomenon. Locals and foreigners alike seemed to agree on one single point: *tarantismo* was something that belonged to the historical past of Salento, not to its present. It was, so to speak, part of its local patrimony.[19] This performance, which locals connected to the official world of *pizzica* music in Salento received with some consternation and even indignation as an irreverent "fake," was intended by the people of the Orchestrina Terapeutica as an authentic healing ritual; a ritual, though, that somehow complied with the expectations and imaginaries of anthropologically informed tourists, and with the "patrimonializing" goals of the people from the Club UNESCO of Galatina.

The festival of St. Peter and St. Paul in Galatina is one of the most important attractions of contemporary Salento for tourists and locals alike. It is also one of the "anthropological tourism" destinations (Apolito 2007, 13–14) that has developed in this area since the end of the 1990s. Salento, as a matter of fact, has been drawing the attention of ethnologists, musicologists, anthropologists, and folklorists for a long time, and it is well known in Italy and abroad especially from the work of the ethnographer Ernesto de Martino.[20] While a "place" in Western anthropological and intellectual histories (Pizza 2015, 201–202, 214), Salento is more than a "place of memory" of (especially) Italian ethnographic tradition, though. It is also "more than a historical site of production of exoticism internal to Italy, *las Indias de por acà* of the missionaries" (Pizza 2015). Pursuing Salento's cultural, economic, and political production *today* can give ethnologists, tourists, locals, intellectuals, politicians, and *amatours* the "possibility of doing anthropology at home" (2015, 190). In this respect, *tarantismo* and *pizzica* (including their multiple constructions, understandings, and representations) are not, today, just part of the scholarly idiolect of intellectuals who read about these topics, in particular in the works of the well-known Italian ethnographer. Rather, the latter are part of everyday understandings, constructions, and negotiations about "being Salentinians"—in Salento and beyond.

The legacy of the work of de Martino is undoubtedly at the core of the development of the "anthropological tourism" that flourished, in particular, after the establishment of the yearly event called *Notte della Taranta* (Night of the Tarantula Spider).[21] As Apolito points out, this "anthropological tourism" is generative: linked to a "symbolic market," it "is not limited to passive fruition" but generates "forms of participation that sometimes trigger debates, tensions, contestations, refashioning, instabilities, movements" (2007, 13).

Within such a framework, one of the most important dimensions in contemporary Salento, both in reference to the scholarly literature on the area and to the Italian "Southern Question," is the constant attempt of local, national, and international agents to participate in "making/doing tradition"—both online and not.[22] The process of making/doing tradition, similar to what is claimed by Apolito for "making/doing local" (in Salento as elsewhere), is imbricated in processes of *patrimonializzazione* (patrimonialization), which have cultural, social, and economic implications.[23] In contemporary Italy, as elsewhere, patrimonialization is not just linked to material objects but, following UNESCO's definition of intangible cultural heritage, extended to immaterial objects such as local gastronomic traditions and, in this case, *tarantismo* and *pizzica* music.[24] For this reason, Italian anthropologists read some local phenomena as examples of *merci-patrimonializzazione* (a neologism that merges the words *commercialization* and *patrimonialization*), that is, "the construction of local cultural specificities in terms of patrimonial goods" (Palumbo quoted in Pizza 2015, 106n6). An important example of this, in the Salentine context, is the musical event known as *Notte della Taranta* or "Night of the Tarantula Spider."

Since 1999, Melpignano, one of the municipalities of the Grecìa salentina, has become known for hosting the "The Night of the Tarantula Spider" every August. Broadcast both on TV and on the web, this event is preceded by smaller ones organized throughout the Grecìa over the previous two weeks.[25] During the final concert of the *Notte della Taranta*, local musicians perform variations of the traditional *pizzica* music, often featuring national and international guests. Yet, at the dawn of the twenty-first century, indeed increasingly being understood locally as either a fiction or a synonym for cultural backwardness, *tarantismo* was reframed and reconstructed in a new socioeconomical and temporal perspective (Lüdtke 2008). As the old *tarantismo* was eclipsed, new *tarantismi* emerged (idem; see also Nacci 2001, 2004; Pizza 1999, 2004, 2015; Daboo 2010). These new evolutions of *tarantismi* revolve around the ancestral origins of the *pizzica*, the "musical DNA of the Salentinians" (Lüdtke 2008, 15), around a fairly recent development of Salento as a preferred tourist destination, and around local reframings of both the phenomenon of *tarantismo* and its anthropological and historical analyses. The latter are key elements of processes of "making/doing local" (and often, I claim, of "making/doing traditional") in contemporary Salento and, to a certain extent, they can have a role in the *merci-patrimonializzazione* of *pizzica* and *tarantismo*.

Salento as an Iperluogo *(Hyperplace): Toward a Sensory Politics*

The "concentric juncture of time and spaces" (Pizza 2015, 180), hinted to above, that characterizes contemporary Salento, I argue, allows for its conception as a "hyperplace." This notion was developed over the past twenty years by the Italian anthropologist Berardino Palumbo, who used it in reference to Sicily. Following his elaborations on this concept, a hyperplace can be described as a "narrative place" (Palumbo 2006, 45; see also Sorge, Padwe, and Shneiderman 2015 for a comparison) or a "place of places" (Palumbo 2006, 46). It is a space continuously created and narrated, a "total space of the senses (social, political, emotional)" (46), a place, in other words, where objects and signs of the past, together with poetics, practices, and techniques of the body, are continuously manipulated and reinterpreted in an "endless production of sense" (Badii 2012, 9). In this Salentine hyperplace, bodies are subjects/objects—*(s)oggetti*, as I claim in chapter 6—and, I add, the web and the media are dimensions of its locality, too. They are places where dynamics of both the past and the present are inscribed, reinvented, and put into action in different directions, at local and global levels. Together with artistic and cultural objects, through *pizzica* and *tarantismo*, for example, bodies also become *patrimonio*. Bearers of intangible heritage, they are at loci where the local, national, and global interfuse.

In a place like Salento, and in the context I studied for this research in particular, Rancière's understanding of politics becomes especially relevant, taking perhaps peculiar connotations, since the sensory aspects of the "endless production of *sense*" (emphasis mine) become, de facto, a political field. Rancière is among the scholars interested in the connections and tensions between the political and the emotional, between power relations and sensory/aesthetic experiences.[26] Rancière (2004b, 10) suggests that "politics is first of all a way of framing, among sensory data, a specific sphere of experience. It is a partition of the sensible, of the visible and the sayable, which allows (or does not allow) some specific data to appear; which allows (or does not allow) some specific subjects to designate them and speak about them. It is a specific intertwining of ways of being, ways of doing and ways of speaking."

This partition of the sensible, which might also be referred to as regimes of perceptions (Panagia 2009, 7), is what is generally called common sense. The aim of politics, as well as of art, is a reconfiguration of the sensible. By sensible, Rancière understands both what makes sense and what can be sensed (Panagia 2009, 3). Following a definition of aesthetics that encompasses both the original and the current meanings, Rancière develops a philosophy that puts the aesthetic and sensory experiences at the center of political action. In particular, his understanding of democracy lies in the phenomenon of *dissensus* (in Latin, sensing differently). Dissensus is the moment in which the experiences "of those who have no part"—those who are not recognized by the majority and are not included in the political "distribution of the sensible"—are inscribed in society (Rancière 1999, 123). In other words, dissensus (which includes both cognitive and affective dimensions) is intrinsically political in as much as it challenges common sense by broadening the sensorium at a given time and space.

This is the context in which the feminist women with whom I worked operated. Their battles of and for representation aimed at promoting dissensus, at changing the practices of seeing and sensing (and of making "sense") around women and violence—their own, and the ones of their actual or imagined publics, ethnographers included. Their political enterprise was an affective one.[27] Following Mazzarella, I believe that "any social project that is not imposed through force alone must be affective in order to be effective" (2009, 299), and it is his use of the affect theory that is particularly relevant for my research.[28] As I show in this book, the story of the legitimization of the word *femminicidio*, of the world that it depicts, and of the political struggle around representations of women that I have observed can give ethnographic substance to such an approach, and to an understanding of politics as a "sensible" enterprise (see, for a comparison, McLagan and McKee 2012). The same can be said about the ways the women I met aimed at contrasting the commonsensical understandings of their status and roles within hegemonic "patriarchal" discourses that define who women are or should be in contemporary Italy. These exemplify the role of dissensus—as a complement to disagreement—in political action, understood as a reconfiguration of the sensible. In doing so, they engage with multiple dimensions of the "place of places" that is contemporary Salento.

The Fieldwork

I arrived in Salento for the first time in September 2011 and started to follow the UDI women of the group "UDI Macare Salento" in my first week of fieldwork, during the *Scuola della Differenza* (School of Difference). The latter, a weeklong conference on Italian feminisms organized by the *Università del Salento*, connected me to different Italian feminist groups—active in and beyond Salento.

Macare, as I have already explained, is one word for witches in the local dialect. The town of Soleto, in particular, is known locally as the "town of the macare."[29] This reputation depends on the legend that the impressive bell tower of Soleto was constructed in a single night by an army of demons and witches, orchestrated by the alchemist Matteo Tafuri.[30] Macare, though, were not just symbolic presences in Salento. During my stay, I found out that many people referred to macare (or to *sciare/striare*, two other local words for witches) as concrete presences. Generally, their "being witches" was associated with these women's ethical and social marginality. Their popular depiction differed from the one of the well-known legend of the witches of Benevento (a town in the Campania region, described by a legend as the locus of huge gatherings of demon-lovers and witches). While some considered these macare as some type of healer that used (and still uses) herbs and natural remedies to heal (or harm), and *striare* as witches who worked "with other energies, with the subtle ones" (*lavorano con altre energie, con il sottile*), others considered them simply to be socially and ethically challenging persons. According to Cecilia, for example, an elderly lady who lives in Otranto, "*macara ete 'na cristiana fiacca, ca nun ete socievole, ca face jettature, macarie fiacche. Le striare erane puru pesciu. Erane brutte de carattere . . . Iddhe venene de Vaste o de Disu.*"[31] That there are different understandings of the status and the roles of macare in contemporary Salento is also supported by the (unpublished) interviews gathered by a local intellectual, Francesco Manni, who kindly shared his material with me.

Yet other people considered macare to be women who have remedies for *lu 'nfàscinu*, a local version of the evil eye. I met an old woman in the Grecìa salentina who was referred to as a macara, meaning "a woman who practices 'the art'" (i.e., magic).[32] Costantina is the grandmother of a feminist friend's hairdresser called Paola. I met her granddaughter once in her hair salon with my friend Marcella, and again when she and her mother (one of Costantina's daughters) drove me and my feminist friend to her grandmother's place. At that time, Marcella suffered from back pain, and since she liked experimenting with alternative medicine to alleviate the pain, she thought she would give this ritual a try. Knowing my interests in Salento and *macaria* (magic), she was pleased to try Costantina's remedies in front of me. In spite of the fact that Marcella was born in Salento and had spent the majority of her life there, she had never before met a macara. We arrived at Costantina's house late one November evening. Her granddaughter had explained to her that a friend needed some help with back pain, and, as Paola later explained to me during a visit to her hair salon, a macara not only cannot refuse to treat someone who asks for her help; she also cannot accept money or other rewards for her healing therapies. Costantina's house was quite old and small, and its structure was similar to many other Salentine houses I visited. Located at street level, we accessed it through a French door protected by shutters. During the Salentine summer months one can see many men and women in the evenings, sitting just outside doors like these to find some relief from the heat. The first room we accessed was the dining/living room; old furniture and ancient white lace textiles furnished the room, probably the patient and meticulous work of generations of women of the family. The walls of the room were crammed with old family pictures and dolls that had probably been untouched for decades. Costantina received us in the kitchen, which could be reached only by exiting the living room and walking through the lone bedroom. The kitchen was small and full of dark brown furniture and a number of old furnishings, including a table with four chairs in the middle of the room. The TV was on, and remained so throughout our visit, broadcasting a TV quiz show hosted by Gerry Scotti, a popular Italian anchorman. A big fireplace was located in a corner of the room; it was so big that a person could sit in it. And indeed, as we entered the kitchen, Paola took a small bench and placed herself *in* the fireplace, half a meter away from the fire. That had been "her place" since she was a kid. A big iron brazier full of burning coals had been placed on the floor, near Costantina, who sat at the kitchen's table. The house had no other heating system, and the evening was quite chilly by Salentine standards. Costantina's husband, who is six years her junior and in his early eighties stood in the kitchen with his rain jacket and *coppola* hat on. She had married him when she was thirty and he was twenty-four; Paola claimed that her grandma had "wanted to have someone who would drive her around as she aged, instead of having an older husband she should have to look after." Both Costantina's marital choices and their justifications are quite uncommon in Salento, especially for a woman of that age. This, together with macaria and other aspects of her behavior, signaled her eccentricity in relation to Salentine standard. Costantina's husband did not say a word during our visit. In fact, even the old woman did not speak much before and during the ritual. She looked at us with a serious expression and quietly listened to Paola while she introduced us and explained Marcella's problem. I was introduced as a friend who had come from Boston, a city Costantina had clearly never heard of. In fact, probably puzzled by my northern Italian accent, I heard her asking my friend in dialect "*percé iddha sta cunta cussì? Rumena ete?*" (Why is that one talking like that? Is she Romanian?) I understood that she liked me, though, since she looked at me and almost smiled on a couple of occasions: maybe, as I did, she felt a connection between us precisely in virtue of our common unconventionality with regard to the Salentine context. Nonna Costantina remained composed, silent, and aloof in the time preceding the ritual, while her daughter and granddaughter kept asking me questions about my life and work. After some twenty minutes of chatting, the ritual began and unfolded quite smoothly. It was unmarked, treated like a very ordinary activity, with Gerry Scotti's TV program continuing in the background. The old woman told Marcella to sit on a chair randomly situated next to the TV, and she put some oil in a small cup and some water in a bigger one. Then, while pronouncing some unintelligible words, she drew crosses all over my friend's body. We all remained in the room: while I was observing the macara, Costantina's husband continued to watch the TV show, and Paola and her mother kept chatting about ordinary topics such as what to buy at the grocery store and gossiping about some acquaintances. When Costantina finished her ritual, she asked all of us women to join her, and put her index finger in the cup of oil and let a drop of oil fall into the water. She repeated this action silently six or seven times. Since the first three drops of oil spread when they touched the water, she interpreted this as a sign that my friend was affected by a weak *'nfàscinu*. The other drops of oil did not disseminate when they fell into the water, and that is the reason why Costantina talked about it as weak. Nonetheless, she said she had to start over with the ritual. When she had completed it for the second time, she asked us, again, to join her. Now, none of the oil drops that fell into the water spread. This she interpreted as a sign that the *'nfàscinu* was gone. She put some salt into the water and poured everything into the kitchen sink. After the ritual, Costantina felt much more relaxed, became more talkative, and even offered us some of the food that she had prepared on the stove located in the corridor that connected the kitchen to the garage. The dish, *pezzetti di cavallo al sugo*, was a typical and traditional Salentine dish prepared with horse meat, tomatoes, and spices. She chatted a bit with us and even laughed when, amused by the coincidence, she discovered that she and I were born on the same day, fifty years apart, and that she and I had an identically shaped sunspot close to our right eyes. "It's going to get darker," she said directly to me, this time, before we left. Then she added, with a warm and benevolent smile, *"te dicu ca me nomini"* (in dialect, "I tell you that you'll mention me," meaning "you'll remember what I said and will quote my words").

The mysterious aura around macare/witches, their uncanny abilities, and their social nonconformity were indeed appealing aspects for the Macare/feminists. In such a context, it was no coincidence that the feminist activists I met chose to call themselves Macare.[33] They did so in order to signal their desire to be represented and perceived as disruptive of societal values and order, as (marginal) examples of different ways of being women, and, at the same time, as bearers of particular arts and qualities. Traditional macare/witches were, similar to the Macare/feminists, "queer" (*eccentrici*, see De Lauretis 1990) subjects. They were nonconformist, and their "being different"—pursued through the ability of mastering the "arts" (the latter being magic, traditional medicine, artisan or artistic skills)—was well rooted in the history of their territory.[34]

The Macare have been both very generous with me since my arrival in Salento and extremely important in my research. When I started my fieldwork, about fifteen women were part of that group. Their ages ranged from twenty to sixty years old, and they were all white, educated, middle-class women. Some of them worked or studied; some did not. Among those who worked, only a minority had a full-time job. Most of the Macare, at that time, lived a somewhat economically precarious life, like many other women (and men) in Italy. Some of them were married or in stable relationships, others were single (either looking for a long-term relationship or happily into dating). Some were interested in heterosexual relations, others in homosexual ones, and some in both. Nobody, though, used or recognized herself in the term *lesbian*. With a few exceptions, the same also applied to other UDI women with whom I have worked. According to most of them, sexual orientation was not a political dimension of their activism. In spite of the fact that there are, in Italy, politically active groups of lesbian-feminists and of queer activists, terms such as *queer, lesbian, heterosexual, bisexual, intersexual,* and *asexual* were largely missing from the vocabulary of my informants—both personally and politically. However, eroticism—understood freely and independent of sexual identity, sexual orientation, normative practices, and objects—was part of their political agenda. Following Carla Lonzi's distinction between clitoral women and vaginal women (1974), autoeroticism, more than sexual relations with others, was a key political practice and a matter of political speculation for the activists with whom I worked. Moreover, I witnessed frequent reflections on the erotic dimensions of women's relations, understood as a wide experiential field. The latter comprised—but was not reduced to or primarily defined by—sexual intercourse. This was evident, for example, in my informants' theorizations of *erotico diffuso* (diffused eroticism) as a dimension of women's relations (independent of sexual orientations). As the collective *Femministe Nove* (see chaps. 2 and 3) put it: "We consider eroticism something broader than sexual intercourse. The eroticisms of our bodies want to flow in freedom. Let's open the space and the imagination to an expanded eroticism, one that touches all the places that our body touches." This eroticism did not depend on fixed binaries but instead was defined as "expanded sexuality."[35]

The Macare represented the core of my ethnographic research in this book, though I gathered data from other sources as well, including other ethnographic contexts and other materials found on the internet or on other media. The latter material was not independent of the Salentine context; on the contrary, it contributed to shaping the everyday context in which the Salentine activists acted and to which they reacted. Their everyday experiences were indissolubly interconnected with local and national media representations of women that I consider in this book. What happened in Rome, on the web, and in other media, for example, was inextricably connected with and constitutive of the lives of the Salentine activists I followed. I did participant observation by joining the Macare in their everyday activities. At the time, this included the start-up of a feminist bookstore in Lecce. There, between books, cigarettes, and coffees, I got to know and appreciate them. They taught me a substantial part of what I know about Italian feminisms, their jargon, and their practices. They allowed me to observe them, and patiently schooled me in their visualities and perceptions, for which I am deeply honored and grateful. All of them shared with me narratives about their lives and their pasts, which I reciprocated; some of them devoted a great deal of time and energy to this task, allowing me to collect their life histories. With some of them at least, I met daily from September 2011 to March 2012, and less frequently (in physical terms, at least) for the next four years. In addition to looking after a bookstore, our daily activities included also organizing and attending meetings in preparation for the 2011 UDI Congress, recording and editing videos in response to the UDI internal political opponents or to *restituire* (lit., "give back") the political experiences that involved the Macare, organizing events, attending meetings of other feminist groups, eating, reading, chatting, and, on a more general level, participating in one another's ordinary lives.

Following my time with the Macare, I joined the historical Italian UDI feminist group (see below) at an important point in their history—right before their Fifteenth Congress. This represented a turning point for the association. I followed the Macare from the last months of the precongress period through the congress, on the occasion of the *autoconvocazioni* (self-convocations) of the UDI, and during the mourning period following the congress. During those weeks, I also met other UDI women from other parts of Italy, who expanded my horizons in terms of Italian feminisms and feminist practices. In the aftermath of the Fifteenth Congress, Pina Nuzzo (a woman from Salento, a reference point for my informants, and the former national delegate of the UDI) was not reelected, and she first created the group Udichesiamo, and then Laboratorio Donnae, which I started following. The Macare joined her in her transition from being a national delegate of the UDI to engaging political activism outside the association in which she had served for decades—and I did, as well. I attended their meetings in person, when possible, and I followed their work at a distance, through the activities of their blogs and of their Facebook pages. Mostly, though, while away from Salento, I kept in contact with some of my informants on a regular basis through Skype, emails, WhatsApp messages, and Facebook. I joined the Macare in their trips to Bologna and Rome, traveling, living, and sharing time and space with them. These precious moments included an eight-hour trip in a small car with five other women (one of us traveled in the trunk with the luggage), sleeping on the floor of tiny rooms with them (with way too few pillows and mattresses), and borrowing a cart from a store for the feminist cause. Mostly, whether beside the Ionian or the Adriatic

Seas with wine and *frise*, or just accomplishing everyday chores, I spent with them memorable moments of "women's sociality."[36]

As often happens to anthropologists, the small group of people I started following in September 2011 rapidly grew by including acquaintances, friends, and families, as well as their acquaintances, friends, and families, in what is known as a snowball reaction. Accordingly, especially from mid-2012 onward, I expanded my research beyond the city of Lecce, where the Macare used to meet, into the southern, less urban, part of Salento. During my stay in the Salento area of Italy, I was able to connect with many people, including some men but mostly women.[37] Some of them were engaged formally in women's politics, thought of themselves as feminists, and belonged to different women's groups working in the area or outside Salento. Some of them did not identify as feminist but worked or volunteered in structures such as women's shelters (I did some participant observation in two of them in the province of Lecce) or in associations whose aim was to promote the well-being of women (both in Apulia and in other regions of Italy). Some other women did not think of themselves as feminists at all (*feminism* being a term they hardly knew) and were not involved in any type of women's politics or association. I was able to conduct open-ended interviews and photo-elicited interviews, both off-line and online, with many women. I also had the chance to live for three months in an informant's house with her husband, two daughters, mother, father, brother, two dogs, a cat, two hens, and a rooster. The magnitude of their generosity is rivaled only by the amount of insight into the everyday life in Salento that I received from that experience.

From September 2011 to March 2012, in July, August, and November 2013, for another ten weeks in 2014, in January 2015, from June to December 2015, and in the first months of 2016, I did participant observation in person in Salento. For the rest of the time, I kept in constant touch with my informants in various internet-based ways: from Facebook to Skype, email to blogs. My exchanges with some of them were very intense in the periods I spent in North America: I heard from some of them daily and talked with others weekly or monthly. This allowed me to cultivate my connections with some of my informants (who also became my friends), to remain up to date on what was happening in Salento and in their lives and to discuss with them their positions vis-à-vis the changing Italian cultural climate, especially in reference to violence against women and femminicidio. As I will explain in chapters 1 and 3, I had the chance to witness the gradual legitimization of the emergency of femminicidio within Italian public opinion, from being an unknown word and phenomenon to making it to the front page of newspapers.

Along with the Salento-based online and off-line fieldwork, I monitored daily what was happening online within Italian feminist circles. By following my Salento informants, I made contact with other feminists in other parts of Italy and started cultivating those connections mainly through Facebook. The internet space was a very important dimension of contemporary feminist political activism in Italy and an important arena for my research. While I tended not to intervene directly on Facebook—for example, by openly commenting on the posts, statuses, and images uploaded by the feminists with whom I worked online—I realized I could not avoid participating to some extent in their online activities; if my ethnography was to be successful, I had to be trusted. I accepted every tag (even the ones I did not agree with) and used the "like" feature as a way to communicate my support for their cause. Occasionally, I shared some links or posts (mostly, as a way to give audience to the initiatives of the activists with whom I worked). Thoughtfully and contextually, at times I used Facebook's privacy settings to put a distance between activists' online activities and my other Facebook friends.

Given the situation I have described, the multiple fields, and the disparity of women's practices, it will be evident that choosing whether to use the adjective *feminist* to describe the experiences of the individual women I met became theoretically challenging. On the one hand, adopting a too-strict definition of what constitutes a feminist woman would erase from the picture other more nuanced experiences. On the other hand, dismissing the possibility of using this adjective at all would be disrespectful of the context of my research. In order to overcome these problems, I decided to distinguish between feminist women and women (in general) in this book. By the former I mean those who problematize the representations and roles of women in their society and who want to challenge and change the current status quo, according to their own personal paths, idiosyncrasies, and reference points. This definition of *feminism* is quite loose, and certainly my more radical informants would not go along with it. Being feminist, in this sense, does not imply belonging either to the left or to the right; it is neither an exclusive feature of members of feminist associations nor a characteristic that could be applied solely to intellectuals or educated women, and it potentially includes men, too. It is worth noting that many of the persons involved in what I identify as feminist activism may be indifferent to the use (or lack thereof) of this word to describe their political engagement. While applying such a loose definition of being feminist might be theoretically weak, I nonetheless believe that it is heuristically useful, for it includes the complexity of experiences linked to the emergence of a new women's question in Italy. The latter, which I followed at a distance, started to appear on the Italian scene in the early months of 2011 (see below). By contrast, the term *women* signifies two different things in this book. When used contrastively, it refers to individuals who were *not* feminists; that is, it indicates women who did not problematize their status in Italian society, or at least not to the extent that they attempted to challenge and change the patriarchal system. They preferred to try to find their own compromises with the situations they were facing, occasionally expressing a certain uneasiness with being associated with feminism. Instead, when the term *women* is used alone, following the emic representation of my informants, informed by the pensiero della differenza sessuale, it refers to female subjects.

Overview of Chapters

In chapter 1, I discuss violence as the object of this book. I explain how I encountered the topic of violence in my fieldwork, and how I came to theorize it in reference to and beyond current anthropological debates on violence. While Italian women today do experience structural, symbolic, and physical aggression, these aspects of violence are not specifically the ones that affect the lives of my informants, my ethnography, and my anthropological reflections. Violence against women, in this book, is conceptualized primarily as a cluster of discursive and affective elements and formations inflected in rhetorical and representational terms. These inhabited my informants' everyday lives: what violence against women did, and how, is at the center of my ethnography. In particular, I analyze how violence, its possibility, and the struggle against it became battlefields in struggles of and for representation for the women I met—nationally and, especially, locally.

In chapter 2, I sketch the background historical dimensions of Italian feminisms as a circumstantial yet fundamental frame in order to give prominence to contemporary developments, in particular as they unfolded in my ethnographic experiences. I will narrate them filtered through a particular lens: that of the issues around visibility, which will represent the *fil rouge* of the chapter. The metaphor of vision brings together multiple dimensions relevant to my informants' lives, at both a personal and a political level, posing questions about who sees what, how, and, ultimately, why.

In chapter 3, I discuss the commonsensical understandings and feelings that link women and victims in contemporary Italy. My claim is that for many Italian women and in different manners violence against women worked as a way to think about, understand, and represent their being in the world. I claim that the dominant framework used to represent women in Italy when I carried out my fieldwork put women in the role of victims in relation to violence. This language and images of victimhood dominated the media and political campaigns against "sexed violence" alike.

In chapter 4, and in the following ones, I focus specifically on the Salentine activists with whom I worked and address how the "women-as-victims" trope was understood locally in relation to weeping and to Salentine "traditional" values associated with women and men within the so-called honor and shame complex. After describing how UDI women started drawing an explicit connection between representation, imagination, and political action, I concentrate on the issue of dignity in their representational struggle. I claim that in my field, dignity was not a unitary concept; on the contrary, I found it to be multivalent and malleable. Dignity in Salento was adopted in a way that resonated with certain dimensions of the traditional notion of honor, as a measure of social worth, and, at the same time, as a reference point for a wider discourse on human rights; in my ethnographic field, it was a way to perform modern feminist womanhood, to be "witnesses."

In chapter 5, I focus on the ethical dimensions of the representational struggle that I have previously described. Through representation, my informants aimed to challenge the patriarchal constraints that associated women with (suffering) victims and to promote interpretations of women as empowered, socially relevant, and worthy/dignified (*degne*) witnesses. Moreover, it also aimed to produce witnesses, both among their publics and as a result of practices of autopoiesis. By engaging bodies, senses, and emotions and not only ideas and discourses, my informants wanted to promote dissensus; theirs was a form of "sensible politics" (McLagan and McKee 2012).

In chapter 6, I trace another explicit connection between the aesthetic (sensory and artistic) enterprises of Salentine activists and the ethical dimension. I argue that performing modern feminist womanhood is a form of autopoiesis, or of ascesis (in Foucauldian terms). In particular, in dialogue with the so-called anthropology of ethics, I present the political, ethical, and aesthetic practice of *fare-come-se* (doing-as-if) that I have encountered during my ethnography. Doing-as-if, which I understand as an ethos of becoming (Ziarek 2001; Ibrahim 2014; Dave 2014), is not teleologically oriented and aims at imagining (Andriolo 2006) new practices and criteria to judge and understand them. This process is a form of dissensus and yet another example of how the ethical and aesthetic realms are intermingled in my ethnographic field (and beyond).

If not otherwise stated, all translations from Italian are mine and the names used to refer to my informants are pseudonyms. I am aware that the choice to use the term *informant* might unsettle some of the readers of this book, but it is, culturally, the more appropriate choice in reference to my particular field.

From my interlocutors' point of view, the use of the term *informant* does imply a power differential between their knowledge and expertise and my learning position and standpoint.

Notes

1. Giulia Torlone, "Ogni due giorni una donna viene uccisa dal compagno. I numeri della violenza di genere," *L'Espresso*, http://espresso.repubblica.it/attualita/2017/06/19/news /femminicidi-1.304466 (accessed March 21, 2019).

2. "Femminicidio," Treccani, http://www.treccani.it/vocabolario/femminicidio _(Neologismi)/ (accessed March 21, 2019).

3. Maria Rosaria Iovinella, "10 parole che dovremmo conoscere meglio," *Wired*, http:// www.wired.it/play/cultura/2014/10/17/10-parole-consocere-meglio/ (accessed March 21, 2019). On femminicidio in South America, see Fregoso and Bejarano 2010; Panther 2008; Domínguez Ruvalcaba and Corona 2010; Radford and Russell 1992; Russell and Harmes 2001; Payan, Kruszewskim, and Staudt 2009; Gaspar de Alba and Guzmán 2010. On femminicidio in Turkey, see Arin 2001.
According to the website of the prestigious *Accademia della Crusca*, femminicidio appeared in the dictionary Devoto-Oli for the first time in 2009, in ZINGARELLI from 2010, in the Vocabolario Treccani online, and in Neologismi Treccani in 2012 (as "femmicidio o femicidio"). See "Femminicidio: i perché di una parola," Accademia della Crusca, http:// www.accademiadellacrusca.it/it/lingua-italiana/consulenza-linguistica/domande-risposte /femminicidio-perch-parola (accessed March 21, 2019). In spite of this official recognition, there is occasional resistance to its adoption, as seen in this article published in the left-wing newspaper *La Repubblica*, which caused strong reactions among feminists online: Guido Ceronetti, "Care donne, abolite la parola femminicidio," http://www.repubblica.it/la -repubblica-delle-idee/societa/2013/12/27/news/care_donne_abolite_la_parola_femminicidio -74585204/ (accessed March 21, 2019).

4. See, for example, Spinelli 2008, 2011, 2013, 2014; Abis and Orrù 2016; Violi 2015; Pramstrahler 2015; Gamberi 2015; Bandelli 2017; Bandelli and Porcelli 2016.

5. It is enough to go to the Italian Amazon website and search the term *femminicidio* and see the number of results. Though they are likely only partial results, they are nonetheless relevant for supporting my claim. See, for example, *FEMMINICIDIO, Feminicide, Femicidio*, http://femminicidio.blogspot.com/ (accessed March 21, 2019); and *Femicidio*, http:// femicidiocasadonne.wordpress.com/2014/01/24/stop-al-femminicidio/ (accessed March 21, 2019). On Dandini's *Ferite a Morte*, see the website: http://www.feriteamorte.it/ (accessed March 21, 2019).

6. Presa Diretta 24/02. 2013, RaiPlay, http://www.rai.tv/dl/RaiTV/programmi/media /ContentItem-f3293d14-8b95-40c5-b333-957340103241.html (accessed March 21, 2019). On violence against women and the Italian cinema and media, see Laviosa 2015. On the "Law against Femminicidio," see *Conversione in legge, con modificazioni, del decreto-legge 14 agosto 2013, n. 93, recante disposizioni urgenti in materia di sicurezza e per il contrasto della violenza di genere, nonché in tema di protezione civile e di commissariamento delle province: Gazzetta Ufficiale*, http://www.gazzettaufficiale.it/eli/id/2013/10/15/13G00163/sg (accessed March 21, 2109).

The contestations came from many feminist groups. Notably, the Paestum 2013 meeting produced a collection of signatures against it entitled Not in My Name.

Information on the Commission of Inquiry at the Italian Senate can be accessed at https://www.senato.it/4731 (accessed March 21, 2019).

7. On the politics of becoming, see, for example, Dave 2014; Ziarek 2001; Ibrahim 2014; Pearce et al. 2012.

8. The Apulian people gained visibility in the international media during the 1990s for their geographic—and affective—proximity to these troubled areas of the world. On the occasion of the first migrations of mostly illegal immigrants from Albania reaching the Italian shores, in search of a better life (such as the one they could watch on Italian TV shows), the people of Apulia were able to face this unexpected humanitarian emergency. Because Italy and Europe, to a certain extent, were unprepared at that time in particular for these immigration waves (see, e.g., King and Mai 2004; Zinn 1996; on migrations in Italy today, see, e.g., Tuckett 2018), the people of Apulia and its territorial administrators took charge of the emergency and mobilized local networks to provide shelter and first aid to the thousands of migrants who kept reaching their shores. These collective efforts clashed with the harsh formal responses of the Italian government and touched the hearts of millions of (not just Italian) TV viewers, in particular the arrival of the ship Vlora with its fifteen thousand passengers at the port of Bari in August 1991.

9. On Berlusconi and "*berlusconismo*," see, for example, chapter 3, as well as Ginsborg 2004; Ginsborg and Asquer 2011; Tuccari and Bongiovanni 2004; Molé 2013b; D'Arcais 2011; Repetto 2015; Dei 2011; Herzfeld 2008.

10. Besides having been Apulia's governor for ten years, Nichi Vendola was the president of the far-left party Sinistra Ecologia e Libertà (Left, Ecology, and Freedom). He defines himself as being Catholic and Communist—something that challenges recent conservative developments of Italian Catholicisms. On Catholicism in Italy, see Garelli 2007a, 2007b, 2013; Turina 2011, 2013; Faggioli 2012; Muehlebach 2012, 2013; Pace 2013; Diotallevi 1999; Palmisano 2010; Napolitano 2016. See also the important development of the phenomenon of the *Sentinelle in Piedi* (Standing Sentinels) and their protests against LGBT+ rights, http://sentinelleinpiedi.it (accessed March 21, 2019).

The understanding of Vendola as the "anti-Berlusconi" is partially the result both of a tendency of the Italian Left of defining itself, somewhat unsuccessfully, in distinction to the former Italian prime minister and his entourage and of Vendola's life choices. In a country where newspapers and TV programs indulged in detailed descriptions of the macho skills of Berlusconi, where the Catholic heritage and the presence of the Vatican was so influential in everyday life, and in a political environment where obtaining a legal abortion seemed almost impossible, being a public man who loves men represented a nonconformist political stance. On the Italian Left, see, for example, Tuccari and Bongiovanni 2004; Muehlebach 2009; Però 2007. On Berlusconi and machismo, see, for example, Molé 2012, 2013a, 2013b; Ferrero, Camoletto, and Bertone 2012; Crowhurst and Bertone 2012. On Italian machismo, see Seymour 2005; Bellassai 2005; Guano 2007; Plesset 2006; Passerini 1996.

Although abortion is legal in Italy (Law 194), it is widely acknowledged that the current Italian bureaucratic apparatus that should guarantee this legal right to women is often able to dissuade women from interrupting their pregnancies. Besides the fact that the overwhelming majority of physicians employed in public hospitals are objectors and do not perform abortions, in certain regions just one hospital in six is able to offer a woman the possibility of meeting a physician who is not an objector. See, for example, "Io e il mio aborto impossibile,"

L'Espresso, http://espresso.repubblica.it/attualita/2013/10/14/news/io-e-il-mio-aborto
-impossibile-1.137446 (accessed March 21, 2019), and "Aborto, il Pd: in un reparto su 6 impossibile applicare la legge," *Chronicle* (Milan), http://milano.corriere.it/milano/notizie/cronaca
/13_settembre_4/aborto-medici-obiettori-coscienza-ospedali-legge-2222898889738.shtml
(accessed March 31, 2019).

11. "Prevenzione e contrasto alla violenza di genere," La Puglia delle Pari Opportunità,
http://www.pariopportunita.regione.puglia.it/contro-la-violenza-sulle-donne-e
-minori (accessed March 21, 2019); "Chi siamo," La Puglia delle Pari Opportunità, http://
www.pariopportunita.regione.puglia.it/chi-siamo (accessed March 21, 2019). For example,
in 2014 the Apulian region decided to bring a civil action in the criminal proceedings in a
case of femminicidio and to create a regional watchdog against violence against women. See,
for example, "In Puglia l'osservatorio regionale per le vittime di violenza," Spazio Speciale,
http://www.spaziosociale.it/articolo.asp?id_art=1921 (accessed March 21, 2019); Consigliera
parità Puglia, http://www.consparitapuglia.it/newsite/consigliera (accessed March 21, 2019).
While the Consigliere are present in every Italian region, not all of them take their mandate
with the same zeal as Serenella Molendini.

12. The UDI, first of all, was present in the region. More recently, though, Apulia in general, and Salento in particular, witnessed the establishment of a Women's House and various
other feminist and queer-feminist groups.

13. See, for example, Trono and Pesare 2013; Santoro and Torsello 2002, 2005; and Santoro
2010. See also "È morta Cristina Conchiglia, guidò le lotte delle tabacchine," Rassegna, http://
www.rassegna.it/articoli/2013/05/6/99995/e-morta-cristina-conchiglia-guido-le-lotte-delle
-tabacchine (accessed March 21, 2109).

Salento's economy was linked for centuries and until fairly recently to agriculture
and to the presence of latifundia: large landed estates owned by a landlord, often worked by
a large number of (often underpaid) peasants. Traces of this economic history can still be
found in the local language and social structure. It is not uncommon to meet people who
refer to the parcel of land they own and cultivate—mostly as a leisure activity—as *fundu* (a
term in the Salentino dialect clearly linked to the term *latifondo*). The cultivation and handling of tobacco, in particular, played an important economic and political role in this area
until the past century: as Santoro and Torsello point out, in fact, "an endemic class conflict
between the rich owners . . . and the masses of peasants and female workers (*operaie tabacchine*) also developed around the tobacco economy" (2005, 28; on the cultivation of tobacco
in Salento, see also Barletta 1994).

14. On "*presenza*," see, for example, de Martino [1961] 1976; Pandolfi 1990; Saunders 1995.

15. The woman who was interpreting the role of the helper told me, in a personal conversation (December 2015), that she was asked by one of the *tarantate* to be the macara in the
performance. When I asked her why she thought the dancer used this term, she told me she
did not know. Another woman of the group claims that they use the term *macara* to refer to
someone who helps, who gives strength, often by using magic.

16. "World Heritage List," UN Educational, Scientific and Culture Organization
(UNESCO), http://whc.unesco.org/en/list/ (accessed March 21, 2019).

17. In using the verb *interpret* rather than *perform*, I follow Lambek 2014. Also see "Festa
San Pietro e Paolo 2104 Galatina (LE)," http://www.youtube.com/watch?v=wwyR3JTkTos
(accessed March 21, 2019), and "Galatina, la guarigione delle tarantate," http://www.youtube
.com/watch?v=RIkZ_uRcuAM (accessed March 21, 2019).

18. La Taranta: https://www.youtube.com/watch?v=wmbXOdI1yhE.

19. In addition to the already quoted references, on *tarantismo*, see Lapassade 1994; Lanternari 1995, 2000; Mina and Torsello 2006.

20. On Salento, see, for example, de Martino [1961] 1976; Lapassade 1994; Daboo 2010; Del Giudice 2005; Lüdtke 2008; Pizza 2015, 2016; Laviosa 2010, 2011; Minghelli 2016; Nicolescu 2016; Rossi 2000; Signorelli 1996; De Giorgi 1999, 2008. On de Martino, see, among many others, Pizza 1999, 2004, 2013, 2015; Ferrari 2012; Di Nola 1998; Lanternari 1995, 1997, 2000; Seppilli 1995; Gallini and Massenzio 1997; Baba 2010; Zinn 2015; Massenzio 2005.

21. On the Night of the Tarantula Spider, see, for example, Lüdtke 2008; Blackstone 2009; Pizza 1999, 2004, 2015; Daboo 2010. See also La Notte della Taranta, http://www.lanottedellataranta.it (accessed March 21, 2019).

22. On the Italian south, see, for example, Schneider 1998; Inserra 2017; Lumley and Morris 1997; Apolito 2000, de Martino 1959. My expression "making/doing tradition" was coined in intellectual conversation with Apolito's expression "making /doing local" (e.g., 2007, 15). For a comparison see, on Sardinia, Sorge et al. 2015 and Sorge 2015.

23. On *patrimonializzazione*, see, for example, Palumbo 2003, 2009; Pizza 2015; Apolito 2007; Badii 2012; Ballacchino 2013.

24. "Lists," Intangible Heritage, UN Educational, Scientific and Culture Organization (UNESCO), http://www.unesco.org/culture/ich/index.php?pg=00011. See also "Comitato Scientifico per la Valorizzazione delle Tradizioni Italiane," *Antropologia Museale* 17:18–22.

25. The Griko dialect is taught today in schools in the Grecìa. In spite of the cultural policies of valorization of this neo-Greek dialect, supported also by Regional Law 5/2012 entitled "Norms for the Promotion and Tutelage of Minority Languages in Apulia," the younger generations do not seem to be mastering this language for everyday use. Nonetheless, as claimed by Manuela Pellegrino (2015, 2016), the recent florescence of Griko "beyond death" in artistic and performative contexts makes of this language a "performative post-linguistic vernacular." On neo-Greek dialect and communities in southern Italy, see Pellegrino 2013, 2015, 2016; Pipyrou 2012, 2014b, 2016. See also D. Costa 2011; Bosio and Longhini 2007.

While standard Italian is the official language of Salento and the use of Griko is not widespread, the local dialect (*Salentino*) is ubiquitous among older and younger generations, in both urban and rural settings, regardless of the social status and class of the speaker. As a northern Italian born at the border with Switzerland, I found that the use of regional dialect was much more prominent in Salento than in the area from which I come. As a newcomer to Salento in 2011, though, everybody addressed me in standard Italian. Gradually, over the years, especially during my stays in southern Salento, the *Salentino* dialect became dominant in our conversations, especially during informal interactions with my informants. When addressed in dialect, I still tend to reply in a version of standard Italian interspersed with some dialect forms/words and syntax. In addition to standard Italian, the Salentino dialect, and Griko, a fourth language, is also spoken in the Salento area. The latter is linked to the nonmigratory Roma community that is thought to have lived in some areas of Salento since the 1700s. This language, in my experience, is currently spoken especially among elders. Unlike the neo-Greek dialect, though, it is not considered a "historical minority language," neither by the Italian state nor by the Region of Apulia. This latter element might be read together with some of the discriminatory attitudes, widespread in Italy at a popular level, against Roma communities (see, for example, Sigona 2005; Marinaro 2003. On issues about immigration in Italy in general, see, for example, Angel-Ajani 2000; Ambrosini 2013; Barberis and Boccagni 2014; Capussotti 2010).

26. See, for example, Aretxaga 2003; Taussig 1992, 1997; Williams 1977; Massumi 2015; Panagia 2009; Mazzarella 2003; Rancière 1992, 1995, 2000, 2004a, 2004b, 2006; Muehlebach 2011; U. Linke 2006; Žižek 1989; Ahmed 2004; Gorton 2007; Staiger, Cvetkovich, and Reynolds 2010; Napolitano 2016; Hinderliter et al. 2009; McLagan and McKee 2012; Butler 2012, 2015.

27. In an oft-quoted article, Brian Massumi distinguishes between affect and emotion. He defines the former as "intensity" (2002, 7) and the latter as "qualified intensity" (2002, 88).

28. In a 2009 book, Panagia explored the possibility of putting the philosophy of Rancière in conversation with the recent philosophical investigations on affects. On affects, see, for example, Thrift 2004, 2008; Navaro-Yashin 2009, 2012; Massumi 2002, 2015; Mazzarella 2003, 2004, 2009; Clough and O'Malley Halley 2007; Gregg and Seigworth 2010; Stewart 2007; Panagia 2009; Brennan 2004; Rutherford 2012; Salazàr Parreñas 2012; De Sousa 2001; Muehlebach 2011; Napolitano 2009; Gould 2010; Gorton 2007; Staiger, Cvetkovich, and Reynolds 2010; Tambar 2011; Cvetkovich 1992, 2007, 2010.

29. In this book, I refer to UDI activists as Macare and to witches as macare.

30. The story of Matteo Tafuri, a well-known Apulian alchemist who lived between the fifteenth and the sixteenth centuries, is one of medicine and Inquisition. Well known beyond Apulia, and now celebrated in Soleto, his birth town, also during the yearly event *Notte in Noir* (Night in Noir), he studied in Paris and Spain before returning home and living the last years of his life facing accusations of magic and sorcery.

31. Personal conversation in dialect, December 2015. "Macara is a bad woman, one who is not sociable, who makes curses, evil magic. Striare are even worse. They are bad tempered. . . . They come from Vaste and Diso" (two localities in the province of Lecce). For a comparison, see Pizza 2012. On "witches," see, for example, Favret-Saada 1981; Federici 2004, 2008; Sempruch 2004, 2008.

32. The union of the municipalities of the Grecìa salentina (*Unione dei comuni della Grecìa salentina*) is a consortium founded in 2000 as a result of Legislative Decree 267/2000. The Unione comprises the municipalities of Calimera, Castrignano dei Greci, Corigliano d'Otranto, Martano, Martignano, Melpignano, Soleto, Sternatia, and Zollino and was established after the recognition of Griko as a "historical minority language" (Law 482/1999) by the Italian state.

33. Another local group of feminist women founded a community of women for women, called *Le Sciare*, in a mansion in Melendugno: "Le Sciare homepage," http://www.alvearelesciare.org (accessed on March 21, 2019); "Dal Salento al Navigliarrivano le Sciare, un posto per donne," *La 27esima Ora* (blog), http://27esimaora.corriere.it/articolo/dal-salento-al-naviglio-arrivano-le-sciare-un-posto-per-donne-dove-inventare-chiacchierare/ (accessed on March 31, 2019). For folk theories on macare, see also Codacci-Pisanelli 2009.

34. On artisans, see Herzfeld 2004.

35. "Manifest@F9," *Femministe Nova* (blog), https://femministenove.wordpress.com/manifestofemministenove/ (accessed on March 21, 2019).

36. Frisa is a bread typical of Salento.

37. The feminists with whom I worked strongly believe in *separatismo*; that is, they not only do not want to involve men in their political activism but even prefer not to share space with them.

1

LOCATING VIOLENCE IN SALENTO AND BEYOND

In this chapter, I discuss violence as the object of this book. I explain how I encountered the topic of violence in my fieldwork and how I came to theorize it in reference to and beyond current anthropological debates on violence. While Italian women today do experience structural and symbolic violence, and physical aggression, these aspects of violence are not specifically the ones that affect the lives of my informants, my ethnography, and my anthropological reflections. My particular ethnographic encounters led me to frame violence in ways that do not completely overlap with those that have been commonly used in the past two decades of anthropological literature on this topic. Instead, the main area of my interest is violence against women conceptualized primarily as a cluster of discursive and affective elements and formations inflected in rhetorical and representational terms. These inhabited my informants' everyday lives. What the consequences of violence against women were and where and how they occurred are at the center of my ethnography. In particular, I analyze how violence, its possibility, and the struggle against it became battlefields in struggles of and for representation for the women I met—locally, nationally, and on the internet and other media.

Rosa

It was a nice and sunny Saturday morning in late November, and, because of the *scirocco* (a warm southern wind), the temperature was mild. Everyday life in Salento, the southeastern fringe of the Italian peninsula, is characterized by references to the winds. A popular saying of Salento defines it as the land of sun, sea, and wind (in dialect: *Salentu. Lu sule, lu mare, lu jentu*). Hardly a day passes without references to winds being made. Almost uniquely, in my experience, Salentinians refer to the *scirocco* and *tramontana*. Occasionally, people mention *faugno*, a condition experienced as an extreme version of *scirocco*. The latter is a hot, humid wind that blows from the southeast and is often blamed for feelings of oppression and irritability—and for never-drying laundry. *Tramontana*, by contrast, is a cold, dry wind that blows from the north, and, according to the people of Salento, it is responsible for rapid changes in temperature, especially in the winter, but is generally appreciated as a relief from *scirocco*.

Rosa, Veronica, and I were in a Fiat Punto, performing one of the most common activities in Salento: commenting on the change in the wind. "*Ete votatu sciroccu . . . ca pare faugnu*" (the wind has changed into *scirocco*, it seems *faugno*), Veronica said as soon as we got into the car, relying on the local vernacular to break our initial silence. For the rest of our trip the conversation went on enjoyably. We were headed to a beautiful *masseria* (mansion) surrounded by olive trees for a two-day women's sociality (*socialità femminile*) organized in honor of Carla. Rosa was a middle-aged lesbian woman who drove to Lecce, an Apulian city in the southeastern part of Italy, from another Italian region specifically for this event. Unlike most of the other women I met during my fieldwork who were engaged in homosexual and/or homoemotional relationships (see Kirtsoglou 2004), Rosa chose to define herself as a lesbian. The adoption of this identity marker was probably related to her particular history: unlike the majority of the women I met, she had been politically active in different movements, including groups that were known to be lesbian-feminist. Given the particularity of her standpoint, her experience in different sectors of Italian feminisms, and her position on the governing board of the UDI (Union of Women in Italy), I was eager to use our time together in the car to hear her perspectives on both that historical feminist association and the events of its Fifteenth Congress in Bologna.[1]

At that time, I was curious about whom the UDI women considered to be a "woman." I knew that the name of the organization had been changed from *Unione delle Donne Italiane* (Union of Italian Women) to *Unione delle Donne in Italia* (Union of the Women in Italy) some years earlier explicitly to recognize immigrants—that is, nonnative women who live in Italy—as part of the movement. However, a month earlier while attending the Bologna congress, I noticed a striking uniformity in social status, class belonging, and geographic origin among the UDI women. Moreover, I remembered that, in Bologna, it was strictly forbidden for men, including journalists, to participate or even to sit in the Farnese Chapel of the D'Accursio palace, where the congress was held. I witnessed some women escorting a male journalist out and others commenting on the inappropriateness of his presence in the room. By contrast, even if they were not members of the UDI, women could attend the meetings freely. I decided to introduce the topic semiseriously: "So, Rosa, I have a question for you, as a member of the governing board of the UDI. Am I entitled to be a member of the

UDI? You know, I am Italian, but I live in Boston . . . if the UDI is the Union of the Women in Italy . . . well, technically, it might not be possible for me to be a member." Rosa and Veronica laughed, and both offered me some reassurance: I could indeed be considered part of the UDI. I laughed as well, reciprocating their affection. I continued, "Seriously, Rosa. Who is a woman for the UDI? For example, could a transgendered or a transsexual woman be part of the UDI?" In formulating this question, I paid close and explicit attention to talking about transgendered and transsexual women. This choice, which seems obvious in English, was not in Italian (the difference between "transgendered" and "trans-sexual" was not perceived by the vast majority of Italians). In everyday language, *transessuale* was preceded almost exclusively by the masculine article *il*, even when referring to a male-to-female transsexual. By using the feminine indefinite article *una* in my question, and by adding the word *woman*, I made it obvious I wanted to take a particular stand. Rosa replied brusquely, almost with irritation: "I would not give a UDI membership card to a trans. They were not raised as women and were not exposed to the violence and to the possibility of violence in the same ways young girls are." I was surprised. Given her political past, I did not expect this answer from her. Our conversation continued gently and respectfully for the remainder of our trip, and Rosa proposed that I organize a panel with her to discuss this topic with other UDI women. That discussion never took place, and, when this topic was taken up later in front of other members of the group, it was once again dismissed in a few sentences. Nonetheless, Rosa's answer moved me deeply, and I could not get over it. In particular, I could not get over the abrupt change of ambience that my question had provoked—from friendly warmth to huffy distance. I had apparently touched a sore spot. I admit that I had felt disturbed by the implications of Rosa's line of reasoning. It was the first time as an Italian woman that I had heard such a narrative. Didn't her response marginalize or conceal the experience of violence of other human beings? Wasn't it a way to give violence additional power, that of defining who I am? How could Rosa not see this? As Koyama writes in her *Transfeminist Manifesto*, I knew that "some feminists, particularly radical lesbian feminists, have accused trans women and men of benefiting from male privilege. Male-to-female transsexuals, they argue, are socialized as boys and are thus given male privilege" (2003, 247).[2] Yet in the conversation with Rosa, what surprised me was that this gender privilege was inflected with a language of violence. According to Rosa, what made a woman a "woman" was not described in terms of the lack of particular privileges or particular rights. Not surprisingly, in our conversation in the car that day, Rosa refused to accept my understanding of "woman" as whoever defines herself as such, regardless of the criteria she uses to define herself. What was interesting to me was that she disagreed with me not primarily in the name of a biological understanding of genders, typical of Italian mainstream feminisms that follow the *pensiero della differenza sessuale*, nor on the basis of women's lack of opportunities compared to men's (including, for example, the fact of being so routinely exposed to violence). Rosa seemed to be saying that *it was violence itself and its possibility that made women "women."* At a minimum, violence constructed an imagined community of women (Anderson 1991), a "community of sense" (see Hinderliter et al. 2009; Parmigiani 2018) around being women.[3] This violence was understood as a particular type of violence, one that the UDI women rather awkwardly called *violenza sessuata* (sexed violence). The expression "sexed violence" is not widespread in the Italian language. It was coined by the UDI.[4] This sexed violence did not seem to be comparable to that to which transgendered and transsexual persons are often tragically exposed, according to Rosa. The ambivalence of constructing women as (potentially) violated women was evident to me, but not fully to her. On the one hand, it liberated new possibilities for some women, and, on the other hand, it exploited the discriminatory violence of language (Butler 2006) that defined whose violence was meaningful and whose lives were worth grieving—in Rancière's words, who "had part" and who "had no part" in society. It decided who counted as human and whose lives counted as lives (Butler 2004; see also Rancière 1999, 124; 2010, 62–75).

After having unexpectedly encountered violence early on in my fieldwork, as my ethnography unfolded, "violence" appeared as a ubiquitous reference point in what I witnessed about the ways in which Italian women, and Salentine women in particular, thought (and learned to think) about themselves.

Violence against Women in Italy: Some (Contested) Data

Narratives around violence against women and *femminicidio* were quite contested in Italy at the time of my fieldwork, and unsurprisingly the debates about them tended to be quite animated.[5] On the one hand, the emergence of these themes in the media and in Italian public opinion as a national problem presented these issues as facts (see Herzfeld 1998, 2008) about which politicians and intellectuals, in particular, were required to have an opinion. On the other hand, these opinions were far from unanimous and tended to align themselves along preexistent political party lines. In the absence of a national research organization on violence against women and *femminicidio* in Italy, gathering data on these topics required comparing the results of different sources: some of them national and some international.

According to the 2011 Global Gender Gap report, for example, which describes well-established international parameters of the World Economic

Forum, Italy ranked seventy-fourth in the world for gender equality, a particularly poor result for a country that is among the founding members of the European Union.[6] Such principally economic data are better understood when read in conjunction with other international reports, such as the UN's CEDAW (the Convention on the Elimination of All Forms of Discrimination against Women) shadow report. This shadow report on Italy, from 2011, makes the following remarks, confirmed in UN Human Rights Council special rapporteur Rashida Manjoo's report[7] on her visit to Italy in 2012: "The government formal approach to gender equality makes it impossible to adopt comprehensive and long-term strategy to combat structural discrimination against gender and sexual orientation-based discrimination. . . . Machismo attitudes are widely tolerated. The mass media and the political debate have reinforced them through frequent sexual references, stereotyped expressions and a degrading representation of the body and the role of women in society."[8]

The effects of gender discrimination and high levels of tolerance of male chauvinism in Italian society could be observed in many aspects of women's lives: from the difference in salaries between men and women and the percentage of unemployment among women compared to men (almost 45 percent of women in Italy did not have paid work) to how women were represented on TV and in other media and the 2007 ISTAT data on violence against women.[9] According to the latter, published by the Italian National Institute of Statistics, in 2006 more than one million women in Italy were the victims of male violence, which in 90 percent of the cases went unreported. In particular, the constant increase in the numbers of femminicidi—that is, the murder of women by men for reasons of gender—in Italy in the past ten years seemed particularly worrisome. According to a study by the Casa delle Donne per non Subire Violenza of Bologna, in 2010 there were 129 femminicidi—8 more than in 2009 and 45 more than in 2005. In 2011, reportedly, the number of victims of femminicidio was 129, and in 2012, 126.[10] According to the same source, which is currently one of the few organizations that tracks the number of victims, the data indicate, in 2014, 115 victims and 101 attempts of femminicidio; in 2015, 117 victims; and in 2016, 121 victims.[11] The 2013 data recorded 134 victims and 86 attempts.[12]

According to the aforementioned sources, some of the problems that Italian women faced, when involved in violence against them, were cultural and others were more directly linked to the structure of the Italian juridical system. The laws on abortion, in 1974, and divorce, in 1970 (see Molé 2013a, 84; Plesset 2006), together with the abolition of honor killings, in 1981, and the reinterpretation of sexual violence as a crime against the person, in 1996, are some examples of important achievements around women's rights in Italy. Nonetheless, as the CEDAW shadow report (2011) points out and the report of the

UN's special rapporteur for the Human Right Council (2012) confirms, these improvements failed to coalesce into an organic legal corpus of norms. The existence of an integrated system of laws on these matters could provide protection to women victims of violence and related situations (CEDAW, General Recommendation 19).[13]

In spite of the wide circulation of these data and their interpretation in Italy, in the absence of a national watchdog on femminicidio and violence against women, these data were contested. Organizations involved in reporting violence against women could not agree on the numbers, the methodologies of data collection, or the statistical analyses of these data. While some referred to these numbers to document a national problem around femminicidi and violence against women, others referred to the same data to question the reality of these phenomena. According to the Catholic online newspaper *Tempi*, for example, "while the absolute figure [of homicides in Italy] was declining, . . . the decrease was way sharper [among men] . . . [and therefore] the incidence of murders of women, that in the past was around 10–15%, [instead] increased to 25% more or less. But the numbers [of murdered women] are not increasing: they are decreasing, at least if one gives more importance to the data from *Istat* [i.e., the Italian National Institute of Statistics] rather than from those of *Casa delle Donne*, and *Telefono Rosa* [i.e., Pink line against violence against women]."[14]

The divide between those who supported and those who rejected the existence of femminicidio as a societal problem was not the only rift in relation to the perception of violence against women in Italy. Even among those who recognized violence against women as a minor (nonetheless important) issue, talking about it too often became merely a pretext for voicing political rivalries and polemicizing with political competitors.[15] My informants' activism unfolded precisely in response to such ambivalence about the reality of violence against women and femminicidi, to the use of those topics as pretexts for other political goals, and to the (transversal) framing of women as victims in need of protection. My informants told me that there was often violence even in antiviolence political stances. The so-called Law against Femminicidio (Law 119/2013) is one example of this.

Locating Violence

The women I met in Italy, like most women, certainly suffered from the effects of widespread sexism (see, for example, Guano 2007; Plesset 2006; Passerini 1996; Molé 2012), from economic precariousness and unemployment (see, e.g., Molé 2012; Muehlebach 2012; Fantoni 2007), and from an economic gender gap.[16]

They were indeed the objects of various forms of violence, discrimination, and sexual harassment. Nonetheless, in their everyday lives violence typically took on other connotations. Similar to what Pesmen claimed of the "Russian soul," I found that what the women I met called sexed violence—that is, the violence perpetrated by one gender on the other, as they told me in several occasions, was in fact a "deceptive lexical item: *not just* a notion, image, or entity but" something that involved "an aesthetics, a way of feeling about and being in the world, a shifting focus and repertoire of discourses, rituals, beliefs, and practices more and less available" to them (2000, 9). I encountered violence and its phantoms (Aretxaga 2003) and phantasmic dimensions (Navaro-Yashin 2012) as elements that could "dominate a speech act, performance, work of art, or image without . . . being present."[17] They could "lurk in other terms, in a tone of a voice, in a gesture, expression, or pause" (Pesmen 2000, 12). This does not mean that violence was not a concrete experience for my informants. On the contrary, violence, the possibility of violence, and the ways one reacted to it did have tangible and important roles in the lives of the feminist women I met. These roles could be affective, emotional, practical, aesthetic, and ethical. Mostly, though, these roles tended to be framed beyond an understanding of violence in terms of physical and psychological trauma (for a comparison, see Fassin and Rechtman 2009; Stringer 2014).[18] As I illustrate in this book, violence-as-suffering did affect my informants, but suffering was just one aspect of what violence against women meant and did in their lives. Violence against women, and the ways they reacted to it, was extremely important to the women I met, in shaping their lives. Violence and reactions to violence set women's political agendas by influencing discourses and practices around women's activism and its political goals, by structuring the ways in which the women thought about themselves, and by informing practices, performances, and representations of specific inflections of what I call "modern feminist womanhood." In my ethnographic experience, in other words, I could witness and experience forms, somehow unexpected, of what Scheper-Hughes and Bourgois (2004, 1) call the "productive" and "reproductive" dimensions of violence.

The discovery early on in my fieldwork that my informants spoke of and felt violence in their lives and discourses primarily but not only as an existential experience—that is, as a traumatic condition of suffering that was the result of certain particular acts or relationships—came as a surprise to me. Even more surprising, and somewhat unsettling, was acknowledging the power that my informants were giving to violence. The latter emerged clearly, and not only in the aforementioned vignette as a decisive dimension in their attempts to define what being a woman was and was not in contemporary Italy. As women, the circumstance of being potential objects of violence and systematically also objects of *representational* violence (see chap. 3), became the kernel around which my informants started to think about themselves. This produced a community of sense of women, who gathered together not in the name of shared ideals or ideal-types but primarily around the *feeling* of being (potentially) violated. This new political subject, I claim, first began to appear in Italy in 2008, with the UDI's national campaign against sexed violence, and developed particularly since 2011, setting the stage for the emergence of a new women's question around femminicidio and violence against women.

If my informants did not frame violence primarily as something to which women are subjected, nonetheless they considered it as structuring, in a fundamental, almost ontological manner, the particular ways of their being in the world, and of "being women" in general. In this framework, how one reacted to (and not just dealt with) violence played a central role in the ethical and aesthetic axiologies (i.e., systems of values) of my informants. My particular ethnographic encounters led me to frame violence in ways that do not completely overlap with those that have been commonly used in the past three decades of anthropological literature on this topic.[19] Although some scholars have not hesitated to mention the possible problems of using violence as an anthropological analytical tool (see Jeganathan 1997), many others have been feeling the urge to put violence at the center of their ethnographic accounts and anthropological analyses.[20] Heuristically, since often the two dimensions are imbricated, as some of the literature on violence shows (see, for example, Taussig 1986; Sluka 2000; and the literature on state terror), one can divide the scholarly production into two broad areas.[21] On the one hand, some scholars have tried to make sense of specific traumatic events or troubled areas.[22] On the other hand, there are academics who have instead focused on more structural (see, for example, Farmer 2003; Farmer and Haun 2010) or symbolic (see Bourdieu and Wacquant 2004) types of violence.[23] Among other topics, in this latter corpus of research, researchers investigated the violent dimensions of illness, disease, bureaucracy, media images, and the state and showed how "social suffering results from what political, economic, and institutional power does to people and, reciprocally, from how these forms of power themselves influence responses to social problems" (Das et al. 2000, ix).[24] Within this perspective, "personal problems" are inextricably linked to "societal problems": "If suffering is a social experience," then violence can be found "within the structure of society as part of our ordinary lives" (ix).[25] This latter corpus of research is important for my ethnography, in particular in order to understand the role of potential violence in my informants' lives.[26] The acknowledgment of the dynamics and effects of structural and symbolic violence—the latter being "the violence which is exercised upon a social agent with his or her complicity" (Bourdieu and Wacquant 2004,

272)—helps redefine not just the loci where violence can be found but also the times defined and redefined by violence.[27] As Scheper-Hughes and Bourgois point out, "Positing a violence continuum comprised of a multitude of 'small wars and invisible genocides'" (19) that goes beyond specific states of exception and comprises both times of war and peace "allows us to see the capacity and the willingness—if not enthusiasm—of ordinary people, the practical technicians of the social consensus, to enforce genocidal-like crimes against categories of rubbish people" (20). In my ethnographic experience, the emergence of a community of sense around violence against women did precisely this: it created an understanding of violence against women within a continuum that had femminicidio as its extreme manifestation.

Within such a framework, the initiatives that aimed at fighting violence against women (whether carried out by institutions or by other women's groups) became central in my informants' political practice. The discursive and semiotic aspects of antiviolence campaigns were seen as pivotal in their struggle against "patriarchy."[28] In this respect, the way violence was understood by my informants resonated with Hartman's reading of the language on slaves' rights in *Scenes of Subjection*. In this book, the author inquires into "the ways that the recognition of humanity and individuality acted to tether, bind, and oppress," by focusing on "the encroachment of power that takes place through notions of reform, consent, and protection" behind declarations of "slave humanity" (1997, 5). Hartman's argument speaks to my ethnographic material in as much as it points out that there are forms of "domination enabled by the recognition of humanity, licensed by the invocation of rights, and justified by the grounds of liberty and freedom" (6).

In sum, I am certainly interested in the forms and incidence of violent behaviors against women in contemporary Italy and in the cultural constructions and genealogies of what is considered violent in this particular area of the world, as Whitehead (2004) suggests. Yet the focus of my interest revolves around violence against women conceptualized primarily as a cluster of discursive and affective elements and formations inflected in rhetorical and representational terms. These inhabited my informants' everyday lives.[29] Hence, what violence against women did, and how, is at the center of my ethnography. In particular, I analyze how violence—its possibility and the struggle against it—became central in struggles of and for representation. This representational struggle played an important role in directing and shaping the lives of the women I met, as well as in shaping this book. My interpretive move does not aim to deny the personal and collective experiences of violence that my informants and women in Italy suffer: I do not question the reality of these dimensions (both in the women's narratives and in the statistical data available).

My ethnographic encounters, instead, revealed how "violence is a slippery concept—nonlinear, productive, destructive, and reproductive" (Scheper-Hughes and Bourgois 2004, 1), and how, as a discursive device "interfused" (Das, Kleinman, and Lock 1997, ix) with affective overtones, it shapes the personal and political lives of the Italian women I met.

Eugenia

I met Eugenia on the first day of my fieldwork, in September 2011. The temperatures were still summery, and she was working with Mena at the feminist bookstore's stall at the yearly meeting of the Scuola della Differenza organized by the University of Salento. Her dark hair and eyes and warm smile caught my attention as she was trying to sell books to a couple of women who, like me, were attending the meeting and had stopped by. I started looking at the bookstall, too, realizing that it was the first time I had seen so many books on feminist themes written in Italian. I immediately smiled at Eugenia and Mena and asked for information on the different Italian feminist journals: *DWF* (Donna Woman Femme), *Via Dogana* (the journal edited by the Women's Bookstore of Milan), and *Diotima* (a journal connected with the University of Verona). At that time, I was unaware of the existence of so many written materials on feminism and women's issues in Italy. I immediately started asking questions of Mena and Eugenia, whose passion for feminist themes animated their social interactions. Eugenia explained to me many of the issues around the UDI and pensiero della differenza sessuale and pointed out to me the feminist "celebrities" who were attending the Scuola della Differenza (whom I did not know): Luisa Muraro, Lia Cigarini, but especially Pina Nuzzo. The latter, a Salentine woman raised in Galatina, was at the time the national delegate of the UDI and a close friend of—and a political, emotional, and existential reference point for—all the Macare. She had been part of the UDI for decades: in Modena, first, where she had moved after high school, and later in Lecce and Rome. Eugenia and I spent a long time chatting that day, both at the bookstall and during a couple of coffee breaks. It did not take much for us to become friends, and while Eugenia talked to me about the UDI and her personal story within it, Mena introduced me to all of the other Macare and invited me to their events. Which of them was the first to introduce me to the UDI is still a matter of playful debate between the two.

Eugenia was a woman in her thirties. She lived with her parents in a small town a few kilometers from Lecce. She had been living there since she was born, although she spent some time in the north during her college years. She had graduated a few years before I met her in 2011 and, I learned, had only worked off and on since she had completed her MA. When I met her, she was enrolled in a computer-programming course—one of the many courses she attended since her graduation—that she seemed to enjoy very much. She was single at that time and willing to share with me information about her recent personal life. Our chats included a fair amount of picture browsing and comment reading on Facebook and discussions on the romantic pasts of common acquaintances and of women she knew but I did not. Mostly, our conversations on her romantic life seemed to me to have the performative effect of distancing her personal history and narrative from the failing emotional lives of other women. It was a way of allowing me to become acquainted with her by finding out what she thought she was not, or what she did not want to be. In the course of this book, it becomes clear that her performance was a political practice, but I did not realize that at the time. One night, early in our relationship, Eugenia drove me home. I was sitting in her car in front of my apartment. It was late for me, as I was not yet acquainted with the rhythms of life in Salento. I felt anxious since, before leaving home, I had promised my three-year-old son that I would be back in time to put him to bed, and it was already way past his regular bedtime. For Eugenia, though, immersed in Salentine habits, it was early (just late afternoon), so she felt that it was perfectly appropriate to continue to indulge in conversation and to give voice to the flow of her thoughts.[30] "Giovanna, you don't know how many girls around here think that jealousy is a sign of *true* love. I know many girls who justify and even look for a jealous, violent man." This sentence came out of the blue, without—or so it seemed to me—any connection with the previous one. Retrospectively, I think that the connection was very clear: we were talking about feminism. Feminism was a strong motivational element and identity marker in Eugenia's life, and a pretty unusual one for Italian women, especially of her age. When we talked about feminism, Eugenia loved quoting her grandmother, who, given her poor origins and lack of education (a very frequent feature in Italian women of her age and economic class), could be defined as a feminist (*femminista*) in all but name. Apparently, having heard the word *femminista* for the first time from Eugenia, the old woman had asked her: "What is this being *femminista* about?" Eugenia claims to have answered: "Being *femminista* is fighting for the dignity of women, *nonna* (grandma)!" At this point the old woman apparently replied, with a bit of disillusionment: "Oooh, I see. So . . . I have been *femminista* for my whole life without knowing it!"

Dignity, violence, and (the absence of) intimate relationships: all these seemed to be at the core of Eugenia's experience of what being a feminist was and what it was not. If, on the one hand, it was obvious that she was looking for romance in her life, she also appeared to be proud of not being in a situation like those of the many women she talked about: involved in abusive (hetero-sexual) relationships. If violent relationships were so ubiquitous, she implied, not having one was a mark of a feminist in a "patriarchal" context, and a way to respect one's own dignity (see below). On more than one occasion, Eugenia seemed to be particularly sensitive to the topic of women and violence; every time she mentioned this subject she became quite emotional. She would lower her voice, incline her head, and move her hands nervously. On one occasion, I recall, she described how she felt physically sick and psychologically unsta-ble as a result of the marital problems of a person she knew well (a relative, perhaps).

* * *

It was now the beginning of 2012, and the first time Eugenia and I had met in a couple of months. She had been quite busy with a temporary job, and we did not have the chance to see each other or talk by phone. She asked me, "Giovanna, did you hear the news?" I did not respond as I was not sure to what she was referring. Given her bodily expressions, I thought it might be better to wait for her to continue. "Did you hear about that girl who was murdered?" She was referring to one of the many femminicidi that took place in Italy in the first days of 2012. Neither of us knew the murdered woman personally, and the homicide had taken place in another city, far from Salento. Nonetheless, it appeared clear to me that this news affected her personally—though, I confess, I did not respond that way myself. Of course, I was sorry to hear about another femminicidio, but the news did not have the same effect on me as it did on her, for it did not touch me personally. Nonetheless, I felt compelled to show concern and I found myself mimicking her body gestures: I frowned, lowered my voice, started to talk slowly, and occasionally shook my head. I also found myself wondering whether I was being cynical, insensitive, or, even worse, compliant with patriarchal hegemonic discourses: Eugenia's reaction (rather than the news itself) affected me deeply.

Why did our responses to the murder of a woman appear to be so different? What was all this about? I was puzzled: I had seen Eugenia in various circum-stances before and thought I could recognize when she was worried, angry, stressed, or sad. Her behavior and expressions that day did not easily fit into any of those categories.

After a few months of silence, I contacted Eugenia by email. Some per-sonal circumstances had distanced her from the group, and I had not had the chance to meet her in person for a long time. I found Eugenia as I had left her: busy dealing with family relations, concerned about her life as a woman, and extremely warm and generous in her exchange with me. On that occasion, I asked her what she feels, emotionally and physically, when she hears about a femminicidio or about episodes of violence on women. This is what she said:

> At the beginning it is as if someone has punched me in the stomach and my first thought is: "No, it happened again." Then, I feel I can't breathe (*mi sento mancare l'aria*). This reaction comes from the fact that I have suffered from asthma since I was in elementary school. The allergist explained to me that asthma is my mechanism of self-defense against intense emotional shocks. Then goose bumps. I can't control any of these [reactions]. It is as if my body reacts independently to the input: femminicidio. This is not something new for me, though, since I've always experienced violence in a visceral way. When the war in Iraq started, I couldn't sleep for a week, since I kept thinking about the number of persons that would have been killed by the bombings. However, when a woman is murdered, the feeling is more immediate for me. I don't know if I can explain it properly, but it is as if I feel I'm right next to her and myself a potential victim of a violent man. I imagine her smile that's no longer there, especially when I see her picture. And I feel as if I didn't do enough to stop the violence from happening.

Eugenia continued by referring to a recent (2013) dramatic event involving the killing of someone she knew personally, an event that touched her deeply. She concluded: "Before all this, talking about violence against women, for me, was something that still had not touched me 'directly.' Now it is different; it is even more visceral than in the past. Because I have seen with my own eyes the results of this [i.e., men's] sick possessiveness."

Eugenia's reactions and words moved me: I found the affective intensity she felt when talking about femminicidio and violence against women almost palpable. I found it overwhelming; the various shades of her affective tones pierced me so deeply that, somehow, they affected my own perceptions. In fact, I was so overwhelmed that I was no longer sure of what I was really perceiving. I felt confused but curious to understand what was happening to her—and to myself, too. Only months later, I realized that all this had to do with political practices.[31] While Eugenia's sensitivity might be considered exceptional, her reactions to the news of femminicidi and of violence against women did not seem to me to be idiosyncratic behavior at all. Often, in the field, I noticed that every single time a reference to a femminicidio or to episodes of violence against women became part of a conversation among the women with whom I was working, I would register a change in the ambience of the conversation and witness affective and bodily performances that I could not easily understand and frame according to the emotional categories I thought I shared with my informants. This happened, for example, while watching the news on the occasion of the 2011 International Day against Violence against Women (November 25) or while women informants were recalling the murder of a woman—whom they did not know personally—that had happened months or years before. On those occasions, every single woman of the group in her own way displayed a particular form of affective involvement that achieved the same results: the marking and performing of a strong discontinuity with the conversation at hand, and a shift in the tone of the communicative verbal and nonverbal exchanges. As a result, while I was always feeling as if I were missing something, I also felt that I was getting closer to the activists, precisely in virtue of this shared, embodied, and relational involvement. This puzzled me, since I could not really *understand* what was going on. The ways I perceived Elisabetta, Marta, Eugenia, and the others reacting to femminicidi and cases of violence against women (enacted or potential) were peculiar in two ways. First, the women of the group performed various mannerisms, each one of them engaging in somewhat different behaviors and bodily gestures. Second, for every single woman of the group, these performances differed from the bodily reactions each one of them showed separately in relation to discrete emotions they (and I) recognized, such as fear, worry, anxiety, and stress. My perceptions were somewhat supported by my informants' own words. When I asked some of them, in private individual conversations, to describe what they felt emotionally and physically in one of those affectively intense circumstances, most of them had some trouble associating their feelings with a discrete emotion. Apparently, there was no single word that could describe their feelings. All the women—even those who mentioned one specific emotion as being prevalent—tended to describe their feelings by describing their bodily reactions. Elisabetta, for example, claimed that she feels "anger with weeping" (*rabbia con pianto*) when she hears about a femminicidio, whereas when a newspaper article justifies a femminicidio as a "crime of passion" she just feels "angry." By contrast, Marta described what she feels when she hears about violence against women as "not really anger" (*rabbia*) but something like a strong emotion that gets her in the gut (*un'emozione molto forte che mi prende nella pancia*), or as "tumult in the gut" (*un tumulto nella pancia*). By contrast, Lucia feels overwhelmed (*mi sento sopraffatta*) and tries to control her anger, which manifests as feelings of being smothered (*sentirsi soffocare*) and not being able to get enough air (*mi manca l'aria*). Veronica describes feeling "like a powerful hurricane, almost devastating, that can't find its way to assert its power over that dark shadow that is violence."[32] There was something confusing to me about their behaviors, something I could not pinpoint precisely but that definitely affected me. This confusion lasted only until I realized that I should not try to *understand* the reactions of the Macare but to *sense* them, in order to *make sense* of what was happening.

Violence was a ubiquitous topic among the feminists I met in Salento in 2011. Directly or indirectly, it popped up, often unexpectedly, in both public and private circumstances. Before debates about violence began to be an every-day topic in the Italian media (as gradually happened over the following cou-ple of years), while I was in Salento, I encountered the topic of violence quite frequently. For example, I heard Pina Nuzzo talking about violence against women; I witnessed Luisa Muraro at a meeting organized by the feminists of *La Casa delle Donne of Lecce* (Lecce women's house) on February 28, 2012, specu-lating on aspects of justifiable violence perpetrated by women; and I watched it act as subtext to a meeting on journalism as civic commitment at a book fair in Campi Salentina. Yet, mostly at that time, femminicidio and violence popped up out of the blue for me, in informal conversations.

My Words Are My Dress: The Web as a Political Platform; Digital Media as a Dimension of the Salento Hyperplace

Carla, Marta, and I had been fantasizing about a trip to Bari's IKEA for weeks, as a break in our Leccese routine. Oddly, it appeared that finding the right day was tougher than expected, due to last-minute obligations or mishaps. Finally, one Thursday morning we met in front of a bar in Lecce and, after drinking our first espresso of the day with a *pasticciotto* (a typical Salentine breakfast treat), our one-day leisure trip started.

The atmosphere was relaxed and joyful: we were clearly very happy to be there together. Nonetheless, as soon as Marta, who was driving, started the car, Carla, who was seated in the back, took her laptop out of her backpack and switched it on. She wanted to check her Facebook profile, and she turned her USB hotspot router on. I thought this would take just a few minutes, and I was eager to exploit the car drive to talk about the UDI and our lives and to get to know each other better. Somehow this still happened, but in ways that I would not have anticipated. Carla spent the whole time (a two-hour drive) on Facebook: what "happened" there was the main topic of the whole trip. Carla told us about her posts, and how and why she published them. She told us about people's comments online, and asked our advice while typing, retyping, edit-ing, and reediting her own comments. She carefully weighed every single word, explaining why she made some choices and not others. She considered very carefully every hidden allusion or possible reading, and these became subjects of our conversation in the car as well. For Carla, taking care of her Facebook profile was a matter of image, of being seen, of being appraised. No detail could be left unconsidered. Similarly, the reactions of others to her comments, and to her and others' comments on comments, were treated with great attention and consideration. Who wrote what, when, and where were dimensions that gave Carla insights not just on the Facebook personas but also on the degree of political feminist engagement of her Facebook friends. This practice clearly produced structures of belonging and contributed to the creation of ethical and aesthetic patterns of modern feminist womanhood.[33]

Smartphones, laptops, notebooks, netbooks, and other devices of the sort were an almost unavoidable part of my everyday life with the feminists in Salento. These technological devices made the connections between the local communities with whom I was working and the broader Italian one quite close. In fact, they were an inescapable reference point for the construction of "senses" in the Salento hyperplace and for my ethnographic research. What happened on Facebook was an inevitable dimension of the ordinary life of the feminist Salentine activists. A few years later, I continue to talk or chat over Skype and through WhatsApp messages with some of the women I met in Salento; now, as then, who wrote, commented, quoted, and posted what and when on Facebook is always part of our exchanges. One of the elements that became immediately evident by hanging out then with the UDI feminists was that a large part of the information, topics, debates, activities, and agendas they were involved with was established by their engagement with the internet—mostly blogs and Facebook. As soon as I started meeting more feminists—for example, by traveling to Bologna and Rome with my UDI informants, following the UDI Congress and self-convocations (*autoconvocazioni*)—and becoming their friend on Facebook, I realized that many of these women put a lot of daily effort and energy into posting, commenting, linking, liking, discussing, glossing, quoting, sharing, and emailing media concerning women's issues from a feminist perspective. This practice involved performances and, I claim, was performative of "modern feminist womanhood" in the Italian context (see below). It was widespread at that time, and it is even more so today. While Facebook seemed to be the preferred platform, some of the UDI feminists (sparingly) used Twitter and YouTube, and wrote on blogs (both personal and collective), sometimes signing the articles with a nickname. The videos posted ranged from video recordings of events to ironic creations, from photo-video narratives of particularly significant experiences to audio-video letters for their political opponents. Yet most of the feminists I met appeared to be regular followers of a number of web pages and blogs, the consultation of which soon became, and still is, part of my own regular internet routine.[34] The daily activities of the Salentine activists, and of others I did not meet but who are friends of friends on Facebook and who I learned to know by virtue of their posts being reposted, repetitively commented upon, requoted, and so on, encompassed many forms. These comprised signing petitions; organizing email-bombings against brands that, according to them, for example, objectify women for the purpose of selling products; bickering with other feminist groups that make claims different from their own; publicly unfriending acquaintances who appear to have views that in their opinion are detrimental to women's self-determination; and posting and reposting viral images in support of women's causes.

Interestingly, as soon as I entered this online feminist world (one that became a second, and very important, field of my research and that I practiced for more than five years), I noticed that much of the daily exchange of this virtual community of feminists revolved around issues of violence against women and femminicidio. Sometimes it popped up around the last woman murdered, sometimes around sexual violence, sometimes against the local and national rendering of this type of news by the media, and sometimes against the public use of images of battered women. In any case, paralleling my off-line experience, the topic of violence was also ubiquitous online. In the absence of a governmental research institution concerned with violence against women in Italy, there were blogs that counted femminicidi; these were and are always quoted and posted, requoted and reposted.[35] The zeal, time, and passion put into these online activities surprised me then, and still does now; the Italian feminists I met spent several hours per day Googling, reading, commenting, writing, and posting materials in favor of the feminist cause against violence, and in so doing demonstrated their serious commitment, fond dedication, and enthusiastic eagerness. Facebook was a serious matter: each comment, like, share, or post was meant and felt to be a political statement.

Facebook, in particular, and the internet, in general, were considered as a field of/for the representation of "feminist womanhood" and as a space for challenging the dominant gazes on women and violence against women. As one of these very politically committed women wrote on Facebook once: "If I think about Facebook as a public square, I do not put on the first clothes I find for going out. Since I know I can be seen, I dress myself with care. My words are my dress." In this public square, "public declarations are a great responsibility."[36] Pina Nuzzo was even more explicit when she wrote on the Facebook page of the Donnae Lab (see chap. 2): "The 'friendships' and the 'shares' on the web re-define the profiles of a political geography that cannot be led back to 'territory.' Thus, through the written word, some individual women and some groups acquired an 'authority' that goes beyond the web" (November 2, 2013).

The affective and aesthetic dimensions of violence against women permeated my days among the Salentine feminist women with whom I worked. Their stories and political activities, though, strongly resonated with what was happening at a more general level in Italy at that time. If this was the situation when I started my fieldwork, in the past five years I have witnessed the progressive shift of this online community from being a self-referential virtual community of feminists to having an impact on Italian media. Moreover, it had an important role in constructing a community of sense of women—specifically of (potentially) violated women—that gradually started to represent women as a political subject vis-à-vis Italian public opinion.[37]

Women, Violence, and "Patriarchy": A Perspective from Italy

The emergence of public concerns around femminicidio in Italy in the past five years has had many consequences. On the one hand, for example, it opened up new possibilities for recognizing nationally the presence and effects of violence against women in contemporary Italy. Yet, on the other hand, public stands to counter violence against women started to be seen as restructuring and reinforcing images of womanhood that, according to my informants, supported "patriarchal" values and imaginaries. This also happened when antiviolence messages were subsumed and spread by other women's groups. It is precisely in this context, where compliance with and resistance to "patriarchy" blended (see, for a parallel, Mankekar 1999; El-Kholy 2002), that I understand the existential and political lives of the feminists with whom I worked and the representational struggle that informs both my ethnographic experience and this book.[38] If the overall claim of this book is, to paraphrase Mankekar (1999), that hegemony and resistance are imbricated phenomena, this claim stems from my experience with and analyses of the discourses, practices, and affects that the feminists I worked with mobilized in order to react to the shape-shifting features of "patriarchy."[39] In particular, it develops around the Salentine activists' imagination and representation of new possibilities of being a woman in contemporary Italy, possibilities constructed in contrast to commonsensical representations of women-as-victims that my informants identified as "patriarchal." I consider the representation of being a woman, which is a practice in the sense of both "work" and "labor" (see Lambek 2010; chap. 6), as an important form of political activism engaged by my informants.

The feminisms I encountered in Italy differed considerably from the ones I had encountered and studied previously in the United Kingdom and afterward in North America. The Italian activists I met adhered to what is called pensiero della differenza sessuale. In spite of the multiracial Italian context, the Italian feminism I encountered was not intersectional, and it rested on an unnuanced conflation of sex and gender. The word *intersectionality* was hardly known among the feminists with whom I worked. The multiracial Italian context only recently seems to have started challenging the mainstream political agenda of Italian feminists, especially with the *Non Una di Meno* movement, a recent development of Italian feminism, not active at the time of my research.[40] This lack of intersectionality concerned different women: from migrants to transsexuals, from transgendered to persons with disabilities (*con disabilità*). The only dimension that might have been taken into account by the Italian feminisms I encountered was economic, since economically precarious workers were starting to raise their voices within the Italian feminist movement.

I found all these elements quite challenging, especially at the beginning of my fieldwork. Trained in gender studies within other feminist traditions, I first strove to find a common language and ideological framework in order to talk about women's issues, and I struggled to follow definitions of *woman* that I found problematic (see, e.g., the vignette on Rosa above). The activists with whom I worked defined women primarily by their biological sex. For them, woman-as-a-political-subject was the result of some specific positionalities: those of white, Italian, middle-class, middle-aged, educated women. Though I personally found them restrictive, these are nonetheless the definitions I use in the descriptions of my informants' points of view in this book. In spite of the limits of such definitions of *woman*, my ethnographic research shows that Salentine activists, through the aesthetic and ethical practices that I am narrating here, were moving toward an opening up of the categories of womanhood, in particular in their focus on becoming (see, in particular, chap. 6). This perspective, I claim, while firmly rooted in the pensiero della differenza sessuale, had undoubtedly generative and expansive effects.

The pensiero della differenza sessuale in Italy is conceived of as a practical philosophy, "a philosophy of those who think through a modification of themselves" (Muraro quoted by Scarparo 2005, 40), a philosophy that is not primarily founded on women's rights but rather on the "activation of female subjectivity in order to produce socio-symbolic change" (Scarparo 2005, 37). Its object of thought "is not the social condition of women, nor the identity, and much less the essence of women. Its subject is a sexed singularity that considers her/himself the other, and [considers] reality outside the prescribed and prescriptive definitions of sexual identity that the symbolic order transmits to us" (Dominijanni 2005, 27–28). For the activists I met, a woman was primarily a sexed person who considered herself as other within a given symbolic order. The latter, which my informants called "patriarchy," was characterized by phallogocentrism and was understood to be historically exclusionary of women's subjectivities. According to the Italian feminists I met—influenced by Luce Irigaray and by the Psych&Po French feminism (see, e.g., Bono and Kemp 1991, 12)—the symbolic dimension of Western society was characterized by phallogocentrism. What was defined as subject, citizen, and human being, and the language used to define them, were each intrinsically masculine. In Carla Lonzi's words, "The feminine problem is the relationship of any woman—deprived as she is of power, of history, of culture, of a role of her own—to any man: his power, his history, his culture, his absolute role" (from *Sputiamo su Hegel*, in Bono and Kemp 1991, 40). According to pensiero della differenza sessuale (and to my informants), sexual difference (taken mostly acritically to be biologically determined) is the "stronger and most basic characteristic of humanity" (Muraro 2012, 62).

In order to pursue their political activity, it was this practical philosophy of difference, rather than equality, to which Italian feminists adhered. According to them, equality with men should not be the goal of feminism. "The world of equality is the world of legalized oppression and one-dimensionality," where "equality between the sexes is merely a mask with which woman's inferiority is disguised" (Lonzi quoted in Bono and Kemp 1991, 41–42). What is meant by woman's equality "is usually her right to share in the exercise of power within society, once it is accepted that she is possessed of the same abilities as man"; therefore, "existing as a woman does not imply participation in male power but calls into question the very concept of power. It is in order to avoid this attack that we are now granted inclusion in the form of equality" (41). For philosophers of the pensiero della differenza sessuale, the reconfiguration of the symbolic order coincides to a certain extent with the pursuit of difference.

Among the most recent developments of the pensiero della differenza sessuale, I find Braidotti's rethinking of sexual difference within a postmodern perspective as the most pertinent that I encountered in my fieldwork for describing the political activity of constructing womanhood. According to Braidotti (2003), in fact, this pursuit of difference entails facing a challenge of nonrepresentability by working on representations, on the collective images of woman—both symbolic *and* embodied, cultural *and* affective, intellectual *and* emotional.[41] Therefore, in Braidotti's understanding of the pensiero della differenza sessuale as well as in my ethnographic observation of the lives of my informants, "women" become "subjects-in process," "mutants," "the other of the Other" (Braidotti 2002, 12; see also Dell'Abate-Çelebi 2016). This subject, rooted in sexual difference but open to becoming and determined to repossess "patriarchal" imaginaries, is the one that I encountered and that I address and narrate in this book. Their *difference* was played in a dimension of becoming—in particular, of becoming "other." As I show in the chapters that follow, the struggle of and for representation of the Salentine activists embodies such a perspective. Their pursuit of sexual difference entailed an openness, rooted in the pensiero della differenza sessuale but open to becoming, that took many forms: from becoming something they could not anticipate to becoming something that they were—only not *yet*, from generating dissensus to "producing witnesses." One of the main examples of this is the subjects-in-process that existed in my informants' peculiar way of understanding political change. The feminists I met, women who upheld a radical understanding of the relationships between the political and the personal, indeed aimed at changing the performances of seeing and sensing around womanhood and violence against women. Yet, they were less concerned with the actual effects of their representations on their publics than with the power of the representations themselves in transforming their own lives from within. The ethical and aesthetic dimensions of their political activism were therefore more focused on their own *becoming* than in catering to actual or imagined publics. This element was *particularly* evident in the difference that exists between the performance of bella figura (see, in particular, Plesset 2006; Nardini 1999; Pipyrou 2014a) and what my informants referred to with the expression fare-come-se (doing-as-if, see chap. 6). While bella figura caters to the expectations of their audience and publics, following clear and shared behaviors and norms, fare-come-se does not. Performances and practices of fare-come-se exist in a space of desire and enact something that it is not there, yet. Performing *as if* has consequences both on the subjects who perform and on their publics: through performances of fare-come-se that were linked to modern feminist womanhood and to being witnesses, my informants both discovered themselves for what they were not yet (and could not foresee before the performances took place) and created dissensus.

The movement toward an opening up of the concept of womanhood and to becoming other that I witnessed during my fieldwork, I argue, might be read also in the recent mainstream elaborations of the intersectional feminism of *Non Una di Meno* and suggests a new development and understanding of pensiero della differenza sessuale.[42] In order to better locate the experiences of the activists that I met, I now offer an overview of the history of the Italian feminisms.

Notes

1. The Fifteenth Congress of the UDI (2011), for many reasons, represented a controversial moment in the history of the UDI. The two main pressure groups in the association had had a harsh and not entirely politically correct confrontation on some issues regarding the present and the future of the group.

2. On the relationship between radical feminism and trans women, see also, for example, Sweeney 2004; Jeffreys 1997.

3. This type of violence is primarily not historically but ontologically conceived. It does not primarily belong to the past, but it is conceived as a condition that defines "being women." For a comparison, see Sorge, Padwe, and Shneiderman 2015; Sorge 2015; and Giordano 2005, 2014.

4. I am not sure why the UDI women did not use the expression "gendered violence" (*violenza di genere*), but they were, in general, not acquainted with the idea of there being a

distinction between sex and gender, and even less so with its critiques. In agreement with the pensiero della differenza sessuale, they considered sexual difference to be a biological and fundamental attribute of being human.

5. To a certain extent, they still are.

6. Sixty-ninth in 2014. See "Rankings," World Economic Forum, http://reports.weforum .org/global-gender-gap-report-2014/rankings/ (accessed March 21, 2019).

7. "Report of the Special Rapporteur on Violence against Women, Its Causes and Conse-quences, on her mission to Italy" (January 15–26, 2012), GE.12-14254, Human Rights Council, United Nations, https://www.ohchr.org/Documents/HRBodies/HRCouncil/RegularSession /Session20/A-HRC-20-16-Add2_en.pdf (accessed April 7, 2019).

8. "Italy Submits CEDAW Shadow Report," *30 Years CEDAW* (blog), http://cedaw30 .wordpress.com/2011/07/13/italy-submits-cedaw-shadow-report/ (accessed March 21, 2019).

9. "I dati dell'Istat sul lavoro femminile: ancora grande divario tra uomini e donne," Winning Women Institute, http://winningwomeninstitute.org/news/i-dati-istat-sul-lavoro -femminile/ (accessed March 21, 2019). See, for example, Lorella Zanardo's documentary "*Il Corpo delle Donne,*" http://www.ilcorpodelledonne.net/; Gribaldo and Zapperi 2010, 2012; Hipkins 2011; "Quasi una donna su due in Italia non lavora e non cerca un posto. L'Istat rileva che a settembre il tasso di inattività femminile è pari al 48,9%," *La Repubblica*, http://d.repubblica.it/frasi/2011/11/01/news/donne_lavoro-630099/ (accessed March 21, 2019); the ISTAT data can be accessed at I.Stat, http://dati.istat.it/ (accessed March 21, 2019). See also Ufficio Statistico della Regione Puglia, 2013. Focus Novembre 2013. Recenti dinamiche del mercato del lavoro femminile in Puglia.

10. The study was based on the information published by national and local press. The numbers are just indicative, since some data, for example, about sex workers and illegal immigrants, are not easy to access. Nonetheless, the numbers outlined in this study are worrisome.

11. "Femicidi in Italia. Dati sintetici 2015," *Femicidio* (blog), https://femicidiocasadonne .wordpress.com/2016/12/01/femicidi-in-italia-dati-sintetici-2015/ (accessed March 21, 2019); "I dati del femicidio in Italia (2016)," *Femicidio* (blog), https://femicidiocasadonne.wordpress .com/2017/11/22/i-dati-del-femicidio-in-italia-2017/ (accessed March 21, 2019).

12. "Femicidi in Italia. Dati sintetici 2015," *Femicidio* (blog), https://femicidiocasadonne .wordpress.com/2016/12/01/femicidi-in-italia-dati-sintetici-2015/ (accessed March 21, 2019); "I dati del 2014. Le donne in Italian continuano ad essere uccise," *Femicidio* (blog), https:// femicidiocasadonne.wordpress.com/2015/11/25/i-dati-del-2014-le-donne-in-italia-continuano -ad-essere-uccise/ (accessed March 21, 2019); "Seminario: 'Femminicidio: una lettura femminista' 29 novembre-Bologna," *Femicidio* (blog), http://femicidiocasadonne.wordpress .com/tag/casa-delle-donne-per-non-subire-violenza/ (accessed March 21, 2019); "Indagine Sui Femicidi in Italia Realizzata Sui Dati Della Stampa Nazionale e Locale: Anno 2014," *Femici-dio* (blog), https://femicidiocasadonne.files.wordpress.com/2015/11/report-femicidi-20141.pdf (accessed March 21, 2019).

13. "General recommendations made by the Committee on the Elimination of Discrimin-ation against Women," UN Entity for Gender Equality and the Empowerment of Women, https://www.un.org/womenwatch/daw/cedaw/recommendations/recomm.htm (accessed April 7, 2019).

14. Rodolfo Casadei, "Gli omicidi contro le donne sono uno scandalo, ma i numeri del "femminicidio" sono gonfiati," *Tempi*, http://www.tempi.it/gli-omicidi-contro-le-donne-sono -uno-scandalo-ma-i-numeri-del-femminicidio-sono-gonfiati#.U2YQ7dzAX_Q (accessed March 21, 2019). See also Facci: il "Femminicidio è moda. C'è già chi ci vuole far soldi," *Libero*

Quotidiano, http://www.liberoquotidiano.it/news/italia/1356906/Facci--il--femminicidio-e
-moda--C-e-gia-chi-ci-vuole-far-soldi.html (accessed March 21, 2019).

15. See, for example, "Femminicidio è moda. C'è già chi ci vuole far soldi," *Il Giornale*,
http://www.ilgiornale.it/news/interni/femminicidio-se-vittima-nonno-nessuno-ci-bada
-970108.html (accessed March 21, 2019).

16. It is worth noting that most of them, during the 2017 #quellavoltache protest—that is,
the Italian version of the #metoo campaign—published posts and Tweets.

17. While Aretxaga and Navaro-Yashin use different terms to refer to the role of fantasy
in their fields, both *phantoms* and *the phantasmatic*, respectively, imply a conceptualization
that merges material and fictional aspects. As Navaro-Yashin puts it: "The phantasmatic has
an object quality, and vice versa. As argued by Begoña Aretxaga, the fictional and the real are
not distinct; one does not precede, antecede, or determine the other. Together they constitute
a kernel" (Navaro-Yashin 2012, 757–760). See also Navaro-Yashin 2007.

18. The point made by Fassin and Rechtman in *The Empire of Trauma* (2009) is significant
to my research in as much as it depicts dominant understandings of the relationship between
violence, trauma, and victimhood that I argue are also generally valid in the Italian context
(see also Giordano 2014; De Luna 2011; and Gribaldo 2014). Their claims are useful, I argue,
in describing the context for understanding the affective, representational, political, and
symbolic resignifications that structure my informants' lives, and, by extension, my book.
The women with whom I worked contest precisely the widespread understanding of the
relations between victimhood (specifically its association with womanhood in the Salentine
context), violence, and trauma by reimagining womanhood and its relationship with violence
through the figure of the witness. The latter also takes on different nuances in this context, in
comparison to the one spelled out in *The Empire of Trauma* and in Fassin (2008).

19. See, for example, Riches 1986; Nagengast 1994; Whitehead 2004; Coronil and Skurski
2006; Aretxaga and Zulaika 2005; Schmidt 2001; Das 2008; Farmer 2003; Taussig 1986, 1999.

20. If, as Whitehead (2004, 5) argues, violence has always been a part of ethnographic
analyses, as embedded, for example, in kin relations, religious rituals, and relationships
between groups (see, e.g., Evans-Pritchard [1937] 1965; Turner 1967; Gluckman 1955; Bloch
1986, 1992), by the end of the past century it became a specific filter used to understand and
describe certain particular and global realities. See also Hinton 2012 on a historical perspective on violence and morality.

21. As Sluka (2000) points out, normally the violence enacted by the state is called terror
while antistate violence is called terrorism.

22. Examples include the Cambodian genocide (see Hinton 1998; Hinton and O'Neill
2009), the Israeli-Palestinian conflict (see Allen 2008, 2013), the Rwandan genocide (see De
Lame 2005; Eltringham 2004), the violence in Northern Ireland (see Feldman 1991; Aretxaga
1997) or the Partition between India and Pakistan (see Das 1990, 2007).

23. See, for example, several contributions in Das, Kleinman, and Lock 1997; Das
et al. 2000; Das et al. 2001; and Scheper-Hughes 1993. See also, for example, Morgan and
Bjorkert 2006.

24. In this respect, the three books edited by Das, Kleinman, and coauthors—*Social Suffering* (1997), *Violence and Subjectivity* (2000), and *Remaking a World* (2001)—represent
milestones in the anthropological understanding of violence. In *Violence and Subjectivity*,
the authors show eloquently "how subjectivity—the felt interior experience of the person that
includes his or her positions in a field of relational power—is produced through the experience of violence and the manner in which global flows involving images, capital, and people

become entangled with local logics in identity formation." Within this perspective, "the processes through which violence is actualized—in the sense that it is both produced and consumed" become central (2).

25. It reveals the interpersonal grounds of suffering, too (ix). See also Al-Mohammad (2012), on intercorporeality; and Hermez (2012). While not specifically anthropological, I see Cavarero's work on "horrorism" as a means of incorporating both ways of looking at violence (see, e.g., Cavarero 2007; Weber 2014).

26. For a possible comparison with the notion of "vulnerability," see, for example, Das 2007; Stringer 2013; and Mackenzie 2014.

27. See, for example, Scheper-Hughes and Bourgois 2004; Hermez 2012, on the anticipation of violence; Carr 2009; and Molé 2010.

28. In this book, I use the term *patriarchy* in the sense my informants used it.

29. For a comparison see, for example, Foucault [1972] 2010. On Foucault and feminism, see, for example, McNay 1992.

30. This remark, which is situated at the very beginning of my fieldwork before I was schooled in the visualities and practices of my informants, is not intended to be judgmental but to express the difference in the perception of time that characterized that initial period of fieldwork. I am not judging the value of her time in reference to mine. I am only describing some of the elements in the field that, in spite of my being a native ethnographer, I needed to learn and adjust to. On this occasion, for example, I realized that my son's bedtime (8:30 p.m.) was considered late afternoon in Salento.

31. In this respect, I was Eugenia's audience, and her performances of dissensus (see below) influenced me deeply.

32. For a comparison, see Ahmed 2004 on the circulation of (affects and) emotions.

33. I agree with Bonilla and Rosa 2015 (see also Postil and Pink 2012) that (social) media ethnography needs to focus also on individual practices, experiences, and uses (both online and off-line) and on the broader, also material context, of social media production. For this reason, I here focus on the context of production of "online modern feminist womanhood" personas.

34. The use of Twitter was not as widespread as Facebook among my informants. Among the feminist blogs mentioned above, I can cite, for example, *Femminismo a Sud*, http://femminismo-a-sud.noblogs.org (accessed April 7, 2019); *Al di là del Buco*, http://abbattoimuri.wordpress.com (accessed April 7, 2019); *La 27esima Ora*, http://27esimaora.corriere.it (accessed April 7, 2019); *Il Corpo delle Donne*, http://www.ilcorpodelledonne.net (accessed April 7, 2019); *Comunicazione di genere*, http://comunicazionedigenere.wordpress.com (accessed April 7, 2019); *Laboratorio Donnae*, http://laboratoriodonnae.wordpress.com (accessed April 7, 2019); *Ci riprovo*, http://ritentasaraipiufortunato.blogspot.com (accessed April 7, 2019); *Vita da streghe*, http://vitadastreghe.blogspot.com (accessed April 7, 2019); *Zeroviolenza.it*, http://www.zeroviolenzadonne.it (accessed April 7, 2019).

35. For example: *Bollettino di Guerra*, http://bollettino-di-guerra.noblogs.org (accessed April 7, 2019); *Femicidio Casa delle Donne*, http://femicidiocasadonne.wordpress.com (accessed April 7, 2019); *Donne in rete contro la violenza*, http://www.direcontrolaviolenza.it (accessed April 7, 2019); *Giuristi democratici per la CEDAW*, http://gdcedaw.blogspot.com (accessed March 21, 2019).

36. September 23, 2013. This claim is better understood when compared to the role of bella figura (making a good impression) in the Italian context. See, for example, Nardini 1999; Plesset 2006; Del Negro 2004; Pipyrou 2014a.

37. See, for example, for a comparison, the #metoo and #quellavoltache campaigns.

38. In 2002, El-Kholy wrote that "it is well established that power and resistance are not autonomous but are intermeshed and continuously shape each other" (22).

39. It is worth noting up front that, among the women I met both off-line and online, these complex clusters around violence were not unambiguous and that they produced ambivalent results. For example, they did not seem to acknowledge consciously both our "exposure to violence and our complicity in it" (Butler 2004, 19).

40. *Non Una di Meno* is a movement founded in Rome in 2017, promoted by the UDI, the Roman network *Io decido*, and by D.i.re—women in network against violence. Inspired by the Mexican *NiUnaMenos*, it pursues the goal, among others, of fighting against violence against women. It promoted very successful manifestations, strikes, and a plan against violence against women. It is an explicitly intersectional and international movement, the first mainstream one of this type in the recent Italian feminist history. See, for example, Bohrer 2015, for an analysis of the autonomist Italian feminism; Bracke 2014, 65, 193–194, for the history of the Italian feminist movement and intersectionality; Rovetto 2015 and von Lurzer and Spataro 2016, on *NiUnaMenos*; and, for example, "Dieci consigli per sopravvivere al femminismo intersezionale," *Pasionaria*, http://pasionaria.it/dieci-consigli-per-sopravvivere -al-femminismo-intersezionale/ (accessed March 21, 2019); "Non Una di Meno in Italia: un movimento intersezionale?," *Dinamo Press*, https://www.dinamopress.it/news/non-una -di-meno-in-italia-un-movimento-intersezionale/ (accessed March 21, 2109); "Non Una di Meno, chi siamo," *Non Una di Meno*, https://nonunadimeno.wordpress.com/2016/11/09/chi -siamo/ (accessed March 21, 2019).

41. "The quest for a point of exit from phallogocentric definitions of Woman requires a strategy of working-through the images and representations that the (masculine) knowing subject has created of Woman as Other. . . . It amounts to a collective re-possession of the images and representations of Woman such as they have been coded in language, culture, science, knowledge and discourse and consequently internalized in the heart, mind, body and lived experience of women. A feminist who wishes to repossess and re-invest images and representations of Woman is really dealing with fragments and figments of the phallogocentric imaginary. Irigaray argues that this imaginary needs to be repossessed by women precisely because it is loaded with phallogocentric assumptions that reduce Woman to unrepresentability" (Braidotti 2003, 45). Braidotti 1996, 2002, 2003, and 2005, offer a contemporary, postmodern understanding of "Woman" within the pensiero della differenza sessuale.

42. What might be worth considering is that this "openness" can as well be seen as rooted in the philosophy of difference and not only as a consequence of the influence of other, international, feminisms.

2

WOMEN BEFORE WOMEN

Italian Feminists and the Struggle for Visibility

IN THIS CHAPTER, I SKETCH THE BACKGROUND HISTORICAL dimensions of Italian feminisms as a circumstantial yet fundamental frame in order to give prominence to contemporary developments, in particular as they unfolded in my ethnographic experiences. I narrate them filtered through the particular lens of the issues around visibility, which will represent the *fil rouge* of the different sections below.[1] While I agree that recognition is a significant dimension of political movements in general (see, e.g., Hobson 2003), in depicting the Italian context through the lens of visibility I intend to focus on collateral dimensions of the need for recognition, such as the construction/addressing of particular audiences, the choice of being visible or invisible, and the need to intercept certain gazes and not others. The metaphor of vision brings together multiple dimensions relevant to my informants' lives, at both a personal and a political level, posing questions about who sees what, how, and, ultimately, why. My narration will unfold as a braid with three plaited threads: the UDI and the lives of the women I met, the Italian feminist movements in general, and the Italian social and political contexts.[2] In the personal and political lives of my informants, the issues around visibility were of paramount importance and inextricably linked to issues of representation. They dealt with women as a political subject and were connected to performances of seeing and sensing womanhood in contemporary Italy. Violence against women, in this respect, became an important dimension in these struggles of and for visibility and representation.

Karstic Rivers

It was a Saturday afternoon early in December 2015. Marta, Sara, and I were cleaning the kitchen of the *sede* (headquarters) of DNA Donna, a counseling center for women, while laughing, chatting, and commenting on the latest news concerning our lives. I had returned just a few days before from a trip where I attended a conference in the United States and had missed the events organized locally for the International Day against Violence against Women, on November 25. Over the years, this date has become one of the most important for feminists, and all the more so for those who work in centers countering violence against women. Marta had attended or intervened at many events in the province of Lecce that year as well. I, therefore, asked her some opinions on those initiatives, and she replied quite bluntly, with mild irritation: "There's still a lot of work to do. In most of the cases, the topic is approached in a really superficial way. It is not possible that members of the equal opportunity committees of local towns greet the assembly by saying *buongiorno a tutti*, by using just the masculine plural for mixed groups, and not by explicitly saying *buongiorno a tutti e buongiorno a tutte*, grammatically, practically, and symbolically including women in the greetings! In particular, it is sad if it happens in occasion of initiatives against violence against women! I cannot believe that the rhetoric against violence against women is still always inflected in patriarchal terms!" Sara joined in by saying, "So many initiatives for November 25 . . . and what about the rest of the year?" and Marta replied, sardonically, with a stentorian voice: "The Italian feminist movement is like a karstic river." We all laughed, thinking about the overused feminist adage, but our laughs were bittersweet.

As a matter of fact, the metaphor of the karstic river is used frequently and ubiquitously among Italian feminists in order to interpret and narrate the history of Italian feminist movements (see also Bonomi Romagnoli 2014). It responds to the need to find a shared historical narrative that comes to terms with the diversification and the divergences between the specific experiences of the different feminisms that have been developing in Italy since the beginning of the past century. As Sega (2005, 1) writes: "The feminine participation in the collective movements does not have a linear trend: it proceeds with alternate phases, between claimed presences and silences; an appearing and a disappearing that resembles more a 'karstic' river than the flowing, sometimes slow and sometimes turbulent, of a river under the light of the sun."[3]

This need to think about Italian feminisms within a common and reconciliatory historical framework also stems from the need to fight against the absence (sometimes actual, but mainly constructed by the hegemonic, historical "patriarchal" narratives) of the acknowledgment of the role of women in important moments of Italian history, such as the *Resistenza* (i.e., the resistance movement that fought against Fascism during the Italian Civil War, 1943–1945). As Sega points out, the construction of the collective memory around anti-Fascism stresses how men "did" the *Resistenza*, while women just "contributed" to it. Interestingly, though, the semantic axis of the karstic metaphor seems to introduce elements of ambivalence in its goals, as the ironic comments of Marta suggest: the *choice* to be invisible risks (partially, at least) compliance with the "patriarchal" narratives that want to hide women from history. If the "invisible is not what is hidden but what is denied" (Fernandez, quoted in Taylor 1997), then hiding from one's own view can be understood and felt as a form of self-sabotage by certain women like Marta and Sara.[4] In other words, the periodical emergence and disappearance of feminist presence in the public arena might be the result of choosing not to be misinterpreted and exploited by others' gazes but also risks looking like a way of not existing or impacting society.

I claim that the adoption of this metaphor, in which the image of the karstic river limits its action by circumscribing a specific role for women *within* ubiquitous "patriarchal" narratives rather than breaking with them tout court, has an ambivalence that is at the core of the contemporary Italian feminist debates I encountered. The ubiquity of this metaphor, pervasive during my fieldwork, describes my ethnographic experience well. In different ways, the issues of visibility, invisibility, and representation emerged as key components of my informants' personal and political lives.

Becoming Invisible as a Choice: The Legacy of the UDI and the Pensiero della Differenza Sessuale—Pulling Back from the Squares

The UDI is the oldest Italian feminist movement and the one around which most of the women I met at the beginning of my fieldwork gravitated.[5] Rooted in the Italian Communist Party (PCI), it was founded in 1944, during World War II, by some women of what Tambor (2014) calls the "Lost Wave" of Italian feminists and was called *Unione delle Donne Italiane* (Union of Italian Women). In 1945, Italian women achieved the right to vote, and twenty-one women became part of the Assembly that wrote the Italian Constitution. As Tambor points out, in spite of Italy's delay in awarding women suffrage in comparison to Britain and the United States, "Italian women had not been backward and unchanging compared to their Anglo-American counterparts; like them, they had organized as feminists throughout the nineteenth and early twentieth century [*sic*], and like them, they had participated in the larger trends of expanding education and employment for women" (6; see also Wilson 2009; Pojmann 2013).[6] The birth of the UDI is one example of this, and its role proved to be central in the emergence of a *new* political subject—that is, the "symbolic woman" that Tambor calls "Constitutional Woman"—in post-Fascist Italy (2014, 4–5; see also Wilson 2009, 142). While the story of this Lost Wave is often forgotten, not acknowledged, and marginalized in mainstream narratives of Italian feminism, it was not by the Macare.[7] As a matter of fact, in 2005, they decided to meet regularly to read the Italian Constitution with a "gendered lens," focusing *specifically* on the role of the twenty-one women in Italy's Constitutional Assembly. As a result of this, they also worked at a website called *Cittadinanze* (Citizenships), on which they published their reflections and comments.[8] This choice, which was not mainstream among Italian feminists, shows the importance of history (and genealogies, see later in this chapter) for the activists I met: if, on the one hand, it represented a way to understand the present by honoring the past of the group to which they belonged, on the other hand, it offered an authoritative reference point and language in the UDI's internal debates of the early 2000s.

During the 1970s and 1980s, the UDI became popular for its prodivorce and abortion rights campaigns, playing an important role in the "Second Wave" of Italian feminism. Many of the older informants I met were very active during this period and participated in the shift from the emancipation politics of the Lost Wave to the politics of difference that I am describing in this book. This transition was not a simple one and involved a symbolic "coming of age rejection of their mothers" (Tambor 2014, 174), the women of the Lost Wave, that culminated in the UDI's Eleventh Congress in 1982. Somehow anticipating the crisis of ideologies yet to come, the women of the organization decided to change the structure of their institution, voting for a separation from the PCI and from any direct link to party politics (see also Tambor 2014, 177). This was a brave choice on the part of one of the most important Italian feminist groups of the time—as brave as it was unpopular. I had the chance to discuss this topic with some of the women who took part in that Eleventh Congress. Both concretely and symbolically, many of them paid the price of this choice personally. The women I interviewed told me that, by virtue of their activity within the UDI before the 1982 congress, many of the group's members used to be functionaries of the party and received a salary from PCI. Earning an income, for a woman, especially in that period, was a sign of emancipation and, for a feminist, even more of a political stance. When the women of the UDI voted for its autonomy from the PCI, this ideological choice of freedom resulted in the loss of economic independence for many of them. By losing their salary, they found themselves dependent on other sources of income; often, paradoxically, on their partner's incomes. Therefore, if, at the ideological level, the adoption of a way of doing politics independent from the parties was somehow an imaginative and innovative choice for that time, this same choice often resulted, at a personal level, in a regression to traditional relational and economic patterns between men and women (or between women and women). Ironically, these were the same ingrained patterns that the feminist activists of the UDI were trying to problematize and dismantle. This regression was often perceived and narrated simply as apparent by the UDI women I interviewed. As an informant of mine told me: "The place of liberty set by the choice of the XI Congress did force some of us to re-negotiate our relationships with our partners, but this did not take our dignity away" (October 2013).

More recently, as I mentioned before, to explicitly recognize immigrants—that is, nonnative women who live in Italy—as part of the movement, the UDI's acronym changed to *Unione delle donne in Italia* (Union of Women in Italy). This first step in the "opening up" of the concept of "woman" gestures toward the changes in feminist politics that I witnessed during my fieldwork (including UDI's Fifteenth Congress in 2011), the emergence of a new women's question that I describe in this book, and the even more recent intersectional developments of the Italian feminisms with *Non Una di Meno*, of which the UDI is one of the organizing groups (see chap. 1). While it is too early to fully assess the nature and outcomes of this—still ambivalent—shift, I intend to suggest a possible trajectory and a framework for describing and understanding, at least partially, the current developments of Italian feminisms. Issues around important themes such as surrogate motherhood, LGBT+ rights, gender, and sexual harassment still generate rifts within the contemporary Italian feminist panorama. Nonetheless, I argue, the voice of a new generation of feminists is being heard more and more. What I witnessed during my fieldwork and address in this book can be seen as a possible step within this "becoming" (postmodern) women and feminists.

* * *

In spite of its long history and ubiquitous presence throughout Italy, I confess I had not heard a single word about the UDI until I met Eugenia and Mena in September 2011 at an annual meeting on the *pensiero della differenza sessuale* in Lecce. While this is certainly an oversight on my part, it is nonetheless true that I went successfully through the training required for a degree in Literature and Philosophy at one of the most progressive and leftist Italian universities (*Università degli Studi di Milano*), before moving abroad, without hearing a single word about the UDI or about Italian feminisms. The first time I heard about a specific *Italian* feminist tradition, I was in Canada, in a graduate course at the Department of Anthropology of the University of Toronto. This remark is not accidental and is consistent with the surprised reaction of my friends and acquaintances concerning the existence of a feminist tradition in Italy. When I spoke about the topic of my research "among feminists in Apulia" to my Italian friends and acquaintances, nearly all of them replied with bewilderment: "Are there feminists in Italy? Today?" These few observations help depict the status of the acknowledgment of a women's question among public opinion in Italy in 2011, at the beginning of my fieldwork. Until then, for my generation at least—people who were born between the late 1970s and the early 1980s—feminist voices, analyses, and discourses had been invisible and had no place in the media, in history textbooks, or in university courses. Why was this so? I have often posed this question to the feminists I met, especially to the ones who belong to the older generation, to those who physically took to the streets in the 1970s and were actively involved in the successful prodivorce and proabortion campaigns. Mostly, they indulged in the narration of anecdotes, in the description of the practices they used in order to reach as many women as possible—such as *giornale parlato* (spoken newspaper) or *riunioni di quartiere* (neighborhood meetings)—depicting, with nostalgia and pride, a period, a context, and even a youth that *are not* anymore. As for the answer to my *why*, I was not able to gather verbal responses that differed very much from the routine ones. As explained to me once by one of the women I met in Milan at the Milan Women's Bookstore (*Libreria delle Donne di Milano*), a historical locus of the production of Italian feminisms, "Italian women in the 1980s decided to stay out of the squares" and "to change societies from within, starting with their own lives." It is widely noted that, in spite of the legal accomplishments of the Italian women's movements during the 1970s and 1980s, the vast majority of the Italian feminist movements, after twenty years of intense political commitment around the legislation on divorce and abortion, chose to continue their political activities in the private rather than in the public sphere and disappeared from public space by the beginning of the 1990s (see, e.g., Plesset 2006; Bono and Kemp 1991).[9] Public protests were substituted mainly by the practice of self-awareness (*autocoscienza*) in small groups and by activity in women's shelters throughout Italy. The Italian feminists who share a radical interpretation of "the personal is political" adage today believe that social change depends on specific political practices, such as the practice of self-awareness (*pratica dell' autocoscienza*; see, e.g., Dominijanni 2005, 26; Bono and Kemp 1991; Cozzi 2011), the practice of entrustment (*affidamento*; see, e.g., Dominijanni 2005, 37; Bono and Kemp 1991), the practice of starting from oneself (*pratica del partire da sé*), and the practice of relations between women (see, e.g., Scarparo 2005, 40–41). In particular, among these four practices, that of relations between women is especially valued for its personal and political implications. Women's political practices and relations happen primarily around the acknowledgment of *disparità* (disparity, see below) among women. While I could not find much evidence in support of the first two among my informants, the last three political practices were part of the everyday experience of the UDI women I met in the field. In particular, I found the practice of starting from oneself to be a key feature of practicing feminism among the UDI feminists I met. This feature is linked to two of the most important—and yet controversial—aspects of the political practice of the UDI: its *separatismo* (women's separatism), and its autonomy from party politics (see below).

The radical interpretation of "the personal is political" adage that considers the personal as *the locus* for the transformation of the public was nonetheless just a (partial) justification of the status quo.[10] While it was often evoked in order to explain the disappearance of feminists from the public scene and while it was consistent with the teachings of the *pensiero della differenza sessuale*, it narrated only part of the story.[11] As a matter of fact, during my ethnography I observed a subtext in action that informed feminist discussions, one that revolved precisely around matters of visibility. In particular, there were two aspects, sometimes intertwined, that seemed to inflame the spirits of the women participating in the debates: the issues around the need to be visible in the public political arena, and those stemming from the need to be acknowledged (*riconosciute*) by other generations of feminists.[12] These aspects, that had both political and personal implications, are narrated in the rest of the chapter by referring to a specific event, interpolated in my ethnographic accounts: the emergence of the Se Non Ora Quando (SNOQ) grassroots women's movement, named after Primo Levi's well-known novel, in February 2011. An analysis of the *appearance*, in the sense of both emergence and external configuration, of this movement helps show how the problems of visibility were differently inflected, among women's groups, in relation to various (imagined) publics and counterpublics (see, e.g., Michael Warner 2002).

La Visibilità che Vogliamo (the Visibility We Want): On Empowering and Disempowering Gazes

On February 13, 2011, allegedly one million protestors, mostly women, took to the streets in more than 250 cities, in Italy and abroad, to, in the words of the SNOQ manifesto, protest against "the model of man-woman relations exhibited by one of the highest state authorities" that "deeply affects" Italy's "lifestyles and culture, justifying behavior detrimental to women's dignity and to the institutions themselves." The demonstration that gathered around the SNOQ women's movement was meant to be politically inclusive and involved women from different contexts and ideological positions. It was the first time in thirty years that Italian women were visible on the streets in such numbers. What triggered this massive reaction, and its media coverage, were some recent events related to the prime minister at the time, Silvio Berlusconi, and what has since been called Rubygate, a sex scandal that involved an underage woman. The media coverage of this event was unprecedented and gave great visibility to women's groups for the first time in many years.[13] It constructed a new political subject as well as a new public able to acknowledge the presence of a women's question in Italy.[14] This visibility, though, did not initiate a dialogue on women's rights or on Italy's poor scores in the Global Gender Gap report, for example. Both among leftist and right-wing journalists and intellectuals, the movement was framed as a possibility or as an attempt to delegitimize Berlusconi *politically*. In other words, by catching the feminist wave, politicians of the left and right (and the national press, which is highly dependent on, and influenced by, political parties) attempted to use a new women's question to accomplish their political goal—Berlusconi's delegitimization. This goal, according to the feminists with whom I worked, was only nominally in the interests of women.

The emergence of SNOQ represented a reappearance of the karstic river that provided an answer to the anxiety around visibility that many feminist women sought. Many committees bloomed spontaneously throughout Italy (and abroad). While for many women this occasion was their first experience with women's politics, many activists found that the visibility of a women's question in the media, even though not framed properly, was indeed something that could be exploited in order to make their voices audible and their bodies visible. It was an occasion they did not want to pass up. This position, present also among some UDI activists, conflicted ideologically with the political stance expressed by the group's national board, which remained loyal to the ideological statements proclaimed by the UDI women in 1982. Interpretations of the Eleventh Congress aside, the retreat to space outside of party politics coincided, temporally and de facto, with the disappearance of the UDI from the public scene. This is why, not surprisingly, in 2011, almost thirty years after the Eleventh Congress and after a decade of regained political leadership within the feminist national scene, the problems of visibility and of the relationships with party politics collided.[15] The emergence of a new women's question in Italy linked to the SNOQ movement, therefore, triggered old and new problems and not just within the UDI. The claims of visibility of SNOQ in the media, for many UDI women, and for those who share their view on the relationship between women's politics and institutional politics, clashed with the choice of nonpartisanship discussed above. Pina Nuzzo, the national delegate of the UDI at that time, wrote in an official notice that the UDI would not participate *as a group* in the demonstration on February 13. Obviously, at the individual level, every woman could decide whether she wanted to take to the streets or not. The reasons for the lack of formal and public support for the SNOQ demonstrations centered on the antigovernmental purposes of the movement and the arguable understanding of "women's self-determination present in the SNOQ's appeal." In the document *noidell'udi, noi con le donne* ("we-who-are-from-the-UDI, we who are with women"; Nuzzo 2011a), a very long public notice meant to be a preparatory document for the Fifteenth Congress, Nuzzo, after recognizing the rift that her position would create within the UDI, writes: "We do not want to play a game where the point of contention is different from us, even if—as usual—it exploits women's bodies." The problem, according to Nuzzo, was one of both *visibility* and *audiences*.

> A demonstration, today, is launched from the internet. . . . In our society, if the media do not talk about you, it seems that you do not exist. A feeling that women know well since they have been fighting against it through feminism . . . : they avoid making their own existence dependent upon the gaze of the other. This principle is valid in life as well as in politics; practicing it requires a strong self-awareness (*senso di sé*), and authoritativeness (*titolarità*) about one's own ideas, actions, and words. Not allowing the gaze of the other to define yourself means disempowering it.[16]

In an email addressed to all the women of the UDI, Pina Nuzzo (2011b) further explained her position, consistent with the post-1982 political orientations of the group:

> We cannot give up our identity in order to present a blurred feminine gender, indignant and anonymous. . . . We never underestimated the importance of exposing ourselves in the squares. . . . Every single time, though, we needed to acknowledge the fact that [institutional] politics does not listen to what women say through women's associations because it does not acknowledge the political aspect of the movement organized by women. Not even the media, which we asked several times to narrate the actions of a civil society that is committed every day in changing an absurd cultural "one-way" model (*a sesso unico*), recognize this. Therefore, it is unbearable that the insistent pleas [of the media] once again leverage an alleged silence [of women] that does not concern us, since we have never been silent. They just silenced us! As we claimed and reclaimed several times.[17]

Yet the UDI's lack of support of the SNOQ's demonstration did not result in an open internal political debate on the role of women's movements and of the UDI in the contemporary Italian political arena. Nuzzo's political claims around the SNOQ demonstration, instead, catalyzed emotions, affects, and thoughts that resonated with old, ill-concealed anxieties around visibility. Nuzzo's position resulted in huge disputes within the UDI that I personally witnessed during my fieldwork and that, eventually, prevented her reelection.

In October 2011, I went to Bologna for the UDI Fifteenth Meeting with the Macare. For many reasons, this meeting represented a controversial moment in the history of the UDI. The two main pressure groups within the association—which ultimately coalesced around different ways to understand the relationship of party politics and the problem of visibility that emerged with the SNOQ demonstration—had a harsh and not completely politically correct confrontation that concerned the present and the future of the UDI and its presence on the Italian political scene. On the last day of the meeting, some women (mostly young and supportive of Nuzzo's positions) decided to form a flash mob in order to protest against the nondemocratic ways in which they perceived the meeting was being administered. Each protestor silently entered the meeting room holding a piece of paper claiming her *indignation* (along with the personal associative number that vouched for her membership in the UDI).[18] After a couple of minutes of silence, the protesters filed out of the room. While I did not have any role in organizing the flash mob, I participated in it, together with the Salento UDI women with whom I was traveling. The fact that I—a newly arrived ethnographer and a newly affiliated member of the UDI and of the Macare—decided to "*mettere la faccia*" (lit., to put my own face, meaning to commit) in this protest was very meaningful to my informants. I had the chance to talk at length with them about this event in the days after the meeting. On those occasions, I realized that what had triggered the flash mob was a strong reaction (that they defined as "emotional") to the feelings of not being considered, seen, interpellated, and, ultimately, acknowledged and recognized as worthy or dignified by the women who were leading the Fifteenth Meeting. In this respect, it is worth noting that some of the women who neither performed nor supported the flash mob during the Congress yelled at us that we, the protestors, were not worthy or dignified (*non degne*) enough to be part of the UDI. Since, according to my informants, this challenge to the flash mobbers' own dignity was not coming from men or a "patriarchal" environment but from feminists of their same group, the Fifteenth Meeting was really an overwhelming and disorienting experience for the Salentine UDI women with whom I was traveling.

On the basis of my participant observation, the fact that these women chose not to speak out but to perform a silent flash mob in this circumstance is extremely significant. Being able to publicly show and express dialectically one's disagreement with another woman is a highly valued practice among Italian feminists and among UDI women. *Confliggere* (conflicting) is considered an important moment of the practice of relations. *Confliggere*, though, presupposes the mutual recognition of the other's value. According to Putino (1987), a Neapolitan feminist philosopher very influential among the women I met:

> Arguing between women is fighting a war. In order to fight this war, one needs to have a deep sense of one's own and of the other's dignity. . . . There are many ways to discourage a war meeting between two women; one of these is to impoverish (*immiserire*) the other at a level where all that happens there is

stripped down by another instance, determined elsewhere. . . . There remains but one she-warrior; the other is a woman of the army. She is a woman who fights without having in her hands the reason for her fighting. Her destiny is not linked to the necessity of something shared, it does not belong to the word of the encounter, it is held by other threads.[19]

Yet war does not happen between only two individuals. In order for this conflict to happen, the two parts need to have a public able to recognize their dignity and to mutually do so. This aspect of *confliggere* leads me right into another dimension of visibility that informs the subtext in action that I was mentioning before: the need to be seen and recognized among different feminist generations. Or, to use my informants' jargon, the need to "weave weavings."

A Gaze That Doesn't Fade but Supports You and Authorizes You to Be

Carmen is a woman in her thirties who, in 2013, was living at her parents' house in the north of Apulia, since her work situation did not allow her to rent a place herself. She nervously touched her bright red hair while Pina Nuzzo introduced the works of the Fourth Laboratorio Donnae (Workshop Donnae, Donnae Lab), a working group founded by Nuzzo in the aftermath of her non-reelection as a national delegate of the UDI.[20] We were some 350 km away from Salento, and the women's association to which Carmen belonged was hosting the meeting. She had been busy preparing the conference room, dealing with the hotel, arranging the meals for the group, and giving directions to those who came from other parts of Italy and were not acquainted with the town. She was visibly nervous and tense, but she had greeted me very warmly when I arrived: with a long, affectionate hug, two kisses, and a bright, open smile. That was probably the second time we had met in person, though. I had had dinner with her and other friends two years before in Lecce, at Elisabetta's apartment. We laughed about this upon my arrival, commenting how, strangely perhaps, we were experiencing closeness by virtue of nothing more than our internet connection.

Donnae Lab is primarily an online platform that has been working since 2012, mainly through a blog and a Facebook page, on which women from various parts of Italy and from various political backgrounds interact throughout the year. Those, together with our own Facebook pages, have been the spaces where Carmen and I built our connection—by sharing statuses, articles, pictures, music, comments, and likes. As Pina Nuzzo puts it, in the internet, "the 'friendships' and the 'sharings' re-define, de facto, the contours of a political geography that it is not ascribable to 'territory' anymore."[21] If the internet is one of the loci of the political today in Italy, Nuzzo claims it does not, however, replace meetings in person (*in presenza*). For this reason, the *donnae* tended to organize two or three self-supported two-day meetings per year, which were prepared for and greatly anticipated by most of the women I met, and by me as well. Donnae Lab, then, in the words of its founder, is "a permanent workshop devoted to research on the thought and representation that women give to themselves in politics, where we may focus on our lives outside given and pre-established readings."[22] "It is called *donnae*," Nuzzo continues, "a word that does not exist in Italian vocabulary because it evokes the Latin origin of *donna*" (Italian for woman) "that derives from *domna*, the syncopated form of *domina*, which means *lady*. It includes both the singular and the plural. Periodically the *donnae* will meet to think and to do projects together" (emphasis in the original).[23]

One of the first accomplishments of the Donnae Lab has been to reflect on a new way of understanding feminism that has been referred to as *femminismo molecolare* (molecular feminism), which describes and fits well with the feminist practices that the Donnae Lab, with its online vocation, is currently building.[24] This neologism—where, as Nuzzo claims, "molecular is not a synonym for fragmentation"—originated from the realization that:

> Women's centrality (*protagonismo*) walks through unconventional paths and it is not ascribable anymore to a single belonging. Feminism, today more than yesterday, cannot be represented as a monolith; [feminism] has always been constituted by a multiplicity of practices and representations. Today it has become, so to speak, molecular—also because of the web. Laboratorio donne took this to be a new fact, unavoidable in politics. . . . Periodically, women's politics return to the idea that being many and united makes us stronger, more visible, more contractual. "*Being all together*," though, does not work on the basis of organizational models and does not work with partisan politics.[25]

Enza Miceli, a woman who gravitated toward Donnae Lab, elaborated this latter point as follows: "Each one of us is the terminal of many other relations, from these we get the necessary strength that drives us to think about new forms and new projects. This allowed me to overcome the feeling of being a lost particle, and to think of myself as a unique particle, taking the liberty of thinking about a project that is mine by involving others. May I say that I feel like a molecular feminist?"[26]

This approach to feminist practices, in other words, relies on the acknowledgment that "there is not a [single] way to be a feminist, but there are the many women that we become thanks to feminism."[27] Women who "are the points of connection of an infinite number of relations, that can be one's own political group, her co-workers, the women whom one meets at the gym, or in front of the school of her children." Each woman is part of a *tessitura* (weaving), as the women of Donnae Lab used to say: "I never liked the word 'web' used in order to give the sense of a more collective dimension of our politics, it is over-used, and it hints of ways of speaking that bother me: to get trapped in a web, to fall into a web, the spider's web. . . . We from Laboratorio Donnae preferred to imagine a weaving of relations, of gestures, to which each one of us contributes in the ways she can" (Donnae Lab, Facebook, March 11, 2013).

For the women of Donnae Lab, the word *tessitura* is central. It evokes an activity traditionally undertaken with skill and prowess by women and gestures toward a connection with history that the women with whom I worked need to trace. Moreover, by concentrating on the role of each thread in composing the final product, this metaphor underlines a commonality, in space and time, of projects and goals.[28] The latter aspect is found also in another keyword for the feminists I met: genealogy. Both of these words, as discussed in this book, rest on the desire and need to be seen, acknowledged, *and* recognized by others.

* * *

Carmen's turn arrived: she needed to address her experience within the asso-ciation and the Donnae Lab and to explain to us her personal interpretation of what *molecolare* means. Yet mostly, and not at all surprisingly, she ended up offering a narrative of her life. The plot of her story did not sound entirely unfamiliar.[29] She started by reading a text in which she spoke about the route (*viaggio*) that brought her there, to the fourth meeting of Donnae Lab. She was born in northern Apulia, not far from the town which was hosting the event, but apparently had spent most of her years trying to escape from there. She had studied in another part of Italy and even lived in another country for a period. When she came back, probably because of a plan that ended up not working as expected, she felt at a loss. Eventually, she found out that:

> Only when you have the *senso di sé* can you truly decide where you want to stay. Otherwise, you just make a series of "smart escapes" that make you wan-der without knowing what your political desire is, and if you ever had one. The escapes bring you to failure. So, I decided to return here to understand why I always demonized my land of origin. I sensed that my "problem" did not have to be sought in a territory that was hostile to me, but in the fact that I felt I had to find my place on a horizon that was already given, already written by others, with dynamics that I did not know, and that were alien to my way of feeling life and politics.[30]

In order to be able to find a horizon not already given, Carmen added, she needed to confront herself with a genealogy.[31] Carmen said, "I did not have the words . . . I was looking for a gaze (*sguardo*) that would acknowledge me (*che mi riconoscesse*), and that would give me authority (*che mi autorizzasse*). . . .

The genealogy gave me the words to name things. A language where I could recognize myself."

This narrative was shared, and renarrated, by Giulia, another woman in her thirties. I had met her, as well, two years before. Giulia, who with Carmen had organized the meeting of Donnae Lab, commented:

> By being away from my birth town, I re-took possession of myself. Before, I could not stay here, and I used to criticize my land, and I did not know that, instead, everything *began with myself.* Putting physical distance between myself and my city would not have changed things. It was me: I was distant from myself. . . . Once you become aware of yourself (*coscienza di te*), you find yourself, you naturally find the energy and the courage to stay and do (*agire*) in any place and to return to the place from where you fled . . . you start to understand that the desire to put down roots it is not so different from that of the women who came before you, starting from the closest. You understand you are in a genealogy that needs to be seen, acknowledged, also when the women who are part of it do not look at you, and do not listen to you.[32]

The fact that every woman is a mirror for other women, as an informant told me once, seemed to be at the core of this interpretation of the genealogical relationships among women.[33] The similarity and the otherness that the metaphor of the mirror evokes were what allowed Carmen and Giulia to find their own horizon within the relational and political fabric (*tessuto*) of their native towns, and within Donnae Lab. The feminist reflections on the relationship to one's mother, informed by the reading of Irigaray (see, e.g., 1985a, 1985b; see also Burke 1994) and received through the intellectual legacy of Luisa Muraro (see, e.g., 1988, 1991, 1994, 2012), were central for most of the women I met. Within these, the genealogical dimension had a special role. According to Muraro, the genealogy among women is twofold: one is "based on procreation," and the other rests on the word, which is something that, first and foremost, has to do with the acknowledgment of "having a history" *through* the women that "left a mark in history" (1994, 322–325). "The first 'genealogical' practice of feminism," Muraro continues, consists "precisely in learning about the women who have affected either our biographical or historical past" (322). This, according to Muraro, is what distinguishes the feminist practices of the 1960s and 1970s from those of her generation. During those two decades, sisterhood was the main framework by which to understand relationships between women. This framework defined even the relationships between mothers and daughters. Conversely, Muraro claims that she and her generation had "experienced the power for change in the practice of genealogical relation," where the "maternal symbolic" and not "sisterhood" is put into action (324, 330).[34]

I listened to Giulia and Carmen's stories with empathy but also with a sense of estrangement. Their words did not resonate with me; they did not give me words to describe *my* life—though it was similar to theirs in many respects, for instance, that of an emigrated Italian woman of their age who defines herself as being feminist. Their narrative did not help me in redefining *my* horizon. To be honest, I had a hard time understanding the linguistic referents of their feminist jargon, for example, expressions such as *senso di sé*, a "gaze that acknowledges and authorizes," and "political desire." I could understand the words, the existential semantic field, but not precisely what they were referring to. While I was listening to Carmen and Giulia and looking at the audience in order to understand, from their faces and comments, how they were receiving the two women's words (which I would describe as one of empathic approval), my mind was going to the anthropological literature on conversion narratives that I had read in my Anthropology of Religion classes years before. While fulfilling the task of being the photographer of the meeting by walking from one side to the other of the conference room taking pictures, I kept thinking about the work of Harding (1987), Saunders (1995), and Stromberg (1993) and about how, at the end, Carmen and Giulia's stories could be framed within similar approaches. *Mutatis mutandis*, the narratives I was hearing in that occasion, de facto, could be considered as *conversion narratives*.[35] I had the impression that, similar to their religious counterparts, Giulia and Carmen's stories were not just telling *about* an experience but also actually *constructing* it, by narrating it to a public that they wanted to emotionally affect. Moreover, they used specific jargon, a language that was as closed as the religious one and shared by those who belonged to those feminist circles. This language, not fully accessible even to a (noninsider) Italian native speaker like me, was shaping their personal events into somehow conventional narratives. This was not the only time I heard about returning to one's place of origin and about finding oneself through an encounter with one's genealogy.[36]

Anthropological resonances aside, the importance of genealogies for the feminists I met was great. For some, it responded to the need to find a meaning in their positions and actions within a broader intellectual and political history. For others, it had more of an existential dimension and represented a relational *tessitura* with specific persons and encounters, an especially important resource in the current times defined by a widespread sense of precariousness. Nonetheless, their adherence to the "women as mirrors for women" narrative revealed a certain need for reciprocity and, together with this, the problem of its negation that I also found in other ethnographic dimensions of my research.

Affect and Conflict: *Sensibili Guerriere*/Sensitive (Sensory) She-Warriors*

Lavinia, a woman in her early thirties, comes from Rome. Nuzzo had invited her to the meeting of Donnae Lab to talk about her experience at DWF (*DonnaWomanFemme*, a historical Italian feminist journal) and about her political experience. This was not the first time that she had participated in the Donnae Lab meetings, although she did not define herself as belonging to the organization. This time, she came with two friends and fellow members of the *Femministe Nove* (*F9*, from now on), a collective that had only very recently been formed and already made the news within Italian feminist circles (see below). This was why we were all waiting, with anticipation, for their presence—and not just because, due to the notorious Italian traffic, they arrived late at the meeting. Lavinia started by thanking Pina Nuzzo and by stating the "importance of acknowledgment between women," in particular of different generations. This represented one of the main topics around which she articulated her narrative: from the open editorial staff (*redazione aperta*) of DWF to her experience with the *collettivo Diversamente Occupate* and her take on the events in Paestum (see below).[37] That was not the first time I realized that the relationship between generations of feminists was framed both as an identity marker and as a source of tension in feminist circles. Two years before, at the beginning of my fieldwork, this had emerged very powerfully in the 2011 *Scuola della Differenza* (School of Difference) that I had attended in Lecce.[38]

It was during this yearly feminist meeting, sponsored by the University of Salento, that I heard, for the first time, Muraro, Cigarini, and other influential historical protagonists of Italian feminisms and that I witnessed an ill-concealed tension between generations of feminist women. While attending the meetings in the beautiful conference room of the Convent of the Saint Benedict Nuns of Lecce, I noticed that the distinction between older and younger feminists appeared to be ubiquitous in the words of most of the speakers, dividing the Italian feminist arena into two, undoubtedly fictional, generational factions. Within such a framework, conflict was praised and reasserted as a key feminist practice: one that, apparently, the young generations did not yet master sufficiently well, according to some of the older speakers.

Having been educated in gender studies within British and North American academia, this was my first contact with the *pensiero della differenza sessuale*, and, I admit, it was a complex experience. I had a hard time, for example, figuring out the meanings of words and expressions within Italian feminist

---

* *Sensibili Guerriere* is the title of a book edited by Giardini (2011).

jargon and overcoming the sense of estrangement that the widespread and grounding belief in the true existence of two sexes was giving me. Moreover, the lack of reference to any notion of gender was puzzling to me, and I struggled with finding the right words (i.e., words understandable to my interlocutors) to talk about my experience as a woman, and as a feminist. Such an external point of view, though, allowed me to notice some elements that in the rest of my fieldwork proved to be central to contemporary Italian feminism: the ubiquity of the warlike metaphors, and the affects around the generational divide. If, on the one hand, I could not completely grasp the implication of this understanding of conflict between women and its rhetorical praise, on the other hand, it was clear to me that this feminist practice had something to do with power differentials and with the public acknowledgment of one's dignity.

Attempting to better understand what was happening around me, I exploited a week of lunch breaks and happy hours to meet women and talk about what I was struggling with. These noninstitutional moments of the school were privileged points of observation. Besides allowing me to collect individual, and much more complex, takes on the status of the art of the generational divide, the more relaxed atmosphere allowed for the expression of some of the emotional dimensions of the conflict that were more restrained during general assemblies. While during public meetings disagreements appeared to occur mainly on intellectual or existential levels—and the ability of not showing apprehension or wariness was considered as performatively effective and as proof of *centratura* (a term that, in the feminist jargon, means being centered, well-balanced, self-aware)—more private settings allowed for the affective aspects of the conflict to emerge. Anger and sorrow definitely appeared to be blurred emotions, and the how-others-make-me-feel sort of statements seemed to overcome the what-they-say ones, both among younger and older women, as my encounter with Carolina shows.

I met Carolina at the back of the conference room of the *Scuola della Differenza*. She looked a bit nervous. I smiled at her and asked her something about the program of the meeting, since I was late and the speakers were already presenting. I smiled and introduced myself. Carolina did the same. She told me she had just finished her PhD with a concentration on feminist studies, and we immediately connected based on our common graduate student status—a status that she was not ready to give up, in spite of her recently accomplished doctorate. We moved into the adjacent room, since our chatting was starting to disturb the women around us who were obviously more interested in the presentations of the speakers than in our personal academic lives. Given that she was an Italian academic who focused on women's studies, I tried to exploit our "common language" to ask Carolina more research-oriented questions. For example, I asked her about the reception of Foucault and Butler in Italy (virtually absent from the debates that I had heard at the school) and expressed my difficulty in finding a common ground between the feminisms I had encountered in the United Kingdom and the United States and the one I had just encountered in Italy. She had read some of Butler's books, and appreciated her focus on "genders," but Carolina's intellectual horizon was clearly not influenced by Butler's work that, in fact, was not well known among the feminists I encountered nor appreciated by most of the "feminist celebrities" present at the meeting. I personally had heard Muraro dismissing Butler's work in a couple of quick sentences that summarized her work as an intellectual desire to erase difference in the attempt to celebrate a utopian lack of differentiation between the sexes. To my surprise, only a Catholic nun who participated at the *Scuola della Differenza* had the courage to challenge and criticize Muraro's take on sexual difference and to try to open up the conversation to include genders rather than just talking to the complementarity between sexes. By "starting from herself," the nun pointed out the risks linked to an overlapping between the thought of sexual difference and the Catholic Church's belief in the complementarity of women and men, as expressed, for instance, in the apostolic letter *Mulieris Dignitatem* written by Pope John Paul II in 1988. Muraro's lines of reasoning, as a matter of fact, supported, at least to a certain extent, the Catholic ecclesiastic understanding of women's complementarity to men and seemed to appreciate then–Cardinal Ratzinger's take on the relations between the sexes. In 2004, she had written a controversial pamphlet endorsing Cardinal Ratzinger's letter on the collaboration between men and women.[39] The nun's criticisms, certainly informed by her personal experience within the Catholic Church, were not fully received nor supported by the participants, Muraro included—at least publicly. These (non)reactions surprised me, and I confessed this to Carolina. We spent some time commenting on this episode, and she continued by telling me that, in spite of the rhetoric about "conflict," according to her, there was no space for real "conflict" over these types of issues among Italian feminists. The elders' feminist legacy was still very active: besides self-celebrating (and requiring younger feminists to acknowledge) their own accomplishments, they demanded that other activists share their same intellectual antagonisms. This was the same criterion used to read, see, judge, and approve who was a "real" feminist, and who was not—something that had political and personal but also quite practical implications. She felt that in order to be seen and approved, she needed to fit with the expectations of older feminists, and this was one of the reasons why she was not sure at that time if she wanted to pursue an academic job and to live an "academic life."

Carolina's struggles with the relationship between being and being recognized as a feminist and its political and personal implications were actually consistent with the concerns I observed also among UDI women. I noted on a few occasions that there were tensions between the feminist moral imperative of "starting from oneself" and the necessity to be recognized as feminists by their fellow activists, especially by elder ones. Since behaviors seen as disregarding the authority of their feminist leaders were understood (sometimes superficially) as variations on the trope of the "killing of the symbolic mother," many UDI women needed to feel "authorized" and "approved" in their personal (and therefore political) choices by Nuzzo or by other authoritative women of the group. The latter were acknowledged and recognized, within a feminist genealogy, as "symbolic mothers," by many of the UDI activists with whom I worked. The "killing of the symbolic mother" trope was used by the symbolic mothers themselves to dismiss their critics and had the performative effect of confirming the worth of the followers by disempowering the criticisms and, with this, the authoritativeness of the critics.

For example, one of the first relational dynamics that I noticed while hanging out with the Macare was linked to their connection with the national delegate at the time, Pina Nuzzo. The latter, a beautiful and charismatic sixty-year-old Salentine lady, was living in another region in 2012. Her trips to Salento were not frequent but always anticipated with great excitement by the Salentine UDI feminists. There was a special connection between Nuzzo and the Macare, something that the latter cherished very much. On our trips to UDI meetings in Rome, for example, we could sleep at Nuzzo's studio for free and often we could benefit from her presence during our dinners and night gatherings. Nuzzo being a very reserved and discrete person, this was quite a big "concession" and a proof of affection. The connections between Nuzzo and the Macare were also expressed in other ways: her advice was sought, almost daily, via cell phone, email, or Skype sessions in order to settle personal issues, romantic relational problems, or existential conundrums. In fact, Macare asked for her approval (*approvazione*) and authorization (*autorizzazione*) in almost every political initiative that they organized and often in relation to issues arising in their personal lives. Moreover, often her approval or disapproval was evoked, in her absence, in order to negotiate authoritativeness among them, or between them and representatives of other feminist groups. In other words, Pina Nuzzo's gaze meant a lot to the Macare, and, in person or not, she was always among their actual or imagined publics.

Thanks to encounters like the one with Carolina, and by participating at the *Scuola della Differenza*, I started hypothesizing that the generational divide was more a matter of dissensus (see, e.g., Rancière 1999, 2000, 2004a, 2004b, 2006; and Panagia 2009) than of disagreement. A few years later, and with many more feminist meetings and circles behind me, my perception of the conflict between generations is more nuanced, but I still find it a meaningful framework by which to understand the situation in Italy. From what I have noticed by hanging out with Italian feminists, older and younger women share two important elements: the need and desire to be recognized/acknowledged by the others, and a sort of dissatisfaction with the responses of the others to their expectations.[40] The older women yearn to be acknowledged as reference points, and the younger to be approved of, and authorized by, "historical" feminists. To a certain extent, though, this need seemed not to be fulfilled and still, quite literally, was at the center of many of the debates I witnessed during my fieldwork.

Diving in Paestum

Paestum is a town in the *Campania* region, well known for its archeological remains from the Greek and Roman periods. In 1976, more than one thousand women met there in what, until a few years ago, was considered the last convention of feminists in Italy. In 2012, thirty-six years after the last convention, some women decided that the historical moment for a new national meeting had arrived. As Dominijanni puts it, "The idea of a national meeting of radical feminism had been accruing for a while, as a counter-melody to the egalitarian, claiming, and moralizing tendency that the discourse around women (and, sometimes, of the women) does not cease to have on the mainstream political and media scene."[41] The title of the 2012 edition was *Primum vivere anche nella crisi* (First of all: living, also within the crisis), a title, in Latin and Italian, that tried to link the ancient past evoked by the setting, the 1976 feminist meeting, and the economic crisis that shapes the lives of many Italians today.[42] Interestingly, the logo of the meeting was a *female* diver: a modification of a local ancient painting.[43] The symbol of the diver was meant to make and reinforce a connection between the past and the future.[44]

This meeting was meant to represent a place where women could meet and listen to each other, a place for sharing and "conflicting." As a matter of fact, the dialogue/conflict between generations was something accounted for, and even anticipated, in the words of the promoters of the meeting. There were even jokes circulating on the web before the gathering. One of them, in the form of a cartoon, represented two women talking. One of them was depicted as saying, "Hundreds of feminists free to conflict!" and the other as replying, "First of all: *surviving* in Paestum."[45]

The 2012 Paestum meeting was organized around work in larger sessions as well as around nine smaller workshops on different aspects of women's politics. Many younger feminists attended Workshop #9, moderated by Muraro, in which the participants discussed "economy, work, and struggle."[46] As Clara, one of the activists who participated in that particular workshop and who later became a member of the *F9* collective, told me one night in Rome, in the women's bookstore where I interviewed her, "we saw each other and recognized/acknowledged each other" (*ci siamo viste e ci siamo riconosciute*).

One of the aspects that emerged during that workshop, in the words of Muraro as well as according to what some of the women who participated said in the sessions, was the mutual recognition not of authority, as Muraro's intellectual legacy would have suggested, but of subjectivity.[47] This need to reframe the relationships between Muraro, what she represents in terms of genealogies and of "authority" within the *pensiero della differenza sessuale*, and the younger women is not just a linguistic issue. As I understand it, it is an attempt to reassess the terms in which *disparità* (disparity) is perceived and lived.

Italian women's political practices and relations have so far been happening primarily around the acknowledgment of *disparità* among women. Solidarity among women is "precious, but it is not enough," since women need "diversified and strong relations . . . into which differences enter into play as enrichment and no longer as a threat" (*Libreria delle Donne di Milano*, quoted in Bono and Kemp 1991, 120; see also Cicioni 1989 on *affidamento* [entrustment]). The construction of these transformative relations is possible, say Italian feminists, only when a woman recognizes that another woman has something extra (*un di più*), a skill that the former does not possess. This acknowledgment of disparity is both an antidote to "the rule of male society according to which . . . all women are definitely equal" (*Libreria delle Donne di Milano*, in Bono and Kemp 1991, 121). It is also the fundamental premise of transformative relations (such as entrustment)—that is, relations that change society while changing oneself.[48]

Disparità, then, is often understood within a perspective influenced by Muraro's *L'Ordine Simbolico Della Madre* (Symbolical Order of the Mother; 1991), for whom authority and power are not synonyms (see, e.g., 1994). What distinguishes the former from the latter is its relational quality, its necessity of mediation: relations and mediations that, clearly, the younger generations do not acknowledge in the practices of the older ones. Nonetheless, the desire to be recognized still guides the actions of many younger feminists who choose not to dispense with the older generations approval and authorization but are quite willing to obtain them. It is from this perspective that I propose to interpret the experience of the *Femministe Nove* (*F9*).

Non Siamo Ereditiere, Siamo Precarie! We Are Not Heiresses; We Are Precarious [Workers]!

According to Clara, in the aftermath of Paestum 2012, fifteen women who had attended Workshop #9 and who, at that time, predominantly lived in or around Rome decided to meet and to produce a manifesto, written using the practice of collective writing. They founded a *collettivo d'azione* (collective of action) named *Femministe Nove*.[49] With this experience behind them—an experience that was "tough and painful," in Clara's words—they went to the 2013 Paestum meeting, which was entitled *Libera Ergo Sum* (in Latin: I am free, hence I am).[50] During the first session, the *F9* took the stage and performed a flash mob.[51] Two of them read some paragraphs of their manifesto, a woman of the group appeared to be directing the applause of the audience with a red fan, and the others held a banner saying *Stato di eccitazione permanente* (Permanent status of excitation/arousal). Here are some parts of the text they read:

> We are *Femministe Nove*. We are not heiresses, we are precarious [workers]. . . . We think about feminism as our possible revolution. And we cannot return it to what has already been said and to what has already been told. Feminism is a becoming, not a "must be." Self-determination is a never-ending struggle. . . . We recognize for ourselves the founding value of our genealogies in feminist thought and practices. We do not want to experience a confrontation between feminist generations, neither in an asymmetry of power and authority, nor in the envy of the epic of a dawning season. We want to start from our lives, from the present that we have in common, in order to build practices of reciprocal empowerment, of liberation from material and symbolic oppression. Self-determination and freedom do not coincide yet. . . . We are historical feminists: the present time scares us. We want to act to change it. Each one is responsible for her own indifference. . . . We feel part of that political generation that does not want to pay the price for the crisis, but that does not have the power to avoid it. . . . Let's do it this way: nobody speaks on behalf of others, of sex, and of the power that she enacts upon the other without having talked about herself. Nobody should talk about relation if she is not really willing to expose herself.[52]

The position of the *F9* was somehow representative of a common feeling among many women I met, who shared with them both the need to be protagonists of their feminist change and to be recognized by the older generations. Fulfilling either one of these needs alone would not have been enough for them. A recognition/acknowledgment without starting from themselves, or a political struggle without recognition by historical feminists, would not have been satisfying options.

It is clear that in the Italian feminist debates the issues of the asymmetry of power and authority played an important role, and it was not at all a coincidence that much of the debate that followed the performance of the *Femministe Nove* in Paestum revolved around the collective taking the stage and the activists presenting themselves as a group (although the names of each member of the *F9* were read at the end of their manifesto).[53] By talking with my informants among and beyond the *F9* group and by going through the videos of the sessions of the 2013 Paestum meetings, the blogs, the Facebook exchanges between feminists, and the press reviews after the meeting, I found that the performance of the *F9* generated a rift in the Italian feminist community. This separation can be described as one between those who acknowledged the flash mob as a political statement and those who, instead, considered it merely as a performance of women who were "showing off."

It was precisely in the fissures, at different levels, between desiring to be seen and recognized and showing off, that the Italian feminist debates were unfolding during my fieldwork. Within these fissures, issues around "representation" of women were central.

Notes

1. On the emergence of this theme, see, for example, the video recordings of the Italian feminists' meetings of Paestum 2012 and 2013 on YouTube: "Assemblea plenaria femminista-Paestum 2012 6/7 ottobre video n°1," http://www.youtube.com/watch?v=Co9bAQjEE_k (accessed March 21, 2019); "Assemblea plenaria femminista-Paestum 2012 6/7 ottobre video n°2," http://www.youtube.com/watch?v=FHGtdft19W8 (accessed March 21, 2019); "Assemblea plenaria femminista-Paestum 2012 6/7 ottobre video n°3," http://www.youtube.com/watch?v=TBFZRm9P5Lk (accessed March 21, 2019); "Paestum 2013-Plenaria 1," https://www.youtube.com/watch?v=e1k2fqgKZIU (accessed March 21, 2019); "Paestum 2013-Plenaria 3," https://www.youtube.com/watch?v=KQt4SEJwl1c (accessed March 21, 2019); "Paestum 2013-Plenaria 4," https://www.youtube.com/watch?v=-CRZf-aZv7Q (accessed March 21, 2019).

2. For the sake of space, I cannot address the specificity of single Italian feminist movements such as the lesbian-feminist traditions, recently founded queer groups, and the feminisms that chose not to engage with the pensiero della differenza sessuale. Without underestimating their importance and their contributions, I feel confident in stating that they were not representative of the majority of the feminist debates in Italy.

3. According to the Merriam-Webster dictionary, Karst is "an irregular limestone region with sink holes, underground streams, and caverns." Geographically, it refers to the "limestone plateau northeast of the Istrian Peninsula in Western Slovenia extending into Eastern Italy." "Karst," http://www.merriam-webster.com/dictionary/karst?show=o&t=1389370436 (accessed March 21, 2019).

4. Recent works on visibility, invisibility, and hypervisibility are, for example, Mowatt, French, and Malebranche 2013; Fleetwood 2011; Kral 2014; and, in the Italian context, Cancellieri and Ostanel 2015.

5. On the UDI, see, for example, Plesset 2006; Michetti, Repetto, and Viviani 1998; Rodano 2010; Wilson 2009; Bracke 2014; Pojmann 2013.

6. "Le donne della Costituente," Biblioteca del Senato Emeroteca, https://www.senato
.it/application/xmanager/projects/leg17/file/repository/relazioni/biblioteca/emeroteca
/Donnedellacostituente.pdf (accessed March 21, 2019).

7. Exceptions to this dominant narrative are, for example, Tambor 2014; Morris 2006.

8. Not currently online, it was called www.cittadinanze.it.

9. The laws on abortion (1974) and divorce (1970; see, e.g., Molé 2012, 84), together with
the abolition of so-called honor crimes in 1981 and the 1996 reinterpretation of sexual violence as a crime against the person—and not against the state—are some examples of important achievements around women's rights in Italy.

10. An important contribution to the historical unfolding of the relationships between
public and private is Michael Warner 2002. See also discussion below on Facebook as a political
platform for the women with whom I worked. Significantly, my informants distinguish between
the personal and the private, claiming that the personal, but not the private, is political.

11. On Italian feminism(s) and pensiero della differenza sessuale, see, for example, De
Lauretis 1990; Bono and Kemp 1991; Dominijanni 2005; Scarparo 2005. See also Plesset 2006,
53–54; Magaraggia and Leone 2010; Parati and West 2002; Milan Women's Bookstore Collective 1990; Dicker 2003; Dalla Torre 2014; Pojmann 2006, 2013; Charlotte Ross 2010; Wilson
2006; Bonomi Romagnoli 2014; Gribaldo and Zapperi 2010, 2012; Cavarero 1987; Ronchetti
2011; Bracke 2013, 2014; Tambor 2014; Malagreca 2006; Dell'Abate-Çelebi 2016; Righi 2013;
Strazzeri 2014; Braidotti 2002, 2003, 2005; Hajek 2018.

12. Following Giordano 2014, I distinguish in the rest of this book between acknowledgment and recognition, arguing that my informants seek both.

13. On the power of images, women, and *berlusconismo*, see, for example, Gribaldo and
Zapperi 2010, 2012.

14. I am not claiming, here, that Italian feminist groups were not active at all on the local
and national public spheres after the 1980s. An important contribution on Italian feminisms
after 2000 is, for example, Bonomi Romagnoli 2014. See also, for example, Orlando: Associazione di Donne, http://orlando.women.it/en/ (accessed March 21, 2019); Casa Internazionale
delle Donne, http://www.casainternazionaledelledonne.org/index.php/it/home (accessed
March 21, 2019); Libreria delle Donne di Milano, http://www.libreriadelledonne.it (accessed
March 21, 2019). In reference to more recent developments of feminisms in Italy, partially as a
reaction to what I describe here, see *Non Una di Meno*, https://nonunadimeno.wordpress.com
(accessed March 21, 2019).

15. During that decade, the UDI promoted three national campaigns: 50e50 Ovunque si
Decide—that is, a collection of signatures for a proposal of a law on women's representation
in institutions; Staffetta di Donne contro la Violenza sulle Donne, a yearlong relay against
violence against women; and Immagini Amiche, a contest for images and ads empowering
women. See Pojmann 2013, 183, and below.

16. While I am aware of the fact that the topic of gazes has been extremely influential for
many psychologically informed scholarly productions—such as those of (and in the legacy
of) Lacan and Irigaray—I choose not to address a reading of "gazes" from these particular
points of view nor to engage primarily with this particular scholarly tradition. While doing
so could potentially be a useful framework for my ethnographic context, I choose instead to
stress other dimensions of gazes and to engage in dialogue with other scholarly genealogies.
Moreover, I choose to talk about gazes, as this word is widely employed by my informants:
that is, my use of it provides evidence of the ways they understand perception rather than
describing what perception is about. I agree with Crary that attention "is much more than a

question of the gaze, of looking, of the subject only as a spectator," and that the "problem of perception" needs to be "extracted from an easy equation with questions of visuality" (1999, 2). See also, on "vision as a metonym for perception, cognition, and aspiration," McLagan and McKee (2012, 22). See also Faeta 2011; Fleetwood 2011; Rose 2012; Christine Ross 2008; Ronzon 2011; Sturken and Cartwright 2009; Berger 1972; Stoller 1989, 1997.

17. Nuzzo makes a pun here, conflating the expression *senso unico* (one way) with *sesso unico* (the only one sex, i.e., the male, which colonizes the symbolic and material aspects of women's lives).

18. It held the words, "I am indignant."

19. "Sulla rappresentanza politica femminile, sull'arte di polemizzare tra donne e sulla rivoluzione scientifica in corso," Sottospora, Libreria delle Donne di Milano, http://www .libreriadelledonne.it/_oldsite/news/articoli/sottosopra87.htm (accessed March 21, 2019).

20. *Laboratorio Donnae*, http://laboratoriodonnae.wordpress.com (accessed March 21, 2019). The fourth meeting was held in Manfredonia, November 16–17, 2013.

21. "Partire da sé, abbiamo detto," *Laboratorio Donnae* (blog), http://laboratoriodonnae .wordpress.com/2012/09/27/partire-da-se-abbiamo-detto/ (accessed March 21, 2019).

22. *Laboratorio Donnae*, http://laboratoriodonnae.wordpress.com (accessed March 21, 2019).

23. *Laboratorio Donnae*, http://laboratoriodonnae.wordpress.com (accessed March 21, 2019).

24. "Femminismo molecolare," *Laboratorio Donnae* (blog), http://laboratoriodonnae .wordpress.com/2013/06/03/femminismo-molecolare/ (accessed March 21, 2019); see also "Una femminista molecolare," *Laboratorio Donnae* (blog), http://laboratoriodonnae .wordpress.com/2013/06/10/una-femminista-molecolare/ (accessed March 21, 2019).

25. It is worth mentioning that *protagonismo* also has a derogatory meaning in Italian, which could be translated as an attention-seeking attitude. "Femminismo molecolare," *Laboratorio Donnae* (blog), http://laboratoriodonnae.wordpress.com/2013/06/03/femminismo -molecolare/ (accessed March 21, 2019).

26. "Una femminista molecolare," *Laboratorio Donnae* (blog), http://laboratoriodonnae .wordpress.com/2013/06/10/una-femminista-molecolare/ (accessed March 21, 2019).

27. Pina Nuzzo, "Partire da sé, abbiamo detto," *Laboratorio Donnae*, (blog) http:// laboratoriodonnae.wordpress.com/2012/09/27/partire-da-se-abbiamo-detto/ (accessed March 21, 2019).

28. The molecular dimension stressed by this way of understanding feminism, and the commonality, in space and time, among different generations of feminists, gestures toward the creations of new feminist spaces and practices that could mend the current rift between feminist generations that I describe below.

29. See Ammirati et al. 2013, 37–56.

30. This text is the author's written revision of the one she read at the meeting.

31. See, for example, Ammirati et al. 2013.

32. This text is the author's written revision of the one she read at the meeting.

33. See also Ammirati et al. 2013, 74–75. Clearly the metaphor of the mirror resonates with the work of Irigaray.

34. Some older informants told me, with a hint of sarcasm, that right after Muraro started to conceive and present her ideas on the maternal symbolic and on the importance of genealogies, the biological mothers of feminist women—who, until then, had endorsed the "never like my mother" slogan—started to appear in feminist meetings.

35. I also found similar narratives in *contro versa*, and in the personal experiences of different women.

36. It is worth noting that genealogies, in their attempt of inclusion, are also exclusionary.

37. "Diversamente Occupate in equilibrio tra lavori e non lavori," *Diversamente Occupate* (blog), http://diversamenteoccupate.blogspot.it/ (accessed March 21, 2019).

38. I noticed this generational aspect also, for example, in the meetings of the UDI, in the meetings organized by the women related to *La Casa delle Donne* of Lecce, in the recordings of the Paestum 2012 and 2013 conventions, and in various comments online (on Facebook, forums, and blogs).

39. "Se il cardinale Ratzinger fosse un mio studente," Libera Università delle Donne, http://www.universitadelledonne.it/muraro-ratz.htm (accessed March 21, 2019).

40. There are, of course, exceptions that do not fit into this schematic interpretation. Donnae Lab and the feminist groups that, at a certain point in their development, ceased to want to be acknowledged by the others and did not answer to the call of the Paestum meeting are just two examples. Nonetheless, in the registrations for the sessions of the 2012 and 2013 meetings in Paestum, it appears that the problems generated by the generational divide and by the lack of *riconoscimento* (acknowledgment/recognition) were still taking space and airtime during Italian feminist debates.

41. "Donne a Paestum. Archeologia del futuro," Libreria delle Donne di Milano, http://www.libreriadelledonne.it/_oldsite/news/articoli/Manifo31012.htm (accessed March 21, 2019).

42. This phrase is probably inspired by the well-known aphorism, popularly attributed to Aristotle: *primum vivere, deinde philosophari* (first, living, then, doing philosophy). This motto is consistent both with the ubiquitous belief among the feminist circles I attended that practices, more than theory, should inform feminist political activism and with the urgent need to concentrate on one's own primary needs in this period of economic instability and precariousness (see, e.g., Molé 2008, 2010, 2012, 2013; Muehlebach 2012).

43. This is the original painting: "Tomba del tuffatore," *Wikipedia*, http://it.wikipedia.org/wiki/Tomba_del_tuffatore (accessed March 21, 2019), and this is the logo of the feminist meeting: http://www.danieladanna.it/xxdonne/2012/12/paestum-primum-vivere/ (accessed March 21, 2019).

44. This element confirms the need for reconciliation with history discussed above in relation to the karstic metaphor.

45. "La rivoluzione si fa per alzata di mano," *La 27esima Ora* (blog), http://27esimaora.corriere.it/articolo/la-rivoluzione-si-fa-per-alzata-di-mano/ (accessed March 21, 2019). The pun concerns the title of the feminist meeting in Paestum *Primum: vivere* (First of all: living).

46. "Paestum 2012: l'autorità come pratica politica delle donne," *Femminile Plurale* (blog), http://femminileplurale.wordpress.com/2012/10/15/paestum-2012-lautorita-come-pratica-politica-delle-donne/ (accessed March 21, 2019).

47. "Assemblea plenaria femminista-Paestum 2012 6/7 ottobre video n°3," https://www.youtube.com/watch?v=TBFZRm9P5Lk (accessed March 21, 2019). See also Muraro, "#paestum2012 luisa muraro by Libreria delle donne di Milano," https://www.youtube.com/watch?v=SwO51eourSE (accessed March 21, 2019).

48. I had the chance to discuss this issue with some older feminist women. It is clear that Muraro's reflections on the authority of the mother, and on disparity, also had the effect of "regulating," of "putting order into relationships between women" that apparently until then had been difficult to manage (Lucia, July 2013).

49. *Nove* means both the number nine—that of the workshop where all those women recognized each other—and "new" in ancient Italian (and in some of its dialectal forms).

50. This title is obviously a modification of the famous latin phrase *"cogito ergo sum,"* coined by philosopher René Descartes in the seventeenth century.

51. See "Assemblea plenaria femminista-Paestum 2012 6/7 ottobre video n°3," https://www.youtube.com/watch?v=TBFZRm9P5Lk (accessed March 21, 2019), around fifty-nine minutes into this video.

52. "F9, Manifesto," *Feministe Nove* (blog), http://femministenove.wordpress.com/ (accessed March 21, 2019).

53. "Sulle Femministe Nove a Paestum," *Femminile Plurale* (blog), http://femminileplurale.wordpress.com/2013/10/12/paestum-2013-femministe-nove/ (accessed March 21, 2019).

3

THE CREATION(S) OF FEMMINICIDIO

IN THIS CHAPTER, I DISCUSS THE COMMONSENSICAL UNDERSTANDINGS and feelings that link women and victims in contemporary Italy. My claim is that for many Italian women, and in different ways, violence against women influenced how they think about, understand, and represent their being in the world. I claim that the dominant framework used to represent women in Italy when I carried out my fieldwork put women in the role of victims in relation to violence against women. This language and these images of victimhood dominated the media and political campaigns against what my informants called "sexed violence." These representations naturalized the connections between women and victims; the consequences of these associations often went unnoticed. Many Italian women, feminist or not, adhered to these representations, too. Sometimes, for example, the precariousness of women's material bodies resonated with the imaginary and experiences linked to economic precariousness, and the traumatized body became "a critical measure of truth" (Molé 2012; see also Petryna 2002), something beyond economic precariousness. In other instances, the commonsensical acknowledgment of the violability of women's bodies instead represented something to exploit vis-à-vis personal and social insecurities or harkened back to more socially acceptable representations of womanhood informed by Italian Catholic heritage.

In this chapter, I indicate some directions one might take to understand how and why this happened. This reading of the existential precariousness of the condition of women also informed the frame of the debates around a women's question in Italy beyond femminicidio and violence against women. By making these remarks, I do not intend to deny the role of self-determination, a key notion, for example, during the pro–abortion rights campaigns in the 1970s, in Italian feminist political activism. I nonetheless want to stress the different overtones—clearly marked by the reference to the existential precariousness of women's bodies—that Italian women's activism showed in promoting different types of campaigns or reflections on the new "women's question" in Italy.

Figure 3.1. Campidoglio, Rome. *ENEL Sole* campaign, 2013. (Photo credit: ANSA.)

ENEL Sole and *Not in My Name:* The Representational Violence of Antiviolence Initiatives

In 2013, on the International Day against Violence against Women, at Campidoglio, the headquarters of the municipality of Rome, the company *ENEL Sole* pointed twenty projectors powered by a 30 kW generator toward the symbol of the city of Rome with the purpose of illuminating it with the (English) words "Stop Violence against Women." In order to "contribute to the perception of such an important issue," the electric company decided to project two images on a red background—the color, the press release claims, was a symbol of that initiative.[1] These images, as appear clearly in figure 3.1, included an open hand and the text: STOP VIOLENCE AGAINST WOMEN. The mission of *ENEL Sole*, a power company that is part of the *ENEL* group (of which the Italian state is the main shareholder) is to "illuminate cities, towns and their distinctive features with efficiency and quality by means of planning, carrying out and managing the systems and services that increase the well-being of the persons who live there."[2] Through this initiative, the company claimed to restate that *ENEL* continuously operates "in respect of people's dignity, their diversity" and that it rejects "any kind of violence" and "supports the mass media and internet campaigns of the Ministry of Labor and Social Policies, and the Council for the Social Policies and Equal Opportunities of the Municipality of Rome."

I ran across the pictures of this installation while surfing the internet on November 25, 2013. I was in Salento at that time and, along with my feminist friends, noticed how much the number of initiatives and the media coverage for the International Day against Violence against Women had increased since 2011, when I first arrived in Salento. I started scrolling through the images of the Campidoglio with some of my Salentine informants, who immediately started frowning. They did so for a reason: the Campidoglio installation in fact represented very well the rhetorical and visually dominant codes linked to the struggle against violence against women and femminicidio in Italy. Its importance was linked to the messages clarified by two different levels of visual and semiotic analysis that correspond to different visualities or ways of seeing (see, e.g., Berger 1972; Mirzoeff 2006) the violence against women in contemporary Italy that I have encountered during my fieldwork. As a matter of fact, these analyses also gesture toward the "karstic" ambivalence of visibility. As Sturken and Cartwright (2009) point out, what is important is not just the image itself but how it is seen by specific audiences who look in particular ways. On the one hand, one cannot deny the visual power of this impressive installation: the bright red color vibrated in the Roman November night, grabbing the attention of passersby. The image was certainly eye-catching. For those who could read and understand English, the words were unambiguous. Without any doubt, such a public and institutional political stance against violence against women would have been difficult to find, and even to imagine, in Italy just two years earlier. Since 2011, the public relevance of femminicidio had changed considerably. From being a topic debated mostly within Italian feminist circles, violence against women gradually started to appear in the mainstream media and make its way into the Italian public scene. In such a reading of the installation, the fact that *ENEL Sole* decided to take this political position in such a *visible* way is indeed an important element per se, a feature of the public relevance that the struggle against violence against women had been increasingly playing in contemporary Italian society. Even the Salentine feminists were recognizing this point. Nonetheless, there was another level of analysis that they were applying to the image of the installation—a much more important one.

Yet a closer analysis of some of the visual and semiotic contents of this installation informed by the visualities of the feminist women I met during my fieldwork adds other relevant dimensions to the issues of womanhood and violence against women in Italy. As I mentioned, while the institutional attention to femminicidio and the visual impact of the Campidoglio initiative were not questioned, a more attentive look at this installation, understood as a representation of the struggle against violence against women by the Salentine feminists, raised different questions on the messages conveyed and on its political efficacy in opposing violence against women in Italy. By looking at the installation through the "way of seeing" I was "schooled in" (see Grasseni

2007, 2011; also Ronzon 2011) by the Salentine activists with whom I worked, it was evident that the image was reinscribing an understanding of women-as-victims—something that the Italian feminists I met strongly opposed. Hence their frowning response. First, it is worth noting that the image projected on the Campidoglio palace appeared to be an example of remediation (see, e.g., Edwards 2012; Sturken and Cartwright 2009, 60): a graphic rearrangement, a visual quotation, of the famous logo of the SVAW (Stop Violence against Women) campaign of Amnesty International. The text and the presence of an open hand were an obvious reference to that image.

Although *ENEL* placed the text on the right, and the open hand on the left, the choice of the fonts and of the size of the texts seemed very similar (i.e., the type size of the word *STOP* is bigger than the ones used for *violence* in both cases). Yet the proportions between the size of the text and that of the hand differed: in the Campidoglio installation, the size of the hand was not as big in comparison to the text as it appeared in the Amnesty logo. The most eye-catching difference in the two images, though, was linked to the silhouettes and shapes of the hands: the one in the Campidoglio installation materialized as a traced contour and not as a stain of color.[3]

The first question that this installation raised to a gaze schooled in the particular Italian feminist circles of which I was a part, especially in the Salento area of Italy, was: Who did the creators of this installation imagine as their audience? Such a question, important in every visual and semiotic analysis, was particularly relevant in this case since the text through which *ENEL Sole* conveyed the explanation of the installation was written in English—a puzzling choice given that few Italians can read and understand this language today, especially among the older generations.[4] Another, perhaps more important, question raised by my schooled gaze was linked to the meaning of the open hand. The latter element, according to my informants, was the more unsettling aspect of the installation. The juxtaposition of an open hand with the words STOP VIOLENCE AGAINST WOMEN certainly was meant to resonate with the authoritative gesture linked to traffic regulations, such as the image of an open hand that appears at some pedestrian crossings. As the Amnesty International campaign shows, this indexical use of the open hand was, and is currently, widely employed in representations of the struggle against violence against women, in Italy and abroad. (See fig. 3.2.)

If this was the shared and dominant (indexical) meaning of the open hand to which the *ENEL Sole* installation was gesturing, an even closer look at the shape and spatial disposition of the hand in the Campidoglio installation reveals some interesting dissonances between the use of *that* particular open hand, and the condemnation of violence against women—at least according

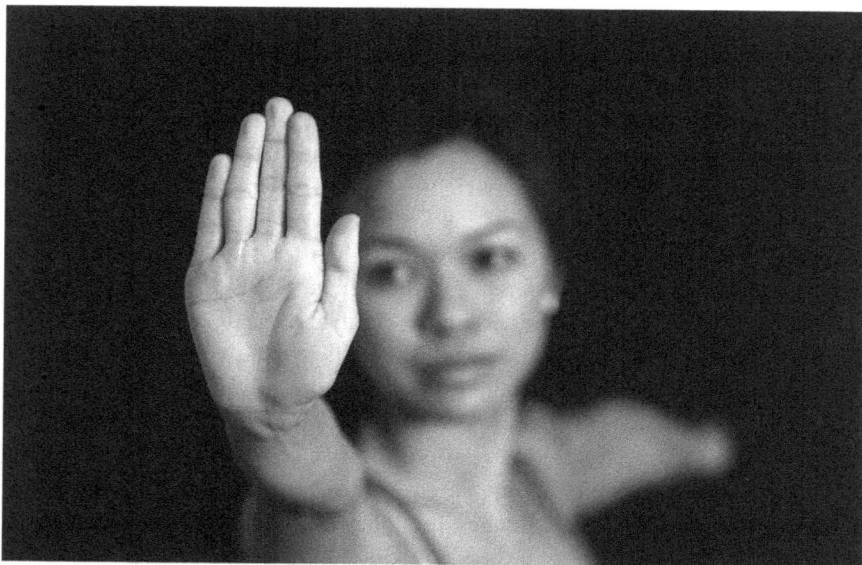

Figure 3.2. Authoritative hand. (Photo credit: Pexels.com.)

to the Italian feminist women with whom I worked. First, in this image the fingers appeared to be slightly parted: they were thin, possibly consistent with a stereotypical female hand. This is what emerged frequently during some photo-elicited interviews I conducted on this Campidoglio installation. Moreover, the hand appeared to be slightly rotated: it was not vertical and perpendicular to the base of the image. In reference to the point of view of the observer, it seemed to originate from a lower position. In other words, aesthetically the hand in the *ENEL Sole* campaign seemed to be (or, at least, was perceived by my informants as) a visual quotation of *these* types of images, images that are rather ubiquitous in relation to the public representation of violence against women in Italy. (See fig. 3.3.)

In sum, according to the way of seeing that I learned during my fieldwork with Italian feminists, it seemed that the open hand in the *ENEL Sole* installation did not have an authoritative function but a *protective* one.[5] The interpretation of the open hand as a protective gesture introduced some questions from my informants' points of view and ways of seeing: Whose voice was saying "stop violence against women"? Who was it being said to? and What were the social effects of this appeal? For the feminists with whom I worked, the semantic visual field to which the image of this particular open hand gestured was consistent with specific and widespread commonsensical understandings

Figure 3.3. Protective hand. (Photo credit: Pexels.com.)

of women in Italian society, understandings that had also been mobilized in connection with the recent issues around femminicidio: namely, with the naturalization of women-as-victims.

From this perspective, while nominally trying to challenge it, the *ENEL* campaign was actually reinscribing one of the features that led to violence against women in the first place: the understanding of women as passive victims in need of (men's) protection. To *these representations* of women as objects of tutelage and as beings in need of protection, my informants reacted strongly. They believed the "commonsensical" interpretations of the roles and places of women conveyed in many campaigns against violence against women to be at odds with their attempt to be and to represent themselves as self-determined, agentive subjects—that is, as witnesses and not as victims, as UDI women strongly claimed. What *they saw* in this installation was not primarily an appeal in support of women's causes but instead a promotional advertisement for the energy company *ENEL Sole*. Therefore, the rhetorical and visual representation of the struggle against femminicidio was not perceived as pertaining to women's empowerment but *primarily* to the company's promotional interests. The women I met perceived the struggle against femminicidio to have been developing into something that helped sell products or services of one type or another in contemporary Italy: this is why my informants often understood the representations of femminicidio as a battlefield for their representational struggle.

The feminists' claim about the violence of antiviolence campaigns was not isolated to the *ENEL Sole* installation. Interestingly, it encompassed other campaigns and initiatives that were meant to be in support of women's causes. Notably, one of those was also the text of the Italian "Law against Femminicidio." In October 2013, the approval by the Italian government of a *Decreto Legge* against *Femminicidio*—the Law against Femminicidio (Law 119/2013)—could be seen both as representing an opportunity to overcome some cultural issues around violence against women and as evidence of the fragmentation of the Italian juridical system around violence against women.[6] This law came after, and complemented, the Anti-Stalking Law (Law 38) that was approved in 2009.[7] Yet, in spite of its intentions, and because of the important media effects that the "Law against Femminicidio" generated, many feminists criticized and contested it vigorously, deeming many aspects of the law to be detrimental to women's causes.[8] First, they read the approval and the structure of this law as being an advertisement for the new government. This interpretation was strengthened by the fact that this specific law was approved in the form of a legislative decree that comprised a so-called package of security reforms, in addition to the articles that aimed at preventing and hindering violence against women. This political move was perceived as an example of notorious Italian slyness, in particular because this package included the legalization of some stricter measures in order to contrast anti-TAV activism—measures that were approved by exploiting the urgency of the antifemminicidio law.[9] Moreover, and most importantly, some feminist women criticized Law 93/2013 since it presented women as weak subjects (*soggetti deboli*), and it was characterized by a security trait (*impronta securitaria*) that favored police control (*controllo poliziesco*) over women's bodies. In particular, the aspect that feminists contested (some of whom started a collection of signatures against this law entitled Not in My Name) was the alleged negation prescribed by Law 93/2013 of the right to rescind the charge a woman has filed at a police station.[10] Paradoxically, then, some feminists understood the antifemminicidio law itself to *represent a form of violence against women* in that it limited their rights and voices. Moreover, this was not an isolated case in reference to initiatives allegedly in support of women's causes.

"Women Cry"

Tonia is a woman in her thirties and comes from Rome. She is one of my Facebook friends and was a UDI woman particularly close to the Macare. One of the most obvious things one noticed by living with the Macare was that the Salentine feminists with whom I worked tended to be quite politically influential and socially popular within the UDI. Their closeness to Nuzzo, their support of political stances they advocated during self-convocation meetings (*autoconvocazioni*), their cheerful attitude, and their sense of humor were some of the characteristics that made them special in the eyes of other UDI women. As a result of their popularity, the Macare tended to have strong opinions on whom to spend time with when they went to national UDI meetings, believing, as the Italian adage goes, that one can tell who someone is by paying attention to the company they keep (*dimmi con chi vai, e ti dirò chi sei*). The presence of some women was particularly welcomed, among them some of the women from Pescara, Calabria, Milan, and Rome, who, occasionally, traveled to Apulia to visit the Macare and to share moments of "women's sociality." Tonia was one of them. We met in person in Bologna, in 2011, at a "Macare & friends" *aperitivo* during the days of the congress, and again a few times in Rome in 2012. Since then, I mostly followed her life and activities through Facebook and her blog: read, commented, and shared on Facebook by UDI Salentine women, too. Tonia defined herself as "communist, feminist, deeply and irreparably anti-fascist, bitter, prone to anger, and long-winded." She was very, very active on the internet. She commented zealously and untiringly on news of women's matters: in politics, media, blogs, and popular culture. She posted, reposted, and commented on many items every single day of the year: as I told her once, jokingly, she should be considered my assistant, since she provided a press review on topics related to women every single day of the year. She was amused by my remarks. On March 25, 2014, in a very much liked post on her Facebook diary (liked also by some of the Macare), she wrote: "From what I understood, in order to show that you are against violence against women you either need to get yourself naked or you need to take a picture of yourself crying with a black eye." Her irony and poignant criticism—a characteristic of her Facebook persona—as usual did not go unnoticed. One of her Facebook friends commented: "Tonia, women are defenseless! Women are weak, women cry. If you beat him, you are not a woman, you are a man. If you file against him, you are not a woman, you are an asshole who wants to get him in trouble. Women CRY, THAT'S IT! . . . If women do not cry, they are not in need of help. They don't need to be assisted and protected but left alone. They do not cry, therefore, they do not suffer. On the contrary, they deserve it [their suffering], or they like it" (emphasis in the original).

This brief exchange gives a sense of some of the issues that were going on inside and outside Italian feminist communities. Tonia and her Facebook friend were gesturing toward the dominant visuality or way of seeing and the hegemonic ways of sensing and representing (potentially violated) women in contemporary Italy. In the past few years, in the aftermath of the SNOQ manifestations (see chap. 2) and in reference to the emergence of femminicidio as a matter of concern in Italy, violence against women became a reference point in sensing and making sense of being women. This was a recent development, and it differed significantly from the one Italian feminist women portrayed in the 1970s and 1980s. At that time, the key phrase in reference to abortion, divorce, and also violence against women was "self-determination." This new interpretation had a representational aspect, too: this particular domain is the terrain of the affective politics that this book describes.

From "Self-Determination" to "Sexed Violence"

This way of understanding what it was to be a woman defined by being potentially exposed to violence was widespread although inflected differently in different circumstances. It was something new and something that differed considerably from the political stances proclaimed in the 1970s and 1980s that had been characterized chiefly by the legal achievements of the Italian women's movements. There are many visual examples of the shift that, I argue, has been characterizing Italian women's movements in the past few years, opening up a space for a new women's question in Italy. By juxtaposing and confronting archival images of women's manifestations during the 1970s and 1980s with contemporary ones, for example, this difference stands out. During the years 2012–2014, one of the main ways to publicly protest was through a version of a "die-in" performance. While it was still relatively easy in 2012 to find women parading with banners and posters, in the 1970s and 1980s, images of women pretending to be dead or identifying with victims of violence and femminicidio are difficult to find, if they exist at all.[11] This can mean either that women in the 1970s and 1980s did not perform "die-in" protests or that the eyes of the photographers who worked for the media at that time did not record or recognize those images as meaningful. In either case, I consider my point supported by this (lack of) evidence: besides the different objectives of the protests, the slogans, and the ways messages were conveyed, the pictures from the 1970s and 1980s differ from contemporary ones. This difference, I claim, supports my reading of a change in the political conceptions of women's bodies that I am presenting in this book. It is my claim that with the Staffetta (see chap. 4) and with the events linked to the SNOQ manifestations, then, violence and the potential exposure to it became the kernel around which many Italian women started to conceive of themselves, both existentially and as political subjects (see Parmigiani 2018). As I illustrated previously, some of my informants certainly did so by thinking about their bodies and their being in the world. However, they were not alone in doing so. In other words, differently from the 1970s and 1980s, the bodies of women in Italy in the early 2010s were not, primarily, the political objects of sexual liberation, or of self-determination.[12] The bodies of women were violated bodies (*corpi violati*), traumatized and/or traumatizable.

This reading of the existential precariousness of the condition of women also informed and expanded the frame of the debates in Italy *beyond* femminicidio and sexed violence. In the 2014 campaign *maipiùclandestine* (never clandestine again), a campaign promoted by the *Femministe Nove* (see above) with Pina Nuzzo in support of the application of Law 194 on abortion, for example, the problem of the enforcement of the law was framed as an attempt of "patriarchy" *to violate* women's bodies. They wrote: "What happens when a woman can decide? What happens is that 'patriarchy' raises it defenses, *forcing a woman* through an obstacle course when things go well, [forcing a woman] on a *via crucis* when they go badly."[13] The warlike metaphors and the reference to the Way of the Cross are eloquent, in this respect, especially when compared to this 1980 flyer by the UDI (see fig. 3.4), when violence and self-determination were inflected quite differently:

> We do not want fear, anguish, and terror.
> We do not want the oppression and the fury
> of the strongest.
> We do not believe in the methods of oppression
> and authoritarianism.
> We do not accept the impunity guaranteed to he who is guilty.
> We won't let [anybody] take away from us all that
> we have conquered
> in many years of struggles, individual and collective
> conflicts
> with the only weapons
> of respect for human values,
> for human life,
> of solidarity and
> of our dignity.
> For freeing us from any form of oppression
> old and new.
> For living a peace marked
> by our liberation.

In the 1980 flyer, which was centered on violence, women's bodies were not represented as potential objects of violence but as loci for liberation. By contrast, in the *maipiùclandestine* public note, the topic of self-determination

8 marzo 1980

NOI NON VOGLIAMO LA PAURA, L'ANGOSCIA, IL TERRORE.
NOI NON VOGLIAMO LA SOPRAFFAZIONE E LA FEROCIA
DEL PIU' FORTE.

NOI NON CREDIAMO AL METODO DELL'OPPRESSIONE
E DELL'AUTORITARISMO.

NOI NON ACCETTIAMO L'IMPUNITA' ASSICURATA
AI COLPEVOLI.

NOI NON PERMETTEREMO CHE CI SIA TOLTO NIENTE
DI TUTTO CIO' CHE ABBIAMO CONQUISTATO
IN TANTI ANNI DI LOTTE, DI CONFLITTI
INDIVIDUALI E COLLETTIVI
CON LE UNICHE ARMI
DEL RISPETTO DEI VALORI UMANI,
DELLA VITA UMANA,
DELLA SOLIDARIETA' E
DELLA NOSTRA DIGNITA'

PER LIBERARCI DA OGNI FORMA DI OPPRESSIONE
VECCHIA E NUOVA.

PER VIVERE UNA PACE SEGNATA
DALLA NOSTRA LIBERAZIONE.

Figure 3.4. UDI's flyer, March 8, 1980. (Courtesy of its author, Pina Nuzzo.)

around the right to choose one's own pregnancy was inflected in a language of suffering and of victimhood (see below).

At first, the reading of the personal and political status of Italian women as a community of potentially violated subjects affected mainly the feminists, especially in the aftermath of the Staffetta. The latter initiative, in fact, helped promote and diffuse awareness around femminicidio and violence against women. With the national emergence of the women's question, after the SNOQ demonstrations, these interpretations of the links between violence and womanhood spilled over to other sectors of Italian society and to nonfeminist women and men. The language of victimhood became dominant also in framing violence against women in the Italian context as a whole (see below). As I show in the next chapters, this national issue presented in particular ways in Salento, where the women-as-victims trope resonated with local understandings of womanhood in relation to the honor and shame complex.

The Creation(s) of Femminicidio: The Emergence of a "Community of Sense" of (Potentially) Violated Women

It was September 2011, and I had just started my fieldwork. I was in Lecce with Eugenia, wanting to get to know both her and the organization (UDI) to which she belonged. I was strolling around Porta Napoli with her when she started talking about the three national campaigns promoted by the UDI since 2002: 50E50, the Staffetta di Donne contro la Violenza sulle Donne, and Immagini Amiche (see chap. 4). She told me that the first one was a bill concerning the percentage of women that should be on Italian governing boards at all political levels, and the third was a campaign to promote awareness of how women and specifically women's bodies were portrayed on TV and in other media.[14] The second national campaign—which Eugenia seemed to consider the most important, the one that exemplified the struggles of the other two campaigns as well—was against what UDI women call "sexed violence" and femminicidio. That was the first time I had ever heard the word *femminicidio*.

Among the first people who used this term *politically*, in the Italian context, apparently were the women of the UDI.[15] Pina Nuzzo, the former national delegate of the UDI, told me in a private conversation that

> the term femminicidio was taken on politically by the UDI during a sit-in in front of the Parliament in June, I think, of 2006, with a banner drawn by me that said Stop Femminicidio. We wanted to involve the women members of Parliament and to direct the attention of institutions to a killing spree (*mattanza*) that seemed, and still seems, unstoppable. From that moment on I always used [the term], and I re-launched it with the *Staffetta* in 2008. There are documents that certify the political choice and the references to the South American context. . . . I chose to push through the use of a term that bothered both men and women in order to force them to see, in many murders classified as generic in the statistical data, the violent death (*morte violenta*) of women at the hands of men. In general, they are relatives and kin.[16]

This linguistic struggle was even more so an ideological one, as Nuzzo clearly pointed out. It was also, I would add, a representational one. The choice of introducing a new word was a conscious attempt to make visible a particular interpretation of the world that, in 2006, was *invisible* to many: it was the emergence of an "incommensurable" (Povinelli 2001).[17] Stressing the fact that *femminicidio* is not a synonym for homicide or for uxoricide was indeed a revolution in men's and women's commonsensical perception, in Rancièrian terms, of what violence against women is.

The story of the process of legitimization of the word *femminicidio*, in this sense, was also the story of its creation, and the steps that describe the endorsement of the term also represented the measures of the passage between the incommensurability of a phenomenon and its recognition by Italian public opinion. It was, to quote Naisargi Dave's pun (2011, 656), the "emergence" of an "emergency." In Dave's ethnography as well, the emergence of a word—lesbian, in that case—coincided with the creation of new possibilities and of an "affective community of women based on the commonality of their desires" (2010b, 598).[18] If one can trace the origin of the public appearance of this word back to 2006, it is not until 2009 and especially until 2012–2013 that non-UDI and explicitly nonfeminist women and men began to embrace and adopt the term *femminicidio*. In this process, the Staffetta delle Donne contro la Violenza sulle Donne, a national campaign against "sexed violence" organized by the UDI in 2008–2009 played a crucial role (see, in particular, chap. 4; Parmigiani 2018). While central, it might be considered only a first step toward the formal and widespread recognition of the word and worlds of femminicidio. Right from the beginning, the Staffetta superimposed the bodies of *violated* women on *all* women. This ideological operation led to the conflation of the violated bodies of *some* women with women's bodies *at large*. It did so by promoting dissensus around sexed violence, which, I claim, contributed to the construction not only of an imagined community (Anderson 1991) of violated (or potentially violated) women but of a community of sense structured around violence against women (Parmigiani 2018). This community of sense was understood as a community that "acknowledges politics to contain a sensuous and aesthetic aspect that is irreducible to ideology and idealization" and that "works toward being-together only through a consistent dismantling of any idealized common ground, form, or figure" (Hinderliter et al. 2009, 2). In the Italian case I am analyzing, this community did not gather around ideas of who a woman is or should be, nor did the community arise from a common acknowledgment of what sexed violence was. Rather, following Rosa's line of reasoning (see chap. 1), it was structured around shared *feelings* and *affects*, triggered by women's sense of being actual or potential objects of sexed violence. With the emergence of this community, a new political subject made its appearance in the Italian context: women. As I have stated before (Parmigiani 2018, 24), in presenting the Staffetta to the press, Nuzzo (2008) wrote, "We want to fight against sexed violence and femicide. In order to do so, we want to say WHO we are, without putting a distance between us and the other [women], because we are not alien [to violence] or privileged and we do not expect one woman alone to do what all of us can't manage to do: stop the violence from which we all suffer! (far smettere la violenza che tutte subiamo!)" (translation mine).

More explicitly, after describing who is "an abused woman" and after highlighting the connection between being the object of violence and "having a precarious job," Nuzzo claimed literally, "QUELLA donna siamo NOI" (WE are ALL THAT woman). Moreover, in the same document Nuzzo wrote that, "We must first of all talk by saying WE, we shouldn't think of ourselves as alien or even privileged, nor should we be tempted (cadere nella tentazione di) to sensitise the women we meet to make them aware of the violence that they certainly suffer, that we all suffer" (Nuzzo 2008).

If the Staffetta was one step in the creation of an (affective, also) community of potentially violated women, of this community of sense of potentially violated women, the events linked to the SNOQ manifestations represented another important benchmark in this process.

"Where Are You, Girls?" Italy's New Women's Question

The Relay, or Staffetta, was a decisive moment in the legitimization of the word *femminicidio*. Nonetheless, it was not until 2012–2013 that this word, the world it conveyed, and the construction of women's bodies as violated (or potentially so) prompted people beyond feminist circles to question the "commonsensical" understanding of the status of women in Italy. As I mentioned in chapter 2, the SNOQ movement developed as a reaction to Berlusconi's sexual scandals. Silvio Berlusconi is a well-known figure of recent Italian political history. He was Italy's prime minister four times, and his party governed Italy for most of the past twenty years.[19] He was the leader of the right-wing party Forza Italia (Onward, Italy! FI) until 2009, and, later, he was the head of Il Popolo delle Libertà (the People of Liberties, PdL). Berlusconi is a billionaire, and his personal and financial interests ranged from the Milan soccer team to the holding company Fininvest S.p.A., from the multimedia production company Mediaset S.p.A. to the famous publishing house Mondadori. Berlusconi's final legislature came to a premature end, in late 2011, as a result of a number of events, including his latest sexual scandal brought to the attention of the Italian media a year before that. The latter had to do not only with Berlusconi's sexual mores; it also now had legal implications. The billionaire was accused of having paid an underaged Moroccan woman, Karima el Mahroug (aka Ruby Rubacuori, meaning heart stealer) for sexual services. He was also accused of exploitation of minors for prostitution and of abuse of office.[20] In the attempt to protect the seventeen-year-old Moroccan woman, who was found by the Milan police without any legal documents or visas, Berlusconi called the police station directly, allegedly asking them to release her, bypassing the standard Italian legal procedures. He then claimed, with an explanation that apparently convinced the majority of the Italian Parliament, that he did so since, at that time, he thought that el Mahroug was the niece/granddaughter (*nipote*) of Egyptian president Hosni Mubarak.[21] The facts presented in el Mahroug's version seemed to be different, though, according to the newspaper *La Repubblica*: she claimed she had been asked by Berlusconi to *pretend* to be linked to the Mubarak family.[22] Legal accusations and verifications aside, Rubygate did not remain an isolated case and deeply affected Italian public opinion: according to some very detailed phone interceptions of the Milan court that somehow reached the newsrooms of the main Italian newspapers, and according to some interviews that appeared in the Italian media, Berlusconi regularly organized *bunga-bunga* parties in his private residences. It is not clear what the term *bunga-bunga* actually means. Regardless of the etymology of the term, it appears that, during these *bunga-bunga* parties, Berlusconi and a couple of male friends used to eat dinner and enjoy postdinner gatherings with many young women (often allegedly thirty or more), many of whom admitted they had received or were said to have received money in exchange for sexual favors, sexy shows, or simply for their presence. While Berlusconi kept referring to these parties as gallant dinners and to the women as friends or girls in need to whom he gave charitable help, the details that emerged around Berlusconi's parties deeply impacted Italian public opinion. Many Italians commented on the details of Berlusconi's sexual exploits with great admiration and some envy. To them, the money, power, and beautiful women with which Berlusconi surrounded himself were a confirmation of, rather than a challenge to, his success as a businessman and as a politician. Berlusconi was someone to emulate rather than to reprimand. Besides these hardcore supporters of Berlusconi, many PdL women engaged in a public defense of their leader. According to them, the problem of the various feminisms and of the leftists was their *moralismo* (moralizing attitude). These PdL women described these others as sad and as lacking joie de vivre, a sense of humor, and sexual freedom. The women who were Berlusconi supporters suggested that the nonsupporters learn from him rather than stigmatize his behaviors. In online forums, on TV shows, and in right-wing newspapers such as *Il Giornale* and *Libero*, men and women of Berlusconi's political persuasion approved of his behaviors and accused their "Communist" opponents of *moralismo*. In particular, among the leftist women, Berlusconi's supporters picked on the women who gathered around the SNOQ movement. Since the latter considered Berlusconi's public and private behavior to be sexist and in conflict with women's dignity, they were accused of being ugly and sad moralists, lacking a sense of humor.

This episode of recent Italian political history is pivotal for its implications about violence against women and femminicidio, and the broader future of women. Rubygate was able to prompt important responses in Italian public opinion. Indeed, as a result of it, a new women's activism grew around it, an audience interested in the conditions of women in Italian society matured, and wider discourses around women's issues developed. If claims in support of women's dignity were at the center of appeals and reflections in the aftermath of the publication of Berlusconi's private phone calls, the discourse moved rapidly in Italian social, political, and media arenas in directions that explicitly included issues around violence against women.

Concita De Gregorio, the former director of the left-wing newspaper *l'Unità* (founded by Antonio Gramsci) strongly supported and endorsed the new feminist cause of SNOQ. Her editorial choices at the time (2011–2012) allowed for the development, expansion, and media success of the movement and for the creation of a public able to acknowledge the new women's question as a "real" and meaningful one. In the aftermath of the emergence of Berlusconi's sexual scandal around el Mahroug and the *bunga-bunga* parties, Concita De Gregorio proposed a collection of signatures. This appeal, that would have merged, later, with the SNOQ manifesto, said:

> I am sure, I know it with certainty, that the majority of Italian women are not in line for the *bunga bunga*. I am sure that conscious prostitution is the choice, if it's a choice under these circumstances, of a very small minority. I am therefore addressing the others, all the other women. This is the time to answer strongly: Where are you, girls? Mothers, grandmothers, daughters, nieces, where are you? Right-wing or left-wing, poor or rich, Northern or Southern women, daughters of a time that other women, before you, made rich with possibilities, equal and free, where are you? Now is the time to say: enough is enough![23]

De Gregorio's contribution to the birth of SNOQ cannot be underestimated. Her work helped mobilize persons, giving voice to, and shaping the attitude of, some sectors of public opinion in reference to the former prime minister's sexual scandals. By doing so, I claim, she not only gathered women and affective response to Berlusconi and the role of women in Italian society; she also helped construct a (counter) public, an audience for the emergence of a new women's question in Italy. In other words, the references to the "other women," to an old-style *familismo* (kinship-centered ideology), and to "patriarchal" values (see Ottonelli 2011) that were evident in her appeal were not at all an idiosyncratic take on Berlusconi's scandals. They were shared by—and, at the same time, triggered in—her readers, the founders of SNOQ, and other intellectuals and political authorities. By underlining these elements, the SNOQ movement was able on the one hand, as Ottonelli argues, to mobilize a particular (although generic) political subject (i.e., the "other women" of De Gregorio's appeal); and on the other hand, I claim that this movement, with the particular help of *l'Unità*, succeeded in creating an audience and a public capable of seeing and recognizing this newly crafted political subject, and the presence of a women's question in Italy, that had been neglected or just absent until then in public opinion. The ability to mobilize the feelings, affects, and thoughts of many Italians and to construct both a political subject and its audience also relied on the fact that, in spite of its being a new movement, SNOQ's ideology did not attempt to introduce a radical change in the frameworks used to interpret reality and contemporary events. In addition to the construction of real women as nonprostitutes, and to the reference to strong kinship-oriented sets of values—which both gesture toward the Catholic origins of such a conception of the honorability, or dignity, of women—there was another element that characterized women's mobilization on February 13, 2011 (Ottonelli 2011, 54–71). This element, ubiquitous in the debates and political discussions during that period of recent Italian political history, can be referred to as the ethics of sacrifice (see also below). According to many women who were clearly influenced by Italy's Catholic past (and present), sacrifice is the feature that defines "true Italian women" (Ottonelli 2011, 22–47; for a comparison, see Tambor 2014). This element emerges powerfully in the speech that Giulia Bongiorno, a lawyer and member of Parliament in the PdL's ranks (a center-right party), gave on the occasion of the February 13 demonstration. As Ottonelli points out, it emerges even more powerfully in the letter Bongiorno sent to the newspaper *La Repubblica* on January 21, 2011. While defending everyone's right of self-determination, referencing Rubygate, she maintained that Berlusconi's personal life was not politically irrelevant:

> Berlusconi, with his words and behaviors, inflicted a wound upon all Italian women: to the women who study and work (often making inadequate money or, as in the case of stay-at-home women, without making any money at all), to all of us who are struggling day after day; to the women who, in order to get prominent positions, not only did not come to certain parties, but, if anything, had to turn down the possibility of seeing friends; to those, who, in spite of looking for shortcuts, walked through the path of commitment and sacrifice with dignity. . . . Upon each one of them—whenever women are picked and "rewarded" not on the basis of merit but on the basis of something else that has nothing to do with professionalism, commitment, intelligence—was poured out the uselessness of her sacrifice.[24]

The audience constructed by SNOQ played an important role both in the consolidation of a community of sense around violence against women in Italy and in that of women as new political subjects. The attention of the media on women's issues, in fact, fueled a renewed interest for public initiatives. While Italy's women's question emerged in connection to concerns around women's dignity, it rapidly shifted to issues of violence and femminicidio. The latter were already discussed within feminist circles even though they had not yet reached the attention of the wider public (on Italian feminism and the karstic river metaphor, see chap. 2).

Many initiatives have taken place since the SNOQ protests. The majority of them have revolved around episodes of violence in which women were injured or killed at the hands of men. In particular, November 25 became a reference point for many women and women's associations. November 25, 2013, for instance, saw a blooming of initiatives against femminicidio and violence against women organized by women throughout Italy, and made the news in national and local newspapers and on TV newscasts. I was in Salento at that time, and I personally attended three public events in the province of Lecce, but I know of many more happening at the same time. This surprised me, since two years earlier that date passed almost unnoticed. Since then, the number of events organized to counter violence against women has been increasing steadily. In addition to the demonstrations on November 25, the imagined community of violated women—the community of sense I have described so far—emerged in the unprecedented media coverage of episodes of femminicidio and violence against women, in the various events organized locally on the occasion of the killing or assault of fellow citizens, and in online and off-line public debates and initiatives, such as the following (see also Parmigiani 2018).

Meno Giallo Più Rosa

In February 2014, the town of Sogliano Cavour in the province of Lecce promoted a campaign condemning violence against women, called *Meno Giallo, più Rosa. Riprendiamoci la scena del delitto* (lit., Less Yellow, More Pink. Let's take the crime scene back). The title is a pun that exploits the Italian categorization of novels. *Gialli*, in Italian, is the adjective that refers to thrillers, while *rosa* is the one that connotes romance novels. The initiative explicitly associates the public spaces customarily associated with men with crime scenes. The aim of the campaign is to encircle with white and pink tape—similar in shape and style to the one used by the Italian police to cordon off murder scenes, but in different colors—the "places with inadequate female presence." The purpose of this taping is to "create a map of the spaces that women cannot access, and where sexist culture is more deep-rooted" (see *Invito*). "There are PLACES where SEXIST CULTURE has always expressed itself in a way that did not respect women. Every woman knows them very well. They are the town

Figure 3.5. *Meno Giallo, Più Rosa.* "Let's take back the murder scene." Against sexist culture, let's take back the places dominated by men. A picture of the initiative in Taurisano. (Photo credit: courtesy of Lucia Sabato.)

BARS, the SQUARES which, after a certain hour we prefer not to cross, the STOPS for [public] transportation that are better not frequented alone. LET'S TAKE BACK all these places, and all the others that are part of your experience. Let's mark them with this tape, before they again become the SCENE OF THE CRIME" (emphasis in the original; from the invitation to this initiative).[25]

On the one hand, the association between these unfriendly places for women and crime scenes underlines the fact that the absence of women from those places represents their symbolic killing. On the other hand, it clearly plays on an imaginary that associates women and women's bodies, indiscriminately, with potential victims of murder.

In my opinion, this initiative summarizes very well the type of discourses, practices, and affects around sexed violence and femminicidio that were circulating in Italy at the time and that I have been describing in detail so far (see fig. 3.5).[26]

In sum, the endorsement of the word *femminicidio*, and the acknowledgment of sexed violence as a meaningful category *beyond feminist circles*, contributed to the emergence of a community of sense of violated women in many ways: First, by focusing on the extreme manifestations of what UDI women called "sexed violence" (i.e., femminicidio), it triggered affects and reflections on a continuum of violence that was believed to characterize women's lives and that started to illuminate other, less visible, structural and symbolic types of violence. In this sense, it became a critical instrument by which feminists could recognize and understand the different forms that violence against women took in their lives.[27] Second, after thirty years of Italian feminist women deciding to withdraw from public squares, it generated a renewed interest in inhabiting squares (see, e.g., Castelli 2013) and in promoting public initiatives as forms of political activism. With the exception of a few groups that remained publicly active—yet not *visible* in the media—even after that period, it was not until the SNOQ demonstration in 2011 that women's activism became *visible* again on a wide scale and on the streets through public demonstrations. Since then, public protests, together with online activism, have become more and more frequent in Italy. This fueled the recognition and self-recognition of women as *visible* political subjects. Third, by affecting the modalities of public protests, it set representation as a battlefield for political activism, as I explain in the next chapters.

Women-as-Victims

If violence, in the past few years, gradually became a reference point for defining who is a woman, some of the women and men interpellated by the SNOQ manifestations started visually, linguistically, symbolically, and affectively to associate violence and suffering with women and victims. In fact, the dominant tendency among Italian women and in campaigns against sexed violence, as Tonia and her friend pointed out, was to represent women's conditions through a grammar of victimhood (or of passivity, as objects of others' gazes). This grammar involved both self-representations and representations of women-as-victims—those who are suffering, helpless, and in need of tutelage and rescue (compare with De Luna 2011). This point is supported visually by many

Figure 3.6. Clendy campaign (Woman). (Photo credit: ANSA.)

images circulating in Italy, at that time as well as today, but it encompasses other dimensions as well, specifically linguistic ones and, in my field, affective and aesthetic ones (see below).

The ubiquity of femminicidio in the media in Italy corresponded to the ubiquity of images of women that related to violence against women representing battered, bruised, and bleeding women (see Gamberi 2015).[28] Such representations were crammed into newspapers and websites, and were very popular in campaigns that were designed to fight against violence against women. Yet, according to the type of audiencing practices of some feminists, including most of the ones I worked with, the effects that they generated were counterproductive

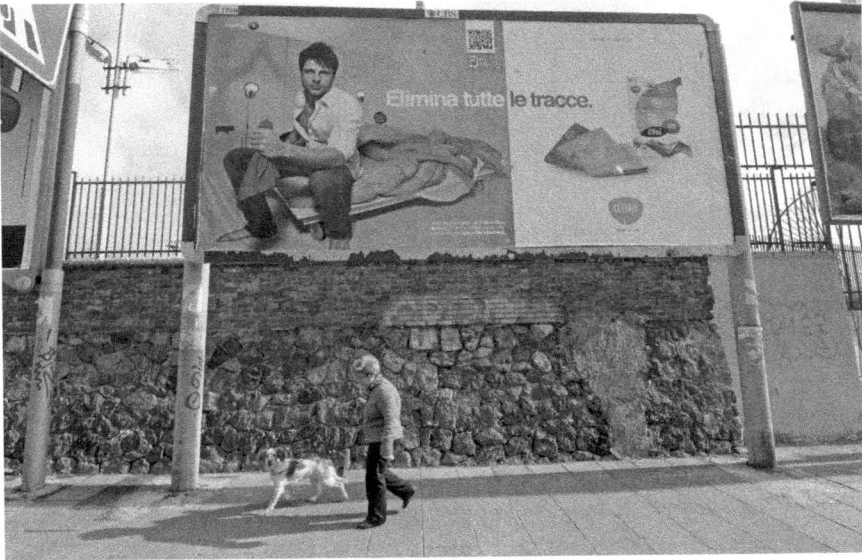

Figure 3.7. Clendy campaign (Man). (Photo credit: ANSA.)

for women's causes. According to feminists, they reinscribed the same "patriarchal" values that women were trying to oppose. According to many of my informants, among other things they overexposed victimized women's bodies, transformed violence against women into media, advertising, and public spectacles, and exploited femminicidio as a marketing vehicle to sell products.[29] Regarding the latter, I find the images in figures 3.6 and 3.7 particularly interesting in reference to my argument: their semiotic analysis shows not only how femminicidio (and the struggle against it) was able to attract the attention of the Italian public but also how women were—both directly and indirectly— represented as victims.

In March 2013, Clendy, a brand of household products, published the ads in figures 3.6 and 3.7.[30] In order to advertise a cleaning rag, the ads showed a picture of the settings and protagonists of two homicides. Two pictures, one slogan: *Elimina tutte le tracce* (It/he/she eliminates all the traces or, as an imperative, "Eliminate all the traces!"). It is not my purpose to discuss the style, efficacy, or the ethics of this ad. Nonetheless, a few observations are worth consideration. First, among the many possible settings of homicides, Clendy staged a *particular* type of murder: one that involved a man and a woman. Presumably, the same slogan could have worked for other types of homicides: for example, an assassination involving a robbery, a killing of a competitor, the murder of a partner's lover. In all these examples, the homicide would have followed a similar pattern: it would have been a homicide for a *reason*—even though a mean and selfish one. Yet apparently the creators of the ads did not think about these options: they probably needed to pick a type of homicide that triggered a sort of ambivalent emotional response in the possible buyers. The murderers needed to be portrayed in a way that could make the act deplorable but also somehow understandable, generating sufficient empathy between the potential buyer and the killer for the former to buy the cleaning product. Evidently, violence against women seemed to be their best option—close enough to the possible buyers to generate empathy and to have them buy the cleaning rag.[31]

Since the target audience of the marketing strategy is wide (most people have a house, car, garden, etc., to clean), the staging of the homicide did not have to represent something *totally* distant from the experience of what was considered the average Italian. I doubt that if the homicides staged had been performed, for instance, by psychopaths, by desperate migrants, or by greedy thieves, the ads would have been as effective. Moreover, the glamorous images, the designer furniture, the stylish outfit, the predominance of the color white, and the presence of a good amount of light helped visually depict the killing as an ordinary, open, and even "glossy" event. The images seemed to imply that this was a clean killing—not gloomy and messy. Clean because of the Clendy's rag but also because of its perceived banality.

The subtext of the images was offered to the viewer by what appears in the shadows. In both cases—in the first image on the upper left, in the other on the right—the shadows depict the shape of an arm with a knife in the act of stabbing (clearly a cinematographic reference). Second, in spite of both being homicides that involve a man and a woman, the two ads showed significant differences in the messages they conveyed. My claim is that the reason there are two versions of the ad—one where the perpetrator is a man, and the other where the protagonist is a woman—was not, as the creators claim, informed (only) by an attempt to pursue equality between the sexes.[32] On the contrary, the indirect (and naturalized) associations between murderer and protagonist, and the particular imaginaries linked to the settings of the two homicides, revealed important information about the links between women and victims and how violence was framed in Italy. This reading is informed by a visuality schooled in the Italian feminist circles I frequented and is supported by several conversations with my feminist informants.

In the ad that presented the man as the aggressor, the setting was a bedroom. The woman (the victim) was naked in the bed. The man was sitting on a corner of the bed, with the rag in his hand, with his clothes on, but without his shoes. His shirt was partly undone—something that hinted both at a previous moment of intimacy and at his stylish look. All these elements clearly referred to a femminicidio for the imagined plot, which was consistent with a "predatory script" (Ferrero Camoletto and Bertone 2012, 2010; Bertone and Ferrero Camoletto 2009; Gilmore 1987). The man/hunter holds the rag as if he had just grabbed it, and the woman/victim lies naked and appears to have been murdered during or after sex.

In the ad that depicts the woman as the aggressor, the setting is very different. There is a chair and a well-dressed man on the floor. The murderer wears elegant clothes and shoes. She is sitting on the chair holding the rag with one hand, and her miniskirt with the other, in the act of covering her legs. Her hair, neatly tied back from her face, looks slightly ruffled. The setting is ambivalent: even though there is no furniture, the location more closely resembles that of an office than a home, and the violence gestures toward a reaction to the attempt of a sexual assault more than a "crime of passion," as the Italian media would call it. This aspect is supported by the fact that the two are dressed, by their wearing elegant clothes, and by the absence of a bed and of any other element connecting the two. The relationship between the protagonist and antagonist seems to be more that of employee/employer rather than of lovers. The fact that the legs of the woman are tilted inward and that the hand on the skirt is trying to cover her legs hints that she is possibly a victim of some kind of sexual harassment or of "mobbing." As described by Molé in her ethnography, the latter is "in its most simplified meaning, psychological and emotional workplace harassment" (2010, 2). In sum, it appears that for the authors of this ad and for their imagined public(s), even when put in the role of the aggressors, women cannot avoid being imagined as victims. Interestingly, in spite of the apparent equality of the treatment of men and women in these ads, in *both cases* the woman is in fact portrayed as a victim—of femminicidio in the first ad, and of harassment, sexed violence, and possibly mobbing in the second.

The ads generated very strong public reactions and were eventually removed and modified.[33] Feminists and nonfeminist men and women reacted through email bombings, the condemnation of this campaign made the news in important national newspapers, and the Minister for Equal Opportunities at the time, Elsa Fornero, took a public stance against it.[34] This is not the place to assess whether, given these strong reactions, the campaign was a success or a failure.[35] Whether the campaign was inspired by the success of news of femminicidi in the media in attracting the attention of the public (as the choice of some newspapers to depict femminicidi as natural deaths shows) or by the ubiquity of a predatory script, it is clear that femminicidio became able to attract the attention of a wider audience in contemporary Italy.[36] Whether the attention was positive or negative, as in this case, is not important; it still mobilized affects and gave *visibility* to Clendy's products that needed to be sold.

In sum, women tended to be represented as victims, not just in many campaigns against femminicidio but also in the Italian media and public scene. They were defined by their suffering—both physical and emotional. They were depicted as powerless and in need of tutelage and rescue. This particular aesthetic might have been intended to trigger feelings of sympathy in the observer—which in itself indirectly tells us something about the type of (imagined) audience to which they were addressed and to the type of visuality they *expected to* prompt. Its effects, however, could also be detrimental to women's causes.[37] Nonetheless, if women were represented by using languages and grammars of victimhood, not all of them considered this to be a problem; many women did feel and choose to adhere uncritically to these types of representations and to promote them, as I show in the rest of this chapter (for a comparison, see Samet 2013).[38]

Precarious Victims

DNA Donna (see chaps. 2, 4, and 5) was a start-up whose mission was to be a counseling center for women who suffer from violence. It was a mixed association: nominally at least, it included both men and women. It was based in Soleto, in the province of Lecce, and was conceived and put together by Eva, a close friend of mine. Trained in women's politics within the UDI, she decided to transfer her knowledge, competence, and network of acquaintances at a local level and, personally, to be actively involved in countering violence against women. She started to talk about her ideas in her geographic area and within just a few months managed to put together a team of experts, all based around Soleto: from psychologists to *Carabinieri* (police), from sexologists to lawyers. By virtue of my close connections to her and most of the team's founding members, I had the privilege of witnessing the transformation of DNA Donna in person for ten weeks and at a distance for more than a year. DNA Donna went from being an idea in the mind of my friend to being practically realized, from being a group of motivated neophytes to one formally recognized by the local authorities and assigned public spaces by the municipality of Soleto. Besides spending time with many of the members in formal and informal gatherings, attending specialized seminars with them, participating in their initiatives and demonstrations, and surrendering to their request to put a picture of my face on their flyers, I was constantly briefed, almost every day (through Skype, email, WhatsApp, or Facebook) on the life and events of the association (and on a selection of topics on the lives and events associated with its members) for years.

On a day in February 2014, a member of the association called to tell me about a meeting she had just had with a person from a union. Apparently, DNA

Donna had been contacted by the local offices of a national Italian workers' union, which looks after the interests of atypical workers, such as immigrants. They had proposed a partnership with DNA Donna for the management of their *Sportello Tutela Donne* (help desk for the tutelage of women). In exchange, they had offered DNA Donna their help and expertise in dealing with contingent cases of mobbing. In describing the meeting, my friend pointed out that she was sorry I was not there, since I would have supported their case with the union's employees, who were bewildered by DNA Donna complaints. According to my friends (I talked about this meeting with another member of the association, too), it was hard to make the union's functionaries understand that it was inappropriate and even detrimental to women to use the word *tutelage* in a service aimed at helping women. According to my informants and friends, "women are not 'impaired' (*inabili*), and do not need any tutelage simply because they are women. Minors need tutelage, women, even violated women, do not." According to them, my presence—the presence, in their eyes, of an expert—would have eased their way through the discussion, since it would have changed the power structure of the exchange. The indignation of my friends did not affect the union's functionaries, and, at present, the name of the service has not changed.

The bewilderment of the union's personnel was probably genuine. Since they were used to finding their way through complicated legal and bureaucratic rubrics in order to take care of the interests of the workers, they had found in the status of a victim of mobbing (i.e., workplace harassment) a quite convenient parameter for offering concrete help to what were often underprivileged women. The partial overlap between mobbing and sexual harassment had triggered their decision to create a help desk for victims of violence, according to my informants at DNA Donna. The union's functionaries could probably not anticipate that, given the success it had in the unions, the "paradigm of the victim" (see De Luna 2011) could be contested in a help-desk for victims of violence. As a matter of fact, as De Luna (2011) explains, the "centrality of the victims"—and therefore their commemoration—is part of the "founding shared principle" of Italy's collective memory, and this cultural element eased the way to the emergence of mobbing as a societal issue. As Molé points out, mobbing emerged in Italy during the 1990s (see, e.g., 2010, 39–40), and it developed into a well-recognized phenomenon to the point that, in 2003, Italy's INAIL (state health institution) recognized it as a possible cause of work-related illnesses. According to Molé, mobbing is a polymorphous and multivalent phenomenon. Among other things, it is a constant threat for workers, a management policy of employers, a cause of illness, and a more legally effective way to prosecute sexual harassment against women. It mobilizes and constructs "practices, images, discourses, fantasies, mechanisms of control, forms of embodied experiences, [and] nodes of affect" (2012, 1) that help redefine biomedical parameters and legal categories as well as the ways Italians think about their being in the world (see, e.g., Molé 2010, 2012, 2013a; for a comparison with the Finnish context, see Funahashi 2013). The overlap between mobbing and sexual harassment (for a detailed description of this, see Molé 2013a), also favored by the lack of organic unity in Italian law in reference to crimes against women, is of particular importance. I claim that the vision of the world introduced and sanctioned by mobbing influenced certain understandings, practices, and affects enabled by the emergence of femminicidio in the Italian public sphere. According to Molé: "The story of 'mobbing' is a social history of what happens when one form of harassment emerges as something considered ethically superior to another and, in turn, becomes the dominant explanatory model for workplace conflict. Mobbing—moral harassment masquerading as a gender-neutral phenomenon—has become an ethical violation worthy of social support and institutionalization on both state and European levels, its victims worthy of social recognition. But when deploying mobbing as a means to dispute the gendered and sexualized abuses of the labor regime, subjects are called upon to mask their full legal and political subjectivities" (2012, 149).

Given the success of mobbing in creating "worthy" victims—in relation to other socially invisible ones—and in becoming a socially recognized, "ethically superior" form of harassment, it is not surprising that violated women (who, from their point of view, suffer from existential precariousness) often sought to be understood and represented as victims, similar to mobbed persons. They described themselves as powerless, passive, and pushed around by the malevolent agency of others to the point of being physically and emotionally damaged.[39] *Precarietà* also emerged, with other specific connotations, in certain discourses, affects, and practices around sexed violence in Italy, especially in the media. Here as well, the traumatized body—that is, the victimized body that appears in the ads and media and that my informants criticize—was understood to be "a critical measure of truth" (Molé 2012; see also Petryna 2002), a way to obtain social recognition and to negotiate one's position in the world (see also Fassin 2008; Fassin and Rechtman 2009).

During my fieldwork, I had the chance to do participant observation in a couple of women's shelters (CAV) in the province of Lecce and to interview some of their staff members: psychologists, educators, administrators, attorneys, and volunteers. One of the elements that they all pointed out in the interviews was that, since the spread of the word and worlds of femminicidio had occurred, they have seen an increase in the numbers of women who ask for their services. While I tended to see this as a positive outcome of media and popular interest in femminicidio—which, from my point of view, was giving a name to something that had not been so clearly identified before—I was surprised to find that this was not the take of the personnel of the CAVs. Instead, they ascribed the increase in the numbers of women asking for help to more and more women trying to exploit the condition of victim of violence in order to obtain social privileges such as a better economic treatment in cases of divorce. While this element speaks about the pervasive "patriarchal" ideology that tends to frame self-determined women according to skeptical biases, it also stresses the fact that like mobbing femminicidio was becoming a socially recognized form of harassment that defined the status of "worthy victims" (see also Gribaldo 2014). The connections between work and existential precariousness that I found in my field were not limited to this example (see also Fantoni 2007 and the special edition on Italian Feminisms of the *Journal Feminist Reviews* 89). For instance, this connection was clearly spelled out in the *Sciopero delle Donne* against femminicidio. On the 2013 International Day against Violence against Women, a group of women—Barbara Romagnoli, Adriana Terzo, and Tiziana Dal Pra—promoted a twenty-four-hour strike (*sciopero*). Women (workers and nonworkers, both at home and at the workplace) were asked to refrain from doing what they normally do for twenty-four hours. This strike was meant to Stop the Culture of Violence in Italy, inflected in various ways. This was: "A 'strike' that demands that the political establishment, the mass media and society as a whole take charge of the daily and relentless killing fury (*furia omicida*) against women that does not show any sign of stopping, not even for a day, since it is the result of a violent and sexist culture" (emphasis in the original).[40] And, "A 'strike' that states an inescapable link between work/care/precariousness/income, that claims that maternity is a choice, that rejects the blackmail of having to sign undated letters of resignation (*dimissioni in bianco*) and that affirms also that the health of women's bodies is a right that cannot be at the mercy of ideological and instrumental objections" (emphasis in the original).[41]

In this case, the overlaps between work and existential precariousness, between victimhood and existential uncertainty, were evident. References to precariousness in relation to violence against women and to women's lives in general also appeared elsewhere, for example, in a 2008 public notice written by the National Coordination of the UDI: "We suffer a substantial precariousness, that, to the present, keeps the circle of the perpetuation of violence unaltered, an extreme and privileged instrument that functions to maintain a relationship of subordination of the 'feminine to the masculine'" (Nuzzo 2008a, 2008b). Moreover, the feminist *Collettivo Diversamente Occupate* (the Differently Occupied Collective), by putting *precarietà* at the center of their political activism, has often referred to women's condition as "precariousness of work and life" (Nuzzo 2011a).[42]

The connections between precariousness, victimhood, mobbing, and violence against women can partially explain the success of the paradigm of victimhood in the media, and among certain Italian women—an attitude that, as I introduced above, the feminists I met especially criticized in moral terms. There is at least another element worth mentioning, though, in relation to the acceptance and adoption of the victim paradigm: the Catholic notion of sacrifice and its connection with womanhood.

Non–Mater Dolorosa: Women, Victims, and Martyrs

On March 1, 2014, the feminist groups *F9* and Donnae Lab (see the Introduction and chaps. 1 and 2) inaugurated the *campagna maipiùclandestine* (never-clandestine-again), a political campaign in support of the application of the Italian law that regulates abortion. After the Spanish government decided to restrict the possibilities for legal abortion (2013), these Italian feminists mobilized to protect the Italian law on abortion (Law 194), asking for the "full implementation of the legal victory of 1978." They wrote that "in our country . . . the problem is not the law but its difficult implementation, given the high numbers of physicians who are conscientious objectors—7 out of 10—in the public health system. Impeding the application of [Law] 194 means putting women in danger, forcing them into a long and painful *via crucis* in search of a structure able to perform abortion or, in the worst cases, into a clandestine abortion."[43]

This *via crucis* (i.e., the Christian way of the cross) was their first public debut one rainy afternoon in Rome.[44] On that occasion, the activists of the *F9* performed a *via crucis*, patterned after the popular representations of the Passion of Christ that inhabit churches and Italian outdoor public spaces on the days before the celebration of Easter. As its main character, it had an object, which the activists named *Pupazza* (the female version of puppet, in Italian), that substituted for the cross, normally used in the religious representations. This metallic doll dressed in violet was shaped in a fashion that resembled the infamous hooks until fairly recently used in Italy for clandestine abortions. During the public performance, the *Pupazza*—which someone in the group also referred to, half joking, as "the other woman who all we women are" (*l'altra che siamo noi*)—was carried through the stations of a medical *via crucis*, which reenacted the obstacles that a self-determined woman who decides to abort her pregnancy often goes through today.

A woman with a megaphone narrated the story of the journey of the *Pupazza*/woman in her attempt to obtain a legal abortion, paralleling the

readings of sacred texts during religious *viae crucis*. One of the activists physically moved the *pupazza* through the *via crucis*'s stations, while other women/
statues held comic-like posters with the typical daunting answers that a woman
who wants to abort her pregnancy receives in Italian hospitals, doctors' offices,
and pharmacies.[45] These responses hinted at the stations of the religious *via
crucis* and at the collective responses that believers attending the procession of
the cross make in the religious liturgy. Determining whether this performance
could be framed as mimetic (Taussig 1992) or as a form of mimicry is not the
aim of my analysis, at least for the time being.

Nonetheless, I want to point out how, in this performance, the *Pupazza*
(i.e., a personified object, see below) was meant to represent women, in a symbolic but easily recognizable journey, that epitomizes the status of victim. The
path that women who seek legal abortions have to negotiate was superimposed
on that of the *via dolorosa* of Jesus.[46] The performance of the *F9* for the *maipiùclandestine* campaign clearly characterized the suffering of the *Pupazza* in
relation to the passion of Jesus, whose story is, par excellence, believed to be
that of an innocent victim of human cruelty and disbelief. In performing the
medical *via crucis*, the *F9* activists did not aim to transcend the status of victim.
Instead, the *Pupazza* was specifically meant to impersonate, represent, and be
recognized as a victim by the extemporaneous public of uninformed pedestri-
ans that were walking in *Piazza del Popolo* at the time of the flash mob.[47] The
Pupazza in the medical *via crucis* represented a special type of victim, one associated with the killing of an innocent (Christ) for the sake of humanity. This
special type of victimhood was connected to a special type of "witnessing": that
of the martyr.[48] The latter term—which means witness in Greek (*testimone*, in
Italian)—has been adopted by the Catholic Church, over the centuries, as a reference point for sanctity. Martyrdom, it is worth stressing, is inflected in terms
of ethical superiority in hagiographic accounts. Martyrs are those Christians
who give their lives for their belief in Christ. Given that the current debates
on the right of abortion in Italy (especially in Rome, due to the presence of the
Vatican) are mainly set by the Catholic pro-life movement (*Movimento per la
Vita*)—which Italian feminists call the *no choice* movement—it is not surprising
that the feminist activists resorted to this type of performance for their political protest.[49] I have to be clear on the fact, though, that these choices were *not*,
by any means, explicitly theorized in this way by the *F9* women, who did not
explicitly recognize *this movement* (no choice) as their privileged (imagined)
audience. This latter point, I believe, might strengthen my argument, since it
indicates that the connections between women and victims were so naturalized in Italian society that they went unnoticed even by feminist activists. In
the rendering of the *F9*, the *Pupazza*/victim mediated relations and testified by

proxy for the women who want to be able to abort their pregnancies according to Law 194. In other words, by subsuming the role of the martyr, the *F9* activists testified to the moral superiority of women/victims persecuted for their belief in self-determination. This identification between martyrs and self-determined women, performed through the representation of the latter as victims/martyrs, aimed to overturn the common understanding fostered by no-choice activists that feminists are "murderers" of fetuses.[50] In this rendering of the medical *via crucis*, women were associated with Jesus: the victim par excellence in the Italian context. They were not represented as murderers, from the point of view of the no-choice movement—that is, as actively promoting the right of abortion.[51] The attempt to show the media an image of feminism that broke with the one pushed by pro-life activists was confirmed by the framing of the *via crucis* portrayed by *F9* women in more than one published interview. On those occasions, spokespersons of the collective specified that as feminists they were not pro-death and that they, as well, believed in the "social tutelage of pregnancy" (i.e., the main forte of antiabortion activists) together with women's right of self-determination.[52]

The connection between the *Pupazza*/women and the redemptive sacrifice of Christ was not the only dimension implied in the use of the *via crucis* metaphor by the *F9* activists. The language of martyrdom used by these activists in their performance is also a *gendered* language in the Catholic tradition: in the history of the Catholic Church it is linked to the formal recognition of (women's) sanctity. It is common knowledge that the overwhelming majority of women-saints canonized by the Vatican belonged to religious groups or died as martyrs (see Ciciliot 2010 on this topic in the papacy of John Paul II; Napolitano and Norget 2011, 255–256). The only exception in recent times is Gianna Beretta Molla, a mother of four who decided not to receive treatment for the cancer diagnosed during her last pregnancy and died to save her child—that is, she chose her own death instead of having an abortion.[53] The exempla set by the Catholic saints match those of the other important protagonist of the popular renderings of *via crucis*: Mary, the mother of Christ, in the particular role of *Mater Dolorosa* (sorrowful mother).[54] Again, this is not the place to delve into the popularity of *Stabat Mater Dolorosa*—the traditional hymn to the Virgin recited on the occasion of the *via crucis*—in the histories of music and arts, nor the place to delve into the overwhelming presence of this particular theme and images in the everyday lives of Italians, through the artistic representations that inhabit Italian public places. Instead, I refer here to the recent analysis by Murgia, in her *Ave Mary*, of the connections between the construction of Italian womanhood and Mary's presence in the *via crucis*. Murgia is a famous Italian writer and a progressive politician; feminist and Catholic, she holds an MA in theology. In 2011, she published the book *Ave Mary: And the Church Invented the Woman* with the aim of accessibly addressing the connections between Catholic heritage and the presence of the women's question in Italy. This book is interesting for my argument since it acknowledges the inevitable confrontations between Italian feminisms and the Catholic Church.[55] *Ave Mary* is the attempt to answer the question: "Why does it seem to be so important to cut women off from the public space of representation of death and suffering, *unless they inhabit the role of victims?*" (2011, 2, emphasis mine). In trying to answer this question, Murgia puts together various types of data: from TV shows to Catholic doctrine, from her own personal experience to iconography, from theology to semiotic analyses of advertisement. She claims that the Christian tradition has a central responsibility in the representation of women/victims, and she offers an explanation. Her general argument is not so dissimilar from Marina Warner's claims (1976) about Mary as a key model—yet an unattainable one—for women. Murgia, though, engages with this general theme in reference to the Italian context, providing interesting insights for better understanding some of the issues I have discussed so far. The aesthetics (and the ethics) of martyrdom, and Mary as *Mater Dolorosa*, are treated in a special way in Murgia's book. Both of these elements can explain some of the dimensions linked to the representations of women-as-victims, as sufferers, and their relation with sacrifice. In reference to the latter, Murgia's claims are analogous to Dubisch's remarks (1995) on the role of the ethics of sacrifice in defining womanhood among Greek women. Murgia writes: "The same bravery, that in the classic epic led heroes to accomplishing great deeds, most of all in war, in Christian aesthetics becomes stoic endurance of pain, up to moral excellence: reaching martyrdom without disavowing one's faith, and without insulting the perpetrator. For centuries, martyrs, first of all, became 'saints' in the Church: excellent emulators of Christ—who died a violent death—and all gloriously protagonists [of their death] with him" (2011, 30). Yet, this same narrative, Murgia continues, does not concern women:

> The suffering of Mary, differently from that of Christ, is never personal, but transferred: it is the echo and consequence of that of her Son. It is an ancillary pain that aims at evidencing the suffering of the Cross. The representation of Mary as sorrowful . . . it is not functional to show the pain of the woman Mary, but to maximize the effect of the death of Jesus; when it becomes a representative model for women, this process ends up permanently legitimizing the suffering of females as a forced path towards the sacrificial obliteration of oneself—a process that Catholicism defines with the specific term "oblation." It gives the sense that the suffering of women—physical or spiritual, deriving from the death of a son or from his birth—does not have any meaning in itself, it does not redeem, and it does not explain why only by suffering an interjected pain, women could hope to obtain the right of consolation. (45)

Murgia's claims are particularly important to better frame the aesthetics of victimhood that I have presented in this chapter, since she illuminates the connections between victimhood, martyrs, and the pervasive ethics of sacrifice that were connected to womanhood in Italy. While I do not want to make a functionalist claim about this, I nonetheless see this dimension as being widespread and active in Italy during my fieldwork: it certainly shaped the construction of imagined audiences among the feminist activists with whom I worked. It is not a coincidence that, in the SNOQ demonstration in 2011, the "real women" were opposed to the ones that were participating in Berlusconi's *bunga-bunga* parties precisely by virtue of the sacrifices that the former tirelessly make every day in comparison to the latter (at home, in their education, in their work, and in their family lives). In this inflection of the so-called *femminismo moralista* (see Ottonelli, earlier in this chapter), the moral superiority of the former was argued precisely by referring to sacrifice: a feature of a representation of womanhood that resonated with the available possibilities, acknowledged both among women and men.

While the aim of this analysis of the performance of the *F9* is certainly not to address the political effectiveness of their medical *via crucis*, it is worth noting that Carla, one of my Salentine informants, in a private conversation voiced her disappointment in relation to the language used by the first political performance of *maipiùclandestine*. Both the name of the campaign and the choice of performing a *via crucis* she considered to speak a "rearguard" language—meaning reactive rather than proactive language. Carla saw them as political choices that did not foster new possibilities of identification for women, but simply exploited and reinforced the range of possibilities *already available* in Italy and manipulated by "patriarchy." Carla's claims exemplified well the relationships between imagination, affects, and feminist womanhood that are discussed in more detail in the next chapters.

Notes

1. "Enel Accende di Rosso il Campidoglio per la Giornata Internazionale Contro la Violenza Sulle Donne," Enel, https://corporate.enel.it/it/media/press/d/2013/11/enel-accende -di-rosso-il-campidoglio-per-la-giornata-internazionale-contro-la-violenza-sulle-donne-- (accessed March 21, 2019); see also "Il Campidoglio si tinge di rossoper dire no al femminicidio," *La Repubblica,* http://roma.repubblica.it/cronaca/2013/11/25/foto/il_campidoglio_si_tinge_di _rosso_per_dire_no_al_femminicidio-71934001/1/#1 (accessed March 21, 2019); "Femminicidio, il Campidoglio s'illumina di rosso poi flash mob, letture e canti," *Il Messaggero,* http:// www.ilmessaggero.it/roma/cronaca/femminicidio_campidoglio_giornata_contro_violenza _donne_cattoi/notizie/369829.shtml (accessed March 21, 2019).

2. Enel, http://www.enel.it/enelsole/it-IT/ (accessed March 21, 2019).

3. If the analytical filter used in this book stresses the role of the visual in my field, it is worth noting that metaphors and practices related to touching were ubiquitous in my field as well and represent a possible further direction of research.

4. It appears, then, that tourists, foreigners, and more educated Italians might have been the main targets of this campaign. If this is the case, this element confirms the false perception that violence against women in Italy today is perpetrated mostly by foreigners and immigrants. The use of the English language, though, appears to be at odds with the general perception that violence against women is something linked with lack of education and traditional values, that is, with backwardness.

Since I wanted to check out the reception of this installation, I used these images in interviews based on the photo-elicitation methodology (see Harper 2002). This collection of data, while not statistically relevant, helped give me a sense of the messages the Campidoglio image conveyed, both within and beyond feminist circles. Older persons and less educated ones were not sure what these images meant and tried to guess what the installation was about.

5. Such an understanding of the position of the hand is informed by my personal acquaintance with the visual world of my informants, and it is confirmed by most of the persons I interviewed about this particular image—men and women, feminists and nonfeminists. Clearly, it resonates with the images I just showed.

6. See, for example, "Il Dl Femminicidio è legge. Braccialetto elettronico anti-stalking," *Guida al Diritto* (blog), http://www.diritto24.ilsole24ore.com/guidaAlDiritto/penale/primiPiani/2013/10/femminicidio-ok-tra-le-polemiche-alla-camera-tempi-stretti-al-senato.php (accessed March 21, 2019).

7. Legge 23 April 2009, n. 38 "Conversione in legge, con modificazioni, del decreto-legge 23 febbraio 2009, n.11, recante misure urgenti in materia di sicurezza pubblica e di contrasto alla violenza sessuale, nonché in tema di atti persecutori," *Gazzetta Ufficiale* n. 95 del 24th April 2009. Interestingly, this law, which passed as a law decree, also included norms regulating immigration in Italy. In particular, it introduced the institution of (unarmed) surveillance patrols and stricter rules on how long nondocumented immigrants could stay in Italy.

8. "Violenza contro donne: si scrive 'decreto femminicidio' ma è una legge omnibus," *Il Fatto Quotidiano*, https://www.ilfattoquotidiano.it/2013/10/11/violenza-contro-donne-si-scrive-decreto-femminicidio-ma-e-legge-omnibus/740552/ (accessed March 21, 2019).

9. The NO-TAV movement contests the building of a high-speed rail from Turin to Lyon, since it is believed it will negatively affect the ecological systems of the Alpine valleys that it would cross, representing a threat to the human, animal, and plant populations of those areas. This radical activism has been strongly opposed by the Italian government for at least the past ten years.

10. See, for example, "Non in mio nome," Casa Internazionale delle Donne, http://www.casainternazionaledelledonne.org/index.php/eventi/non-in-mio-nome-391 (accessed March 21, 2019).

It is worth mentioning that a month after its passage I had the chance to discuss the text of this law with an attorney who works for some women's shelters in the province of Lecce. On that occasion, rather than focusing on the security packet of the legislative decree (the use of which is very common in Italy), or on the obligation to file actions against perpetrators of violence (that she denied exists), she stressed the importance of the law's introduction against femminicidio and of its measure of admonition (*misura dell'ammonimento*)—an improvement in comparison to Law 38 of 2009. While embracing a perspective that understands her role and those of her colleagues who work in and for women's shelters in creating interpretations of the existing laws that could support women's self-determination, she pointed out that this measure, from a lawyer's point of view, could offer more possibilities in this direction. In her opinion, Law 119/2013 might not be perfect, but it was still an improvement on the Anti-Stalking Law, which, in itself, was helpful in the struggle against violence against women in Italy. "Femminicidio, mattanza quotidiana: aumentano denunce e arresti," *Il Sole 24 Ore* (blog), http://www.ilsole24ore.com/art/notizie/2013-06-10/femminicidio-mattanza-quotidiana-aumentano-144153.shtml?uuid=AbjgMj3H (accessed March 21, 2019).

11. The "die-in" manifestations are not a prerogative of Italian feminists. For a comparison, see, among some recent examples, Rovetto 2015, and Nicholas Mirzoeff, "#BlackLivesMatter Is Breathing New Life into the Die-In," https://newrepublic.com/article/122513/blacklivesmatter-breathing-new-life-die (accessed March 21, 2019).

Examples of historical pictures of Italian feminist manifestations can be found here: "All'archivio fotografico di Paola Agosti sul movimento femminista va il premio 'Tempo Ritrovato'- fotografie da non perdere," s.t. foto liberia galleria, https://www.stsenzatitolo.com/st/allarchivio-fotografico-paola-agosti-sul-movimento-femminista-premio-tempo-ritrovato-fotografie-non-perdere/ (accessed March 21, 2019).

12. These topics, though, are still relevant to women's lives, as the constant challenge of Law 194 on abortion shows.

13. "194 maipiùclandestine," *Laboratorio Donnae* (blog), http://laboratoriodonnae.wordpress.com/2014/02/10/1maipiuclandestine/ (accessed March 21, 2019); *F9* (blog), http://femministenove.wordpress.com/ (accessed March 21, 2019).
See also "Quelle che sono nate dopo il 1978," *Lipperatura di Loredana Lipperini* (blog), http://loredanalipperini.blog.kataweb.it/lipperatura/2014/02/14/quelle-che-sono-nate-dopo-il-1978/ (accessed March 21, 2019); "#maipiùclandestine: in difesa della 194," *Giulia Giornaliste*, http://giulia.globalist.it/Detail_News_Display?ID=68540&typeb=0&#maipiuclandestine-in-difesa-della-194 (accessed March 31, 2019).

14. 50E50 was not just a proposal that had to do with quotas but it asked for a more thorough representation of women *ovunque si decide* (in every place where decisions are made).

15. There are some important juridical precedents—such as the work of Barbara Spinelli.

16. Private conversation via email on April 27, 2013. Interestingly, the word that Pina Nuzzo used—"*mattanza*," which I translated as a killing spree—is a term primarily used to designate the harvesting of tuna in the Mediterranean Sea.

17. In her 2001 article, Povinelli deals with incommensurability. With this term, derived from debates in linguistics and philosophy, she indicates those phenomena that the social context in which they are embedded perceives as radical new worlds: totally other and therefore inconceivable. On the relationship between identity, identification, and disidentification, see Asselin, Lamoureux, and Ross 2008, 7.

18. While Dave seems to be more interested in the communitarian aspects of this emergence, and of its transition from an imagined community to a face-to-face one (2010b, 615), my ethnography is more specifically centered on the cultivation of alternative individualities around the issue of being witnesses rather than victims, and it takes representations as a key component of this enterprise.

19. See, for example, Molé 2013b; Ginsborg 2004; Ginsborg and Asquer 2011; Herzfeld 2008.

20. Berlusconi was handed a guilty verdict by the Court of First Instance in 2013, sentenced to seven years of prison, and banned from public office. He was

subsequently acquitted by the Court of Second Instance in 2014, and by the *Cassazione* in 2015. The Italian juridical system has three *gradi di giudizio* (lit., degrees of judgment), which implies that three courts can be involved in a trial: the trial court (Court of First Instance), the appeal court (Court of Second Instance), and the Supreme Court (Cassazione). See, for example, "Ruby, Silvio Berlusconi, assist della Cassazione: la sentenza definitiva slitta a ottobre 2015," *Libero Quotidiano*, http://www.liberoquotidiano.it/news/personaggi/11654063/Ruby--Silvio Berlusconi--assist.html (accessed March 21, 2019); "Ruby, Berlusconi assolto—la Cassazione: 'No concussione'. Grazie a legge Severino," *Il Fatto Quotidiano*, http://www.ilfattoquotidiano.it/2015/05/28/ruby-cassazione-berlusconi-non-sapeva-fosse -minorenne/1727361/ (accessed March 21, 2019); Ruby: "Come nacque la storia di Mubarak," *La Repubblica*, http://video.repubblica.it/dossier/ruby-inchieste/ruby-come-nacque-la -storia-di-mubarak/62401/61117 (accessed March 21, 2019); "Ruby: 'Il bunga bunga e l'harem,'" *La Repubblica*, http://video.repubblica.it/dossier/ruby-inchieste/ruby-il-bunga -bunga-e-l-harem/62407/61123 (accessed March 21, 2019); "Le feste di Ruby e il Bunga Bunga," *Corriere della Sera*, http://www.corriere.it/politica/10_ottobre_28/bunga-bunga -berlusconi-ruby_b7c597ce-e267-11df-8440-00144f02aabc.shtml (accessed March 31, 2019).

21. On February 3, 2011, the Italian Chamber of Deputies voted in favor (314 votes vs. 302 votes) of an appeal to the Italian Court of Appeal regarding Berlusconi's allegations in "Rubygate." The Italian Parliament voted in favor of the conflict of attribution, in order to take the case away from the Court of Milan, considered hostile to Berlusconi. The justification of the request was based on the belief that with his phone call to the Milan police station, Berlusconi acted in the interests of the country, since the prime minister was convinced that Karima el Mahroug was part of the Mubarak family. The Italian Constitutional Court did not accept the appeal.

22. Ruby: "Come nacque la storia di Mubarak," *La Repubblica*, http://video.repubblica.it /dossier/ruby-inchieste/ruby-come-nacque-la-storia-di-mubarak/62401/61117 (accessed on March 21, 2019).

23. My translation. The original statement can be found here: https:// forumcompagnicgilmibac.forumcommunity.net/?t=43454314 (accessed on April 23, 2018).

24. Giulia Bongiorno, "Noi donne calpestate, non possiamo tacere," *La Repubblica*, http:// www.repubblica.it/politica/2011/01/21/news/noi_donne_calpestate_non_possiamo_tacere -11473950/?ref=HRER3-1 (accessed on March 21, 2019).

25. See the page of the initiative on Facebook: "Meno giallo più rosa," https://www .facebook.com/groups/1385816728346175/ (accessed on March 21, 2019).

26. Some pictures of the initiative can be found here: "Particolare Manifestazione per la 'Festa Della Donna a Taurisano,'" http://www.piazzasalento.it/particolare-manifestazione -per-la-festa-della-donna-taurisano-24797 (accessed on March 21, 2019).

27. In their lives and beyond: some Italian feminists described as femminicidio the fall 2014 killing of a female bear named Daniza. Mattia Salvia, "Perché la gente è impazzita per l'orsa Daniza?" *Vice*, http://www.vice.com/it/read/orsa-daniza-reazioni-perche-563 (accessed on March 21, 2019).

28. Image: http://kiaramente1.files.wordpress.com/2010/02/lei.jpg (accessed on March 21, 2019).

Other similar pictures, and a critique of them, can be found here: https:// comunicazionedigenere.wordpress.com/2013/06/18/la-donna-con-locchio-nero/ (accessed on March 21, 2019).

29. See also "Pubblicità&violenza: come fare soldi con il femminicidio," *Fuori Genere* (blog), http://fuorigenere.wordpress.com/2013/03/29/pubblicitaviolenza-come-fare-soldi -con-il-femminicidio/ (accessed on March 21, 2019); "Quando il Femminicidio Diventa 'Da Calendario,'" *Generazione* (blog), http://comunicazionedigenere.wordpress.com/2014/03/02 /quando-il-femminicidio-diventa-da-calendario/ (accessed on March 21, 2019); "#Brand #Femminicidio: Quanto mi paghi se faccio la donna morta?," *Al di là del Buco* (blog), http:// abbattoimuri.wordpress.com/2014/01/15/brand-femminicidio-quanto-mi-paghi-se-faccio -la-donna-morta/ (accessed on March 21, 2019); "#Femminicidio #Brand: book modella e calendario glamour antiviolenza," *Al di là del Buco* (blog), http://abbattoimuri.wordpress .com/2014/01/13/femminicidio-brand-book-modella-e-calendario-glamour-antiviolenza/ (accessed on March 21, 2019); "#Femminicidio come brand: l'industria della moda ci prova!," *Al di là del Buco* (blog), http://abbattoimuri.wordpress.com/2014/06/22/femminicidio-come -brand-lindustria-della-moda-ci-prova/ (accessed on March 21, 2019).

30. See, for example, "Clendy, Fornero: 'Fermare lo spot che istiga il femminicidio,'" TGCOM24, http://www.tgcom24.mediaset.it/cronaca/fotogallery/1019241/clendy-fornero -fermare-lo-spot-che-istiga-il-femminicidio.shtml (accessed on March 21, 2019); "'Lo stro- finaccio che elimina tutte le tracce': Pubblicità e femminicidio, è polemica," *NapoliToday*, http://www.napolitoday.it/cronaca/pubblicita-clendy-femminicidio.html (accessed on March 21, 2019).

31. It could be argued that, for the creators of the ads, the audience needed to be interpel- lated, in the Althusserian sense, by the Clendy's ad.

32. "Pubblicità shock, la Clendy cambia il tiro: 'Non è morta, è solo ubriaca,'" https://www .youtube.com/watch?v=r5SU9SwCM7s (accessed on March 21, 2019).

33. "Pubblicità Clendy, nuovo atto: 'Non è femminicidio, ma solo una sbronza'," *Napoli- Today*, http://www.napolitoday.it/cronaca/pubblicita-clendy-nuova-versione.html (accessed on March 21, 2019). The man and the woman are here represented as victims—not of violence but of a hangover.

34. "CLENDY: Ritira la pubblicità ispirata al femminicidio," Change.org, http:// www.change.org/p/clendy-ritira-la-pubblicità-ispirata-al-femminicidio (accessed on March 21, 2019).

35. See, for example, "Violenza donne pubblicità Clendy è un epic fail," *Melty Buzz* (blog), http://www.melty.it/violenza-donne-pubblicita-clendy-e-un-epic-fail-a109849.html (accessed on April 23, 2018).

36. See, for example, "Se chiamiamo Femminicidio anche le morti per 'malore,'" *Al di là del Buco* (blog), http://abbattoimuri.wordpress.com/2013/05/03/se-chiamiamo-femminicidio -anche-le-morti-per-malore/ (accessed on March 21, 2019).

37. See, for example, "#25novembre: Se il giocattolo si rompe: Campagne sessiste contro la violenza di genere," *Generazione* (blog), http://comunicazionedigenere.wordpress.com /2013/11/21/25novembre-se-il-giocattolo-si-rompe-campagne-sessiste-contro-la-violenza-di -genere/ (accessed on March 21, 2019); "Il sessismo di alcune campagne contro il #femmini- cidio," *Femminismo a Sud* (blog), http://femminismo-a-sud.noblogs.org/post/2013/10/26/il -sessismo-di-alcune-campagne-contro-il-femminicidio/ (accessed on March 21, 2019).

38. It is no coincidence that Clendy's campaigns imagined the woman-aggressor within a sexual harassment/mobbing context: it was intended to trigger empathic reactions from the women-consumers they were addressing with their ad campaign.

39. For a historical analysis of trauma and its political relevance, see Fassin and Rechtman 2009.

40. "Lo sciopero delle donne," *Like @ Rolling Stone* (blog), https://mauropresini.wordpress
.com/2013/10/22/lo-sciopero-delle-donne/ (accessed on March 21, 2019).
41. Ibid.
42. See also Ammirati et al. 2013.
43. "#maipiùclandestine. Campagna in difesa della 194," *Maipiùclandestine* (blog) http://
maipiuclandestine.noblogs.org/files/2014/02/comunicato-stampa-1-marzo.pdf (accessed on
March 21, 2019).
44. On this flash mob, see, for example, "Mai più clandestine, a Roma le donne mani-
festano per la legge 194 ," *Il Manifesto*, http://ilmanifesto.it/mai-piu-clandestine-a-roma
-le-donne-manifestano-per-la-legge-194/ (accessed on March 31, 2019); Valeria Constantini,
"Donne in difesa della legge sull'aborto 'Un fantasma, non si riesce ad applicarla,'" *Corriere
della Sera*, http://roma.corriere.it/roma/notizie/cronaca/14_marzo_01/donne-difesa-la-legge
-sull-aborto-un-fantasma-non-si-riesce-ad-applicarla-ff4d24d8-a14d-11e3-b365-272f64db5437
.shtml (accessed on March 31, 2019); "'Mai più clandestine,' donne in piazza in difesa della
legge 194," Roma, *La Repubblica*, http://roma.repubblica.it/cronaca/2014/03/01/news/mai
_pi_cladestine_donne_in_piazza_in_difesa_della_legge_194_nel_lazio_80_di_medici
_obiettori-79938624/ (accessed on March 31, 2019); Ingrid Colanicchia, "#maipiùclandes-
tine, parte la compagna in difesa dell'aborto," *MicroMega* (blog), http://temi.repubblica.it
/micromega-online/maipiuclandestine-parte-la-campagna-in-difesa-dellaborto/ (accessed
on March 21, 2019); Angela Lamboglia, "Legge 194, 'mai più clandestine': appello a Zinga-
retti," *Il Fatto Quotidiano* (blog). http://www.ilfattoquotidiano.it/2014/02/15/legge-194-mai
-piu-clandestine/881974/ (accessed on March 21, 2019); "#Iodecido mai piu clandestine," *La
27esima Ora* (blog), http://27esimaora.corriere.it/articolo/io-decido-mai-piu-clandestine/
(accessed on March 21, 2019); "TG3 ore 14:20 del 11/03/2014," http://www.rai.tv/dl/RaiTV
/programmi/media/ContentItem-2628376c-5469-4e6a-929f-fe80c6358ff6-tg3.html#p=0 (from
minute 20) (accessed on March 21, 2019).
45. *Mai più clandestine #Campagna 194* (blog), http://maipiuclandestine.noblogs.org/
(accessed on March 21, 2019).
46. This is not the place to engage with the vast literature about performances of the Passion of Christ in Italian religious history and popular culture. For the sake of my interpretation, here it suffices to mention that performances of religious *viae crucis* are very common
in Italy and are, directly or indirectly, part of the experience of nearly every boy or girl who is
socialized in Italy, even if not Catholic or Christian.
47. This attitude of the *maipiùclandestine* activists in representing women-as-victims
is also evident in the fact that *Pupazza*, during the performance, was connoted with
other types of underprivileged marginality within the Italian context, such as that of
migrant women. In this respect, the choice of calling the campaign *maipiùclandestine*—a
name that one of the campaigners that I have interviewed confirmed hinted at clandestine
abortions—is quite ambivalent. In Italy, *clandestine* is a term used primarily to refer to illegal female migrants. The promoters of the campaign confirmed that they were aware of this
connection.
48. Fassin, too, addresses the issue of the witness/martyr. My interpretation, though, in
contrast to his—that is, with an understanding of the latter as the person who testifies without language (2008, 541)—stresses other dimensions of martyrdom. I understand martyrs,
consistent with contemporary Catholic teachings that tend to associate them with the figure
of Christ, as innocent victims. Certainly, in the history of the Church, martyrs have not been
silent.

49. See, for example, Movimento per la Vita, http://www.mpv.org/ (accessed on March 21, 2019); Notizie ProVita, http://www.notizieprovita.it/ (accessed on March 21, 2019); Giovani Prolife, http://www.giovaniprolife.org/ (accessed on March 21, 2019).

50. See, for example, discussion of "nazi-femminismo" at A Voice for Men (http://it .avoiceformen.com/) (accessed on March 21, 2019); "La RU 486 è pericolosa per le donne: parola di femminista," Notizie ProVita, http://www.notizieprovita.it/notizie-dal-mondo/la -ru-486-e-pericolosa-per-le-donne-parola-di-femminista-pro-choice/ (accessed on March 21, 2019); "Io sono la loro custode, non la loro assassina," Papaboys, http://www.papaboys.org/io -sono-la-loro-custode-non-la-loro-assassina/ (accessed on March 21, 2019).

51. On the incommunicability between the "abortion is a right" and the "abortion is a murder" positions, see Luisa Muraro, "Ripaliamo di aborto," Libreria delle Donne di Milano, https://www.libreriadelledonne.it/puntodivista/riparliamo-di-aborto/ (accessed on March 21, 2019).

52. "Mai più clandestine, parte oggi a Roma la campagna in difesa della legge 194," *Il Manifesto*, http://ilmanifesto.it/mai-piu-clandestine-parte-oggi-a-roma-la-campagna-in -difesa-della-legge-194-2/ (accessed on March 31, 2019).

53. It is worth noting that a similar experience, the moving story of Chiara Corbella, has recently caught the attention of Italian Catholics. See Giovanni Fighera, "Spiegare la fede come metodo di conoscenza in classe. E parlare di Chiara Corbella," *Tempi*, http://www .tempi.it/blog/spiegare-la-fede-come-metodo-di-conoscenza-in-classe-e-parlare-di-chiara -corbella#.VHPgYYt1QUZ (accessed on March 21, 2019); Benedetta Frigerio, "Un anno fa moriva Chiara Corbella, la grazia di vivere la grazia," *Tempi*, http://www.tempi.it/chiara -corbella-la-grazia-di-vivere-la-grazia#.VHP7TIt1QUZ (accessed on March 21, 2019).

54. There are other aspects of the figure of Mary that could be stressed. See Tóibín 2012.

55. See the website www.teologhe.org. There are a few Italian women theologians who are very active in trying to change the Church's attitudes toward women. For example, in Lecce I met Benedetta Selene Zorzi. See also Marinella Perroni and Cristina Simonelli.

4

BEING WITNESSES, NOT VICTIMS

On the Affective Politics of Representation

IN THE PREVIOUS CHAPTERS, I CLAIMED THAT, WITH the emergence of a new women's question in Italy, the dimension of representation started (or continued) to be an important one for many feminists and women's movements. I claimed that the women-as-victims trope had been ubiquitous in Italy, at a national level, especially since 2012. In this chapter and in the following ones, I now focus specifically on the Salentine activists with whom I worked and address how this trope was understood locally in relation to weeping and to Salentine "traditional" values associated with women and men within the so-called honor and shame complex. After describing how UDI women started drawing an explicit connection between representation, imagination, and political action, I concentrate on the issue of dignity in their representational struggle. I claim that in my field, dignity was not a unitary concept: on the contrary, I found it to be multivalent and malleable. Dignity in Salento was adopted in a way that resonated with certain dimensions of the traditional notion of honor, as a measure of social worth, and, at the same time, as a reference point for a wider discourse on human rights: in my ethnographic field, it was a way to perform modern feminist womanhood, to be "witnesses."

Basta Lacrime—No More Tears (I)

Obtaining a *sede* (headquarters) was not an easy task for DNA Donna, a start-up counseling center dedicated to countering violence against women based in Soleto, a town in the province of Lecce, in the Salento area of Italy. After I had participated in person in the first steps of establishing the association, I followed remotely the bureaucratic practices that led to this achievement through constant updates (via Skype) from friends who were part of the association. It was the outcome of a long, patient, and stressful negotiation between the members of the association and the municipality of Soleto. It took roughly seven months, and it was the result of much work, including the preparation of documents, management of public relations, and handling of power struggles with local authorities. I waited until the moment my informants told me the keys to the offices were finally in their possession (news that was relayed to me almost in real time through a WhatsApp text message from Italy to the United States) before rejoicing: DNA Donna finally had its own offices! This represented a huge acknowledgment of the value of the project and of the esteem the members were able to elicit among local institutional authorities. I could not wait to receive the promised Skype call with all the details of the final moments of the office handover. Finally, the call came in, and I was able to talk with one of my friends, whose joyful and proud face popped up on my computer screen. We were both so happy about this news that we promised each other we would celebrate together at one of our favorite Galatina restaurants the following summer. Before one of my friends started to brief me about the handover of the keys, she said: "Look at this! I'm sending you a picture. I want to ask Lena to make a poster of this. I absolutely want to hang this on the walls of the *sede*. It needs to be the first thing to be put on those walls." The image my friend sent me was a handwritten note that said: "No more tears. Women's weeping does not change the world; rather, their strength does" (*Basta lacrime, il pianto delle donne non cambia il mondo, la loro forza sì*).

The ideological and political disparagement of women's weeping was not an infrequent element in my fieldwork with Salentine feminists, which I had begun three years before. Among other manifestations of this attitude, in the fall of 2013 I had noticed a picture that was part of the exhibition *Alma de Tierra* in Taurisano (see chap. 5), organized in recognition of the International Day against Violence against Women. In this image, a woman from Taurisano holds a piece of paper that says, "The strongest WOMEN are those who keep smiling in spite of the wounds."

In spite of what I perceived as the lack of novelty of this feminist point of view on the connections between women and weeping, I found my friend's comments quite remarkable. Those precise words she deemed not only relevant but so central to the ethos of the organization that she wanted to frame them as representative of this new counseling center whose focus was countering violence against women. In what follows, I argue that the no-weeping (or smiling) trope had a (metonymic) central role in the ethics and aesthetics of representation of women as nonvictims, which was a central enterprise for my informants. It arose from and depended on local understandings, practices, and feelings about gender proficiencies, and about notions and performances of dignity. Salento is a complex place: in fact, as I mentioned before, it is a "hyperplace."

The "Making/Doing" of "Traditional" Values in Salento:
Honor and Shame Revisited

Marta, a feminist friend, and I were talking about modern womanhood in Salento—that is, about her life. It was the beginning of 2012, and we were sitting on an orange-striped vintage couch in the Lecce feminist bookstore, enjoying our time together. I was some months into my fieldwork, and I was just then starting to ask direct questions to my UDI informants, something I had chosen not to do for a long time. Instead, I had simply lived with the Macare, and had followed them in their everyday activities. We were in Lecce but, since Marta lived in Southern Salento, I was curious about her take on traditional issues. I had not moved much outside Lecce by that point. So, I asked her to tell me more about what she thought were the peculiar "patriarchal" constraints that she, as a feminist Salentine woman, was facing in the area where she lived. Since I had noticed that "patriarchy" was not inflected in local terms but in general "Italian" ones by UDI Salentine activists, I wanted to see whether she felt Salentinians had a particular take on "patriarchy," compared to the experience of other feminist friends we had in common who were living in other parts of Italy, and whom I had met on my trips with the Macare to Rome and Bologna. Since starting with one's own experience is a very common and valued practice among Italian feminists, she seemed to be at ease with this question and offered the following example to locate her own positioning in contrast to what she described as Salentine "traditional" and "patriarchal" constraints on women. She told me what a woman whom she knows, who had lost both her mother and her eight-year-old son within a matter of weeks of each other, had told her a few years ago during a *cùnsulu* (the dialectal form for consolation, a word indicating the practice of visiting the house of a grieving family). During the mother's funeral, the woman had cried, and her weeping went hand in hand with the unfolding of the Catholic ceremony. By contrast, during her son's funeral she felt petrified and could not weep. She had been scolded by some members of the community for not being able to cry for her son, she told my friend. The woman felt guilty and ashamed about not being able to cry at her son's funeral. The experience called into question her worthiness as a mother.

Significantly, my feminist friend did not answer my question by referring to her own personal everyday experience. Instead she reverted to a stereotypical narrative on women and tradition "in the South." Indeed, until recently, like other areas of Italy (see, e.g., de Martino [1958] 1975) and of Greece, Salento still had *prefiche* (*le chiangimuerti*, in the Salento dialect)—women who performed ritual lamentations/weeping during funerals.[1] Whether she reverted to such a narrative because she was too concerned to represent herself and her life as "modern" and "feminist," or whether this happened in order to fulfill what she might have thought were my expectations as a northerner anthropologist I don't know. What I find particularly interesting, though, is that the expectations evoked by her narrative (both in reference to the construction of her "feminist modernity" and in reference to the construction of "tradition") were built around a gloss on the so-called honor and shame complex. In my friend's story and interpretation, the sense of "shame" induced in the woman by social expectations about weeping was a result of "traditional patriarchal" constraints. The latter were a matter of representation and of presentability, not so much of the woman in question but of the "honor" of the family.

It is not surprising, then, that within such a context and interpretive framework, not-weeping *on purpose* could be interpreted (i.e., understood and performed) as a feminist practice. This is what I witnessed, de facto, three years later, when, in January 2015, I attended a wake at a Catholic Church of the Grecìa salentina after the death of a cousin of Marta's. The man's sudden death at a relatively young age was quite shocking; I had met him the year before at a convivial dinner, and his witty sense of humor had impressed me. During the wake, I noticed that the women in the front rows, the closest relatives, were not crying. They certainly looked sad, but they were composed and not crying. However, another woman, who, as a relative of the husband of the dead man's cousin, was only indirectly related, was weeping uncontrollably. During the funeral wake, my friend, who had come to know me well and to read my curiosity perfectly, said to me: "Look at her! They always make dramas (*sceneggiate*) in that family. The women of my family are *orgogliose* (proud), instead. It is a matter of dignity. They do not weep at funerals. One should cry only at home. It is a matter of dignity."

Performing grief differently from expectations was a matter of dignity for Marta, who interpreted the composure of the women of her family as a matter of "modernity" and, possibly, as a feminist practice. As I analyze below, it is significant that the words pride/honor and dignity appear in the same narrative.

Referring to Salento and *tarantismo*, Pizza writes that:

> Anthropological concepts have a complex social life in local contexts: here [in Salento] they contribute, sometimes in a decisive way, to the activation of cultural practices, facilitating their incorporation and naturalization to the point of making them able to interact independently with the same discourses that generated them, to the point of representing themselves as their opponents. Therefore, just as anthropology had a historically central role to play in the production of objects and cultural differences, so too the book, the article, the conference, the documentaries, and the CDs produced by anthropologists and ethnomusicologists are read, judged, and debated not only by the academic community, but also by part of the communities that live in the different sites involved by the ethnographic enquiries, both those conducted over the last century and, even more so, by the contemporary ones. (2015, 181)[2]

If this can be claimed for *tarantismo*, as the performance of the Orchestrina Terapeutica, among other examples, shows (see Introduction), I argue that a similar analysis could apply to other aspects of "making/doing" locality and "tradition" in contemporary Salento. Similarly to what Pizza (2015) claims on the local reception of de Martino and the development of *tarantismi*, my ethnography shows that to a certain extent the social life of anthropological writings impacted the "making" of the "local" and of "tradition," also in relation to the honor and shame complex in so-called Mediterranean societies. As the stories of Marta show, this latter element, if not present in specific, consistent, widespread, and discrete forms, is nonetheless still active in contemporary Salento.

If it is possible to talk about honor and shame in Salento today, I agree with Herzfeld (1980) that this needs to be done by addressing and describing the local specificity of these notions and of the practices associated with these terms. Today, though, differently from the 1980s when Herzfeld's criticisms were formulated, these local understandings and practices are not to be considered as discrete—yet often challenged—behaviors, possibly understood as culturally shared "remains" of past, dominant, hegemonic, or changing axiologies. Maybe paradoxically, in Salento they are usually products of contextual and positional local readings and popularizations of the much-criticized generalist "Mediterraneist" anthropology. The latter corpus of literature became available to locals in the past few years, and its reception can also be envisaged, indirectly, in what is now called *meridianismo*, or *pensiero meridiano* (Cassano 1996; Alcaro 1999; Pizza 2015, 200–202; see also Inserra 2017), and in ubiquitous references to the "Mediterranean" or to "the South" as common identifiers.[3] Whether in reference to traditional music and dance, to moral dispositions, to food culture, or to a shared history, for example, the fact of being Mediterranean is a fairly ubiquitously employed trope. In my experience, as the examples of Marta show, in the Salento hyperplace, "honor and shame" are employed to describe or justify loosely defined traditional behaviors, traceable also *in the present*, that Salentinians think of as *belonging to "the past"* of Salento and of the "Mediterranean." They are very often evoked in a comparative sense in opposition to contemporary, modern, emancipated values. Many Salentine people that I met defined the honor and shame complex not as a particular, specific, and discrete set of values and practices but rather they used it to refer to all that is not *modern*—notwithstanding the particular contextual moral connotation given to this term. The feminists with whom I worked used the terms *honor* and *shame* as a gloss for the notion of "patriarchy" and everything not related to self-determination. In other words, the majority of the people I met share a fictional idea of traditional Salentine values constructed around self-stereotyping notions and practices referred to as belonging to the honor and shame complex in the Mediterranean. The latter was not defined in detail and was influenced by a generally accepted, loose, unchallenged, and uncritical understanding of sometimes inconsistent versions of "honor and shame" as inflected in the generalist "Mediterraneist" literature.[4] The women I met talked mostly about dignity and *orgoglio* (pride), sometimes about shame, but the word *honor* was not generally used to reference contemporary practices and notions but those belonging to an unspecified traditional past. In fact, I heard it used only once, indirectly in reference to something located in the present and not in comparison to modern values. The occasion was this: I was told by a relative of one of the informants I interviewed in Salento that her *zia* (aunt) Maria, who then was ninety years old, had not spoken for more than a month to her unmarried granddaughter who got pregnant. Since her pregnancy was *"un disonore"* (a dishonor) for the family, the old Catholic woman told the young mother-to-be *"'mbàrcalu 'stu piccinnu"* (in dialect, "get rid of this baby").[5] On all the other occasions, honor (*onore*) was not the primary linguistic choice, especially among the feminists with whom I worked, and it was invoked only in response to my requests that the speaker unpack what they had said. In these circumstances, it was described as something associated with *li masculi* (in dialect, the males) and had to do with the display of social worth through economic status, sexual conduct, macho attitudes, an unemotional and sometimes insolent attitude, agonistic behaviors with peers, and practical savoir faire. What was considered to pertain specifically to the rhetorical field of "honor" varied according to the context of the interaction but was associated with stereotypical and one-dimensional understandings of masculinities in Salento. These men were perceived as valuing women on the basis of their attractiveness and sexual modesty, on their ability as mothers, caregivers, cooks, and housewives, and on their performances of social etiquette and hospitality. In sum, for the feminists I met, the traditional notion of "honor" was a gloss on the word "patriarchy," and that of "shame" was reduced to being compliant to men's expectations. In their language, "honor" was a matter of "patriarchy," and "shame" was a matter of accepting being defined by a "patriarchal" gaze. Therefore, "honor" was referred to in order to explain and justify behaviors that clashed with those perceived as "modern" and, in the case of feminists, with the principle of self-determination. The honor and shame complex was therefore evoked, for instance, when pinpointing some women's habit of serving food to men first at mealtimes, to justify the choice of not talking to an "old-fashioned" husband about the recent coming out of a gay teenaged son or daughter, to explain the complicity between a mother and a teenager in the latter's use of contraceptives (without letting the father know), or when someone addressed her own father with the dialectal expression *sirma* (lit., "my lord," a dialectal expression used in Salento to address one's father). In most of these cases the evocation of the honor and shame complex had the performative intention and effect of distancing the informant from the "backwardness" of certain attitudes, and of stressing her "modern feminist womanhood." There was no nostalgia for the past (and for the aspects of the present) identified with the honor and shame society: unlike other pasts, such as the idealized one of *Magna Graecia* or of a pre-Roman supposed matriarchy, this particular one was associated with backwardness, and it was given a negative moral connotation by the feminists I met. For these reasons, figures of noncompliant women of the past such as the Macare/witches (women who were not defined by shame, by men's gazes, or societal expectations) were valued as exempla of self-determination beyond the honor and shame complex.

Therefore, being Macare in the Salento hyperplace also had to do with playing with traditional gendered expectations in relation to the honor and shame complex in order to experience and perform new "disobedient" (*disobbedienti*) ways of being (modern feminist) women. Performing women-who-are-not-ashamed, as I show in more detail below, was achieved by adopting aspects of the poetics of traditional and stereotypical manhood, in order to negotiate authority (i.e., dignity) through the attribution of particular types of (masculine) social worth. This was a necessary condition for feminists to be able to pursue their political goals and for generating dissensus by affecting their publics' performances of seeing and sensing in relation to women in contemporary Italy. Paradoxically, then, by subsuming traditional behaviors and attitudes associated with *men*, they wanted both to be recognized as socially worthy—through an aesthetics of "honor"—and to offer an example of "modern feminist womanhood."

In sum, it is my claim that, in spite of the distance that my interlocutors tended to put between a fictional traditional past and the modern present, elements of the honor and shame set of values, aesthetics, and social expectations were indeed still present, recognized, effective, affective, questioned, and transformed in the ordinary lives of the Salentinians. They were not defined by discrete and specific values and practices but coexisted, at least to certain extents (the degree of which the feminist women I met constantly challenged), with other options that were available and acceptable as being "modern." Obviously, their uses were positional and contextual; as I show below, in spite of the widespread rhetoric I found among Salentine feminists, weeping could also not be associated with "shame," as happened with various celebrations of women's "emotional nature" among the activists with whom I worked. This coexistence was particularly evident in relation to women and weeping. My uses of "honor" (in relation to dignity) and of "shame" (in opposition to self-determination) in describing the practices of feminist womanhood that I encountered in Salento need to be understood within such a multifaceted understanding of this complex—the content of which in Salento was less important (though nonetheless factual in my ethnographic experience; see Herzfeld 1998) than the effects it had in the lives of the persons I describe.

Basta Lacrime—No More Tears (II)

"*Ci morse?*" ("Who died?" in dialect) called a man from a passing car in the center of the town, while my friend, her husband, and I were loading up the trunk of her car with foldable chairs from the funeral home. "Nobody. It's for the inauguration of the DNA center," the funeral director, who had offered to lend his chairs to DNA Donna for the event, promptly replied.

Since this conversation occurred in dialect, my five-year-old son, who until then had been spending his time admiring the number of "sarcophagi" [sic] stacked in the funeral house, looked at me, puzzled: he did not understand why we were all laughing loudly. We were happy that people were helping us and amused by the fact that nothing can really be kept confidential in a town of five thousand. In a few hours, the DNA Donna inauguration event would take place. I had arrived in the area a couple of days before to give my friends a hand with the preparations.

* * *

Now I was sweeping the floor of the headquarters and helping set up the conference room with the chairs we had borrowed, when my friend and Lena came to me. They looked excited. "We have a surprise," they said, and they showed me these panels, the ones that Lena had prepared for the inauguration of the *sede* (see fig. 4.1).

I was excited, too. My friends asked me to help them hang these pictures on the entrance walls of the headquarters. It was a very significant moment for them, and I was honored to be invited. It was just the three of us; I let my friends position the pictures together while I took this photo (see fig. 4.2).

Weeping, as I mentioned above, was still considered the appropriate behavior for a sensitive woman in contemporary Salento. For example, a woman who wept during the Good Friday evening procession that commemorates the death of Christ was thought to be a person who *tene core* (in dialect, "has heart," i.e., good sentiments/good disposition), as I heard people saying in Grecìa salentina. While a range of behaviors in relation to being women and weeping was socially accepted, despite more acceptance of modern and "manly" behaviors, there was still admiration for what was deemed to be women's "natural and appropriate" emotional responses, as we see in the following example.

Figure 4.1. "No more tears. Women's weeping does not change the world; rather, their strength does." (Photo courtesy of the author.)

Figure 4.2. Putting the "No more tears" pictures on the wall. (Photo courtesy of the author.)

In July 2014, Carlo, the husband of one of my feminist friends, returned from the hospital. I had spent the whole day at my friend's house, organizing a meeting. He was in his fifties and worked in the Italian air force; the Italian army has several military bases in Salento, and I met many men there who were in the military. Until recently, working as a *statale* (a person employed by the state)—for example, as a teacher in public schools, in the *Poste* (mail offices), in municipalities, in the police, in the *Arma dei Carabinieri*, or in the army—represented a fairly common choice. Especially in the *Mezzogiorno* (southern Italy), where the rates of industrialization were (and are still) lower, and unemployment was (and still is) higher than in the north, working for the Italian state gave a person and his family some benefits, including a steady income, the possibility of a permanent job, some flexibility in terms of weekly schedule and of paid leave, and a pension.

Carlo, who is the father of two, was the only person who earned an income in his household. In his spare time, not unlike many men I met in Salento, he *"fatica a fore"* (in dialect, works in the fields) in his family's field. This leisure activity was also a source of economic support for his family, and for those of some of his brothers and sisters, the ones who had not migrated to northern Italy. Internal migrations to northern cities such as Bologna, Modena, Turin, Pavia, and Milan, in addition to emigration to foreign countries such as Switzerland and Germany, have been common solutions for Salentinians of his generation.[6]

In July 2014, Carlo, the husband of one of my feminist friends, returned from visiting his mother in the hospital. At first, I thought that Carlo's father, who a few months earlier had fallen from a tree while harvesting, was the reason for Carlo's trip to the hospital. Instead, it was Carlo's mother, a woman in her seventies, who had been taken to the hospital for a heart attack the night before.

I was at home when he arrived, and I immediately greeted him, asking about the old woman's situation. His voice low, and a sad expression on his face, he told me in a mixture of Italian and dialect that he and his sister had just spoken with the doctors. "The doctors said that my mother has *un cuore sofferente* (a suffering heart)." *Sofferente* (lit., suffering) is an expression that physicians in Italy often use *within a biomedical frame of reference* to describe metaphorically the organs affected by a pathological condition. Then Carlo added, with a hint of sadness: "You know, Giovanna, despite the issues with my brother and my sister we never saw our mother weeping or crying at home. We did not realize it, but she must have kept all this [suffering] in for all these years . . . and now you see . . . she had a heart attack." Carlo, who is the oldest of many brothers and sisters, was alluding to his cognitively impaired younger brother and to the leukemia that had affected his sister (before her treatment and cure). I was surprised to realize that Carlo was attributing his mother's heart attack to the worries and concerns that he *retrospectively* linked to the anxiety and sadness his mother must have experienced concerning her offsprings' health.

This emotional pain, he suggested, had affected her heart, understood by Carlo literally and not metaphorically as the locus of sentiments. While he praised her for being brave and proud by keeping her feelings to herself (something typically not considered "womanly" since women are understood as being naturally emotional) and for not wanting to be a burden to the other members of the family, ultimately, he deemed that very behavior to have been responsible for her illness. I had always taken the idiom of suffering as a dead metaphor, and I was really surprised to find that for Carlo it had quite a literal connotation. After the conversation with him, the links between women, weeping, and suffering acquired further meanings and affective resonances for me. The link Carlo described, in fact, was part of the context in which the women of DNA Donna operated.

While a certain variability in the performance of womanhood in reference to weeping was culturally tolerated, it was the constant and explicit challenge of such traditional and "natural" assumptions that characterized my informants' feminism. Their choice to post on their headquarters' walls images that said, "No more tears. Women's weeping does not change the world; rather, their strength does," I think should be understood as an explicit attempt to confront perceived traditional expectations of gender roles and to signal new ways of being women to those who visit the center. In sum, I argue that the connections between the women-as-victims trope and "traditional values" expressed through weeping and its resonances with the honor and shame complex were pivotal for making *sense* of the importance of the poster of DNA Donna and of the representational engagement that characterized the political practice of the feminists I met.

* * *

During the center's inauguration event, my task was to sign up new members and register donations. Because I sat at a table near the entrance to the conference room, while I took care of my duties I also had a privileged perspective on the speeches and readings. The event was a success. The room was full: at least two hundred people (men and women) attended the DNA Donna inauguration, a good result for a new women's shelter in a town of five thousand. About thirty-five of them decided to make a donation, for a total of about $500. Most of the persons I met at the registration table shared some of their thoughts on the initiative and on the purpose of the center. All were enthusiastic. For a few days after the inauguration, people in the town continued to talk about DNA Donna; even my trips to the pharmacy, due to an injured finger, were occasions for the pharmacist to talk about it.

One of the elements that most caught the attention of the audience during the inauguration—according to both my observations and the comments I received while at the registration table—was the reading, accompanied by the music of a harpist, of excerpts of the book *Ferite a Morte* (Wounded to Death), written by the actress Serena Dandini (Dandini and Misiti 2013). This book presents stories of femminicidio, inspired by real events, *from the perspectives of the murdered women.* The voices of the narrators in those texts, in other words, are those of the *victims* that become, in the fiction, *witnesses* of their own murders. In the excerpts chosen by my DNA Donna friends for the inauguration, the murdered women, while tactfully hinting at femicidal events, mainly described the circumstances that led to their murders. Instead of insisting on the gruesome details of their assassinations, the characters focused on their (shifting) interpretations of the events. In the fiction, their deaths—that the victims narrated with surprise, and almost disbelief—represented turning points in their own understandings of the relationships they had had with their killers.

The element that emerged in these narratives, and the reason why my informants had chosen them for the inauguration in the first place, had to do with the ordinary dimensions of these relationships and with the banality of violence in their own lives. The incredulity and the dismay of the women of the book in relation to their murders revolved mostly around the type of connections and engagements they had had with their aggressors: they all seemed to be "ordinary" and from a wide range of social backgrounds. This element was central for the DNA Donna staff: they wanted the women of the book to speak directly to the audience attending the inauguration. They were hoping that the surprise of the murdered women vis-à-vis their own tragic epilogues in the book, and their subsequent postmortem change in the framing of their relationships, could change the way those attending the inauguration and readings perceived, felt, and understood violence against women (see Butler 1997 and Carr 2009 for a comparison). In other words, the book and my friends' use of it represented a firm critique of Italian society, and the recognition that its commonsensical interpretative lenses in relation to sexed violence were quite simply inappropriate. The DNA Donna women called for a change—a change like that narrated by the women in the novel, whose deaths represented a cognitive turning point in their understandings of love, of relationships with men, and of their lives.

By offering these readings to their public, I suggest that my friends wanted not just to present women in positions that differed from that of the victim (namely, quite literally, as witnesses) but also to promote dissensus. By engaging the senses of their public, they meant to trigger and produce, in Rancièrian terms, a different way of sensing and making sense of women and violence against women (see chaps. 5 and 6). Their aim was not only to cognitively challenge their audience but also to *interpellate* it affectively by disregarding the audience's expectation by avoiding a (very much expected) spectacularization of violence. This political move was performed by playing with the expectations of a public that associated women with victimhood and womanhood with suffering and weeping. Apparently, the DNA Donna staff succeeded in their intent, at least for part of their audience, for many of the spectators were visibly moved by the recital. Some of them had tears in their eyes; others commented on the performances, claiming that violence could happen to any of us and that probably these stories were much more frequent than they thought.

The "We Are Witnesses, Not Victims" (*Non più vittime ma testimoni*) motto was something I had encountered many times before among UDI women. In fact, it was Carla, one of my UDI Salentine informants, who had invented the slogan for the Staffetta in 2008–2009. If in UDI's documents the motto appeared mainly in the aforementioned form, the Macare reworked it in other ways such as in a flyer, advertising a sit-in against violence against women in Brindisi on April 13, 2012. The dark purple title of this flyer stated: "one woman by herself is a victim, together we become witnesses of a crime against women."[7]

The Staffetta di Donne contro la Violenza sulle Donne was one of UDI's national campaigns. It was launched on November 25, 2008, in Niscemi, Sicily, where a woman named Lorena had been murdered, and ended exactly one year later in Brescia, Lombardy, where a woman called Hiina had been slaughtered. During that year, an amphora (*Anfora*) designed with two handles "in order to be carried by two women"—to "symbolize the importance of relationships" (Nuzzo 2008a)—traveled throughout Italy. Each city or town that received the amphora welcomed it by organizing public events: from seminars to exhibits, and from shows to public debates. People greeted the amphora in many public places: from schools to jails, and from theaters to city halls. The ritual associated with the amphora's tour was characterized by the public delivery of the amphora by two women to two recipient women. In each town or city, every woman who wanted to could put into the amphora a note with her thoughts, feelings, denunciations, or pictures. The objective of the Staffetta was "to say 'Stop sexed violence and femminicidio'" (Nuzzo 2008a, 2008b), defined variously as "the killing of women by the hands of men," as a "disease" (each "germ" of which needed to be neutralized), and as the act of a man killing a woman in order to feel "*maschio*" (male) (2008a).

In spite of the marginality of publicity about the Staffetta initiatives in the national press, it was a great success. Hundreds of women witnessed the amphora's progress and left messages in it. Besides helping promote and diffuse awareness around femminicidio and violence against women, the Staffetta helped frame violence against women as something beyond trauma and suffering.[8]

In this process, Carla's motto "We Are Witnesses, Not Victims" played a very important role.[9] Carla is a lawyer, and she has been a feminist political activist in the UDI for decades. Since she is from Salento, and one of the first women I met during my fieldwork, I had the chance to talk with her about her ideas on several different occasions. In narrating the origin of the "We Are Witnesses, Not Victims" motto, she told me that she had been impressed by the courage, attitude, and behavior of some women who testified in court during a trial for a case of rape and that she had started to recognize in this striking attitude what it is that "makes the difference" in talking about violence. This is why Carla decided to suggest they construct the Staffetta around the idea of being witnesses—witnessing being something that empowers women without reinscribing the narrative that women are in need of tutelage. Quite bluntly, she told me that "patriarchy" wanted us to be victims and that accepting this identity meant being compliant with it: if there was anything that the latter did not tolerate, according to Carla, it was women's volition (*volitività*) and the inviolability of their bodies. Therefore, it needed to act on both levels in order to control them. From this perspective, coercion and tutelage were just two sides of the same coin, for Carla and for other feminists I met.

Writer and political activist Michela Murgia makes a similar observation. In her *Ave Mary*, she writes:

> Being identified as victims is a condition that should be transitory for everyone, linked to precise circumstances. One is not a victim for the fact of existing as a female, instead of as a male, but one [is a victim] always of something or someone. The attempt to transform people into permanent victims regardless of the circumstances forces victims into the role of victimized. That is another form of violence, more subtle and pervasive, since it imposes a condition of passivity that precludes the ability of self-redemption. The victimized subject cannot try to exit from the condition of victimhood, since around her she has a whole system that prevents her from being something different. (2011, 17)

If, according to Carla and my Salentine informants, "patriarchy" wants to control women, the latter too often reinforce the former by embracing political projects that use the language of victimhood and by embracing the role of victims themselves. On more than one occasion, I heard Carla state that she did not want to talk about violence using passive language, language that affirmed women's political goals only through negation. Language was central for my informants: for this reason, she told me, she proposed to Pina Nuzzo that they call the UDI's third campaign *Immagini Amiche* (Friendly Images) rather than *Immagini nemiche* (Enemy Images), as was first planned. Moreover, she suggested concentrating on positive images of women in media and advertising rather than focusing on their debasement. Words and images were a very serious matter for Carla and the feminist activists I met.

From Violence to Representation: Immagini Amiche and the Power of Imagination

On March 8, 2010, the third of the UDI's national campaigns began. It was indeed entitled Immagini Amiche (Friendly Images). In announcing this initiative, which was described in the document "*8 marzo 2010 SE CI OFFENDI NON VALE*" (8 March, 2010. IF YOU OFFEND US, IT IS UNFAIR),[10] Pina Nuzzo wrote:

> The violent, vulgar images, disrespectful of *women's dignity* do damage to women and to society as a whole. They damage the present and the future that we want because they undermine the basis of the possibility of a respectful and civil coexistence of genders. . . . We want to propose shared, accurate, well-organized political actions that start from the initiative that we already have undertaken, and from others as well, in order to oppose the harmful images and stereotypes of women that are everywhere, not just in commercials. . . . Offensive advertisement is the most visible violation against the feminine gender. . . . The Staffetta showed that women can avoid being subjected to (*possono non subire*) the misery of violence and can make themselves witnesses *(testimoni)* with initiatives that free our creativity and show the path for a civil co-existence between genders. Thousands of women participated [in the Staffetta], they talked about their experiences of victimhood, they reported an unbearable culture of oppression (*sopraffazione*) in the family, at work, and in politics. A culture made of images. WE WANT IMAGES THAT ARE WOMEN'S FRIENDS. In order to give continuity to the *Staffetta*, we propose to the many women that participated in it, and to all the others who want to do so, to get involved.

In this text, the ideological connection between violence and the realm of representations, and between the Staffetta and Immagini Amiche, was spelled out very clearly. Here, UDI women explicitly recognized representation as one of the dimensions in which violence against women operated in contemporary Italy. Yet their political initiative in this phase was still defined by their being, quite literally, *audiences* of these representations. While the ending date of the campaign was set for March 8, 2011, two initiatives appeared to be central to Immagini Amiche. Significantly, both of them took place on the occasion of the International Day against Violence against Women. First, the *Anfora* of the Staffetta and the white notebooks, in which the women who participated in the Campaign Immagini Amiche recorded the virtuous commitments and actions of individuals and of institutions in promoting friendly images of women, went to the European Parliament. The choice of bringing the amphora of the

Staffetta together with the white notebooks to that important institution was meant to "signify a symbolic continuity with the messages that thousands of women chose to give to the witness [*testimone*] of the Staffetta," according to Nuzzo. Second, during a *Cafè Débat* in Rome, the prize Immagini Amiche was announced. UDI activists designated a jury of women who would choose the ads that best promoted a positive image of women. At a table of honor during this presentation sat "the *Anfora* of the Staffetta di donne contro la violenza sulle donne, who on her travels [had] collected many messages in which the relationship between the use of images and violence is spelled out. The *Anfora* continues to be Witness of a path even longer than that begun with the Staffetta" (Nuzzo and Albani 2010). Through the Prize Immagini Amiche, UDI activists, in the role of audience of representations of women in Italy, wanted to negotiate a special place: they wanted *their gaze* to count and for that gaze to be acknowledged as a source of judgment in relation to dominant ones.

The third UDI campaign, however, did not limit its influence to the reconfiguration of women's practices as audiences. It also introduced interesting connections between art, imagination, feelings, representations, and political activism, setting the stage for the development, which I witnessed ethnographically, of a connection between *producing* representations, and political activism. The aim of this political project, I argue, can be framed as an attempt to change the practices and performances of seeing and sensing: of feminists themselves, first, and of their imagined or actual publics, second. In an email sent to the women of the UDI on February 19, 2010, Nuzzo explains the motto "if you offend us, it is unfair." This is a revised quotation of a popular 1976 song by Julio Iglesias *Se mi lasci non vale* (if you leave me, it is unfair). The former national delegate explains:

> The song does not say that it is not right, or legal, that she leaves him. It says it is unfair, since he does not want to admit that the mores are changing, and women are not on board with these anymore. . . . Women cannot be represented in a violent mode that might suggest forms of abuse with impunity. . . . We [UDI women] thought, in order to address this topic without triggering priggish (*bacchettone*) reactions, that the best thing to do would be something positive, by supporting those who sell products without necessarily selling us [women]. . . . Feminists have always tried to undermine stereotypes, inventing forms of opposition that are sometimes very creative.

This creative aspect of political practice, according to Nuzzo (2010), opened up questions among women that were "very dangerous for patriarchy," namely: "What are our fantasies, our imaginaries, our fantastic world(s)? This is the question that had really impaired men's power over women. This was the internal repositioning that involved every single woman and a whole generation, until it became a common feeling (*sentimento diffuso*)." In this campaign, the field of representation was explicitly starting to become a domain of possible political action, framed as an out-and-out struggle. Nuzzo (2010) pointed out that "it is not by chance that cyclically we women return to how genders are represented, since we know that it is crucial if we want to undo the current meanings of signs and symbols and of the imaginary on which the relationship between men and women still rests. The journeys are necessary and sometimes fierce because only making the conflict explicit can lead us to understand how vital is the balance between representations and being representative (*rappresentazione e rappresentanza*)."

The *figura etymologica* in this text was not just a rhetorical device: it conveyed a very important element of how UDI women, and some of the activists I met and followed in Salento, understood the representational struggle against "patriarchy." For them, representation as a political field was not just the locus for showing alternative possibilities of being women: this enterprise was political as long as it generated *rappresentanza* for UDI women—that is, participation in, and sharing of, the administration of the res publica. To use Cristiana Giordano's words, the feminists I followed did not seek only *acknowledgment*, that is, "the political and ethical act of surrendering the desire to know through already established categories and of accepting the challenges of difference and the possibility of not knowing, not understanding, and thus embracing uncertainty" (2014, 9). They *also* looked for recognition, within the new political "common sense," in Rancièrian terms, that they were helping construct through their representational struggle.

I consider representation, in line with its etymology, to be an umbrella term that refers to what is literally placed before something or someone. The English term *representation* (like its Italian equivalent *rappresentazione*) derives from the Latin verb *repraesentare*, where *re* is an intensifying prefix, and *praesentare* means to place in front of. It comprises both temporal and spatial dimensions, as the English words present (versus past and future; in Italian: *presente*) and presence (in Italian: *presenza*) show. According to the Merriam-Webster dictionary, representation means "something that stands for something else." It is not a coincidence, then, that the word present (in Italian: *presente*) is used also as a synonym of gift: it is something that is given and implies both a giver and a receiver. Representing, in other words, implies a mediation, a relation between a body or an object and something else (e.g., an idea, another person, aspects of oneself), one in which something offers itself as a function of something else. The boundaries between the former and the latter are blurred—as the oxymoronic visual grammar I analyze and discuss in the following chapter shows. Representation, though, is often associated with fiction in both its meanings of creation and falsity: an aspect that is consistent with my informants' uneasiness around the issue of visibility. On the one hand, representations were felt and considered as loci to imagine new possibilities of being women; on the other, they felt the anxiety of being perceived as false and inauthentic. Not surprisingly, some of the Salentine women I met considered the term *performance* to be a sort of insult, if used in relation to their political activities. To them it implied a debasement of their political authority. It is also not a coincidence that the Macare followed Carone's elaboration of a distinction (2011) between pretending (*fare finta*) and doing-as-if (fare-come-se; see chap. 6), where the second expression refers to a political praxis, while the former does not.[11] In my ethnographic field, I understand representations as "material symbols" (see, e.g., Herzfeld 2005a, 2005b) that play with what Herzfeld would call "practical essentialisms"—that is, the "pragmatic reification of people as representatives of fixed categories" (2005a)—available both locally and nationally. In this respect, I agree with Herzfeld that "social life consists of processes of reification and essentialism as well as challenges to these processes" (2005a). It is within this understanding of social life that I situate my informants' discourses and practices, and hence also this book. I describe and try to understand how the women with whom I worked challenged "practical essentialisms" (and built new ones) by questioning widespread axiologies (systems of value) around women's role in society (see also Herzfeld 2004). Locally, for the Salentine feminists with whom I worked, they negotiated this enterprise through constructions of traditional gender roles and by performing "poetics of modern feminist womanhood" (see, for a comparison, Herzfeld 1985, 2005a, 2005b; Dubisch 1995; Kirtsoglou 2004; and below).

According to Herzfeld, "poetic principles guide all *effective* social interactions. Such a poetics must also correspond intelligibly with local social theory, with indigenous ideas about meaning, and with criteria of style, relevance, and importance" (1985, xv). According to him, there is therefore "no intrinsic reason to restrict this insight to the purely verbal manifestations of poetic discourse" (11). Poetics "means action" (2005b, 189) and pertains to "all kinds of symbolic expression, including casual talk" (2005a, 23).

The connections between performances and social life have been variously explored by anthropologists. For the reader accustomed to the literature on honor and shame in the Mediterranean, for example, the relations between women, men, and particular ways of ethically and aesthetically inhabiting the private and public realms are not new.[12] These aspects of social life have captured the attention of anthropologists since the 1950s. The traditional literature on honor and shame rests heavily on the (especially gendered) management of these two spheres.[13] It is precisely in reference to these aspects of social life in

Salento that the feminists I met operated. In these processes, performances, practices, and discourses around dignity were central.

Negotiating Feminist Womanhood in Salento: Dignity, Honor, and Human Rights

The small room of the women's bookstore was crowded. Underestimating the last-minute networking ability of my informants, I had not anticipated that so many people would be at the meeting. For the repeat performance of Eve Ensler's *Vagina Monologues* at the local Paisiello Theater, my friends had organized an event at the bookstore entitled "We and Eve: Narratives in Comparison." The subtitle of the meeting was "United against Sexed Violence: A Political Path of Women in Italy." Included on the flyer was the following comment: "From the battle for the recognition of violence as a 'crime against the person' to the national campaigns 'Staffetta di donne contro la violenza sulle donne' (against every form of sexed violence, against 'femminicidio'), and '*Immagini Amiche*' (on the possibility of a positive relationship between women's bodies and advertisement) *videos *readings *documents *comments*."

It was a Sunday afternoon in November, and unusually cool. I regretted the fact that the bookstore lacked a heating system. We were sitting in a circle, most of us on chairs, someone on the floor, someone else standing in the corner of the room. In addition to the Macare, there were other persons that I had not met before: some from Agedo, the theater actresses, and some bookstore clients.[14] Carla started her presentation in front of this heterogeneous public, tracing the connections between violence against women, the national campaigns organized by UDI, and Ensler's famous monologues. She spoke with self-confidence and composure, as an expert on those topics. She was addressing mainly the persons who did not know her (i.e., probably, nonfeminists) and nonchalantly mentioned her experience as a lawyer, her years of activism in the UDI, and her well-read background. She talked off the cuff about herself and her political history, fluently but without a clear outline. Her sentences were apodictic, but the connections between her arguments were not always strong. She dropped some feminist jargon into her speech (which seemed long and confusing to me) all the while looking at the ceiling of the room. She hardly made eye contact with us, her audience, during her speech. She was so different from the Carla I knew: normally, she was very warm and witty but in this situation she seemed distant and aloof. While I was a bit disappointed by her speech, I realized at the end of the event that she was not: on the contrary, she was both very comfortable and happy with her performance and with the event as a whole.

After Carla, it was Renata's turn. Renata is a woman in her early forties with a university degree and a real talent for writing. Carla asked her to explain the meaning of "sexed violence," since this expression, which they expected to be unfamiliar to the audience, appeared in the event's subtitle. I do not know if Renata knew ahead of time that she would have to speak. Nonetheless, she seemed quite comfortable with this task. Coming from a modest family in the Province of Lecce, her former public school teacher, Carla's mother, took her under her wing. Carla and Renata, therefore, lived in the same house during Renata's college years. Carla's mother, as far as I understood, nurtured Renata so that she could study and cultivate her talents.[15] This is probably why, for Renata, being cultivated is really an identity marker: at that time, she was frustrated with working in her husband's shop, since she really desired to become a teacher in Italian public high schools. Renata started explaining the meaning of "sexed violence": it was pretty clear to me that she was completely ignoring the distinction between sex and gender—something that she actually confirmed in a chat we had at the end of the meeting. She talked about men and women, about "patriarchy," and about women's dignity, and pointed out how the role and potentialities of women were smothered by the phallogocentrism of our society.

Finally, Elisabetta spoke. She had prepared a reading from the book *I Am an Emotional Creature* by Eve Ensler and could not wait to perform it in front of us. She read the excerpts she had chosen and commented on the readings, addressing mainly a feminist audience. Elisabetta is always very engaging when she talks in public: she performed a celebration of women in their beings as emotional, nonrational subjects in reference to the banality of men's (stereotypical) composed behaviors. Emotions were good, smart, and fulfilling. Women, who are emotional subjects, should be proud of being so, she said.

I knew that this event was an important moment for my informants: an occasion to proselytize, to show others their feminist womanhood, to be recognized as politically meaningful. Nonetheless, I felt anxious about how the event was unfolding: I was worried that their expectations would not be fulfilled. Yet, according to my friends, the event was a success. When we were alone again in the bookstore after the meeting, they commented with satisfaction on their performances and the public's reactions. I rejoiced with them, even though I had experienced the event differently. After all, they knew their local publics and expectations better than I did. Nonetheless, I was baffled: I had more than a few problems with the contents of my three friends' speeches. Among other things, I wondered how my informants could not see, even if they celebrated emotions over rationality, that adhering to such a binary, stereotypical interpretation of genders might have reinscribed the same patterns that, as Renata explained, lead to violence. Moreover, I asked myself how it was that, during the event, Elisabetta was celebrating emotions, and publicly noting this as a marker of their alternative feminist womanhood—while Carla, for the sake of being recognized as authoritative, was repressing them and behaving so differently from the experience I had of her? Clearly, while the public remained the same for each speaker's presentation, Carla and Elisabetta seemed to be addressing different imagined audiences. To me, all of this had to do with dignity, with feeling *degne* (worthy/dignified), and, especially, with the need to be considered as such.

As was already evident in the previous chapters of this book, *dignity* was a widespread term in my fieldwork context. Dignity appeared, for example, in Eugenia's words and world vision, in her grandmother's understanding of feminism, in the SNOQ appeal, in the flash mob the *indignate* performed in Bologna, in Nuzzo's words, in narratives about funerals in Salento, in Putino's understanding of conflicting, in UDI's 1980 appeal against violence, and in antiviolence ads; it was also associated with weeping/not weeping issues during funerals and was linked to the idea of caring and of being a witness.

Yet, in my fieldwork context, dignity was not a unitary concept; on the contrary, I found it to be multivalent and malleable. On the one hand, when my informants *talked* about dignity, they spoke a global language, one that was related to human rights. In this sense, my informants referred extensively to dignity as a legal category, as an innate quality that belonged to men and women simply by being born, and as a feature of humanity. On the other hand, though, practices and performances—an out-and-out aesthetics—of dignity were sought in their lives as a way to measure, assess, and achieve social worth in front of their local (imagined or actual) publics. In this latter meaning, evident, in particular, in Carla's performance in the "We and Eve" event, I claim, performing dignity resonated with my informants' understandings of traditional local *gendered* inflections of the honor and shame complex (see Introduction).

The widespread association between women and victims in Salento resonated with traditional understandings of gender roles as explained above. Women-as-victims wept, suffered, and were defined by the gaze of men. In order to challenge and overturn these assumptions and to portray their social worth as "witnesses," therefore, the Salentine women with whom I worked performed their being *different* women—that is, they "interpreted" (understood and performed, see Lambek 2014) "modern feminist womanhood." Within the latter, I claim, the performance of dignity took a central role. For my informants, dignity was simultaneously a concept and a set of practices, an ethical perspective, an emotion (i.e., feeling worthy/dignified), and an aesthetic performance. Their quest for dignity seemed to respond both to the need to partake in and to be potentially disruptive of perceived common local and traditional social understandings of womanhood. At one and the same time, performing dignity allowed them to break with the women-as-victims narratives and representations *and* to do so in a *commensurable* way for their (imagined or actual) publics.

The term *dignity* is widely used internationally, mostly in the legal field, ever since it became a reference point in human rights jurisprudence. In spite of its ubiquitous presence in legal and everyday language, its meanings and local understandings are usually not defined or spelled out.[16] If human dignity is something that international jurisprudence grants to every human being, it is surprising that it has not been a widely analyzed object of anthropological research.

According to Cataldi, "Etymologically, the expression dignity is related not only to notions of worth or value, but also (through the Latin *decet* and *dignus*: what is fitting or seemly) to ideas of decency and decorum. Indecorous behavior is im-proper (from *propre*: own), unbecoming or inappropriate—behavior that does not suit one's character or status—behavior that is not one's own (or specific to one's species)" (2002, 113). This interpretation of dignity fits precisely with what I encountered in my ethnographic field: it was something that happened between ethics (value, worth) and aesthetics (decorum), in ways that defined one's being in the (social) world (character or status).[17] Most importantly, dignity was not just something that a person had/did/was/ felt in relation to herself: in order to be enacted, it *needed to be acknowledged by someone else.*

These observations, I claim, are paramount for my ethnographic analyses. Similar to what Kirtsoglou wrote about the practice of *mangia* (2004, 154–155), I noticed that my informants performed "queer" femininity, in the sense explained by Carone (2011; see chap. 6), by fashioning their womanhood around performances of dignity. Dignity, being witnesses, and interpreting modern feminist womanhood in Salento were deeply connected. Performances of womanhood were inflected "according to what is conventionally perceived to be masculine" (Kirtsoglou 2004, 154) in the social world they inhabited, which was constructed, by them, as "traditional" qua "patriarchal" (and vice versa). In the example above, Carla's attitude, I claim, was informed by a similar intention. While in feminist contexts my informants emphatically expressed their emotions and spent a good amount of time celebrating the emotiveness of women in reference to the rationality of men, in nonfeminist settings they did not. As shown above, Elisabetta's attitude differed from Carla's, as did their imagined (or preferred) audiences—this in spite of the fact that the public in front of which they performed was actually made up of the same people.

While I understand this remark as a gloss on Herzfeld's claims that "constant signifiers mark shifting signified" (2005a), I nonetheless noticed a certain uniformity of performance in front of similarly perceived publics. Especially during ordinary transactions with men—for example, at the market, when asking for directions, or when relating to one of the common, abusive collectors of parking fees in the Salento area—the expressions on the faces of my informants, the tone of their voices, and the language choices they made tended to emphasize their being emotionless, self-composed, aloof, and off-putting. These attitudes translated some of the aspects that were locally associated with traditional, stereotypical performances of manhood, through which men were understood to negotiate their social worth and authority. Besides offering an oxymoronic performance of womanhood (see chap. 5), achieved by playing with the gendered expectations of their publics, these performances aimed at negotiating the women activists' worth and authority in relation to their audiences. The particular aesthetics of dignity my informants replicated, I claim, was linked to what has been referred to as honor, as it is lived, understood, and interpreted in this particular place of the so-called Mediterranean.

A similar attitude also emerged in my fieldwork context in connection with violence against women, and in relation to women's suffering. The associations between crying, being emotional, being victims, suffering, being passive, and being women were well established among my Salentine informants. While they relied on hegemonic (essentializing) discourses that were common in Italy as a country, as I have pointed out so far, in this particular area of the peninsula they took on peculiar connotations, linked to what were perceived as traditionally being women's social behaviors. These seemingly banal equations emerged in Carla's words and attitudes and also appeared in Lucia and Rina's excerpts reported below. Moreover, they were an important element among the DNA Donna activists and a message in the Taurisano exhibition (see chap. 5). These associations were as simple as they were paramount to my research. They explicitly traced a link, in culture-specific ways, not just between ethical stances and aesthetic performances but also between not being a victim and being *modern* and *progressive* (changing the world) and between being a victim and being *traditional* and *compliant with* "patriarchy." In other words, they traced a direct connection, not spelled out at a national level, between being a witness of violence against women and being modern and being (only) a victim of violence and being traditional. It is not surprising that dignity, in this particular area of the country, was inflected according to the DNA Donna poster's expectations I discussed above. Weeping (i.e., being emotional) was associated with being victims and being women in the traditional Salento. Not weeping (i.e., being more composed, dignified) was associated instead with being courageous and with "changing the world" (see Rina below).[18] My informants associated this latter feature, in their local area, with men's gendered social expectations and translated it with the aesthetics I discussed above. If women who wept were victims who were compliant with and reproduced the status quo, it is not surprising that, at a local level, embracing *traditional* stereotypical behaviors that were associated with *their opposite* (i.e., with men) was considered a feature of modernity, of "queerness," and ultimately as a political practice that, in Rancièrian terms, aimed to promote dissensus. This "sensing differently," similarly to what I claim in chapter 5, was pursued through the representation of ambiguity.

In sum, the connections between performing and practicing modern feminist womanhood, being *testimoni*, and performing (and pursuing) dignity were very well developed in Salento and were understood as features of being feminist, active, modern, and self-possessed. They were widely employed, locally, in the representational struggle I have addressed so far, as a form of dissensus—that is, of sensing and making sense differently. On the one hand, their uses and performances of dignity clearly resonated aesthetically with the traditional notion of honor as a measure of social worth (see, e.g., Herzfeld 1980; Lever 1986) and spoke about the uneasiness that my informant had in relation to the possibility of being seen as backward. Associations between tradition and womanhood were not neutral ones for the feminists I met in Salento: adhering to the type of gendered performances that they associated with women in the traditional Salento resonated strongly with the paradigm of shame and of victimhood I have discussed above. Being passive was being traditional, being a victim was being compliant with patriarchal values—something they found ethically problematic. By contrast, for them, showing dignity meant being witnesses and interpreting modern feminist womanhood through the ("patriarchal") "traditional" aesthetics of men's honor. Showing dignity, as a measure of social worth, allowed women to be both commensurable to (see Povinelli 2001) and disruptive of the social "patriarchal" context where my informants lived. They framed dignity as a traditional value and behavior, according to categories and aesthetics that might be traced back to those of honor and shame, as described above. On the other hand, since my feminist informants thought of themselves as modern women, they also refused to be *completely* defined by their social context through these traditional parameters, and in particular by those of shame (on the polysemy and polifunctionality of shame in Italy, see, e.g., Plesset 2007). By virtue of their being Italian feminists informed by the pensiero della differenza sessuale, they did not aim to be equal to men. They refused to explicitly adopt the *language* of honor as an identity filter, replacing it with dignity. The adoption of dignity as a measure of social worth resonated also with the *language* of human rights and with a public that went beyond the local communities of Salento, allowing the women to redefine their values in (global) terms that took humanity as their reference point.[19] In this way they transformed and transcended their local social belonging—that is, the local audiences of their performances of womanhood—and framed their feminist identities and experiences according to human categories that were a feature both of modernity and of feminism (on the strategic uses of competing discourses and practices, see Herzfeld 2004).

Both Victims *and* Witnesses: Beyond Victim Blaming

The importance of breaking explicitly with the victim scheme was something that, for different reasons, my informants, as audiences of representations, shared with other Italian feminists, although in doing so they were not among the majority of Italian women's groups. Some of the feminists that actively participated in the Staffetta, or that have for years supported the struggle against femminicidio—like Tonia, who I presented in the previous chapter—in the past couple of years have started to voice their complaints about women being represented as victims.[20] The blogger of *Al di là del Buco* and Michela Murgia are just two other examples of this attitude.[21] As initiators of and participants in the widespread dissemination of discourses and images that depict women in victimizing terms, they, like the Salentine feminist activists, offer critical understandings and analyses of the dominant gazes on women. The latter criticisms emerged mainly on the internet, especially in the form of blog or Facebook posts published, linked, liked, and reposted by an online *tessitura* of relationships (for a comparison, see chap. 2). By framing these gazes through a distinction between victims and witnesses, my informants (most of them trained in their political activities within the UDI) seemed to add to these different practices and performances of being audiences' voices of dissatisfaction with the dominant representations of women (including those used by women's groups). The catchphrase "no more victims, but witnesses," which emerged during the Staffetta, was central to their understanding of women, of their being in the world, and of their political actions as *feminist* women.

As a matter of fact, according to many of the Salentine women activists I met, being (potentially or actually) objects of violence was not synonymous with being victims. If, as the Staffetta made clear, they claimed that women were recipients of violence for the mere fact of being women, this did not mean that they implied that women should consider themselves only as victims, or that, necessarily, they should be defined as such. Many of my informants certainly used passivity and passiveness to describe the status of victims and recognized the injustice of the violent acts perpetrated against women who were not, by any means, considered responsible for the violence they suffered. Interestingly, though, when I asked some of them to be more specific in explaining who they thought victims were, I noticed that they tended to define this condition contrastively—that is, by referring to what being a victim was not and to what being a witness was. Below, I report two of the answers I received when I asked the aforementioned question. These responses summarize very well the issues at stake.

> Women always have to expiate (*espiare*), starting with the fact that they were born [as women]; therefore, violence, rapes, and other vexations are included [in the fact of being born as women]. So, declaring oneself to be a "victim" is perceived as debasing (*sminuente*) the crimes that one suffers (*si subiscono*) and [as being] somehow an "accomplice" to the other [i.e., to men who inflict violence against women]. Becoming a witness [to the crimes] means reporting the felony, the executer, and the instigator: patriarchy. . . . We all are at risk of violence . . . the quality of a political action is determined by the ability of the subject not to allow patriarchy to define her (*di non farsi definire dal patriarcato*) and, at the same time, of not putting ourselves in a position of superiority in reference to those women who cannot do so (Lucia).[22]

> Being witnesses means being witnesses of violence, in front of the World [*sic*] that, otherwise, would not be aware of that [violence]. Generally, witnesses are different from the victims of a crime. In violence, often, they are the same person. Giving testimony to certain facts it is not just an act of personal courage, but a service to humankind. Similarly . . . the witness carries out a public service in the courts. [It is a] civil service, for the good of the community . . . because it is the World that is guilty. [It is the] same World that needs to be saved. [A world] made, in its insides, of different things. The function of the witness it is not just pinpointing who is guilty. But it is also to do a service. To humankind . . . For this reason the function of witness is compulsory by law. If you do not go [to court] to testify, they come to your home to get you, with the *Carabinieri* [i.e., Italian police]. The person who is accused can choose not to speak. The witness cannot do the same. At the very least, s/he gets [an accusation of] perjury (Rina).[23]

In both these answers, as I explained, victims were not characterized well, while witnesses were; the former were described mainly by referring to what they were not, meaning in relation to the latter. What is clear, though, is that victimhood seemed to be the norm in relation to which women imagined new possibilities of being women (i.e., of being witnesses). In other words, for both Rina and Lucia, and for other feminists I met in Salento, the status of the victim was taken to be the norm against which the role of the witness stood out, offering women new perspectives for thinking about their being in the world. According to Rina and Lucia, witnesses testified against "patriarchy," and, in doing so, they pinpointed patriarchy as the ideology that rules the world. By putting their suffering at the center of their self-perception, victims reinscribed the "patriarchal" narrative of women as human beings in need of being controlled and protected. Moreover, witnesses were those who did not concentrate on their own suffering: they were not affected by *protagonismo* (for a clarifying comparison, see chap. 2, and the reactions to the performance of the *F9* in Paestum). Victims, by contrast, did this to attract attention to themselves and deflect it from the crime. Most important of all, witnesses acted ethically while victims did not—at least not in the same way.[24]

Being victims and/or witnesses, then, was described as having moral connotations. According to Lucia, defining oneself as a victim was somehow being an accomplice to a crime: it was allowing "patriarchy" to define women to the point of feeling that, for the fact of being a woman, one needs to expiate through self-sacrifice. To Rina, by contrast, the witnesses acted courageously, but they were also driven by the moral imperative of a civil, collective service to humankind. Remarkably, she pointed out that witnesses were obliged to testify—by law, and not just morally.

The connections between being victims and/or witnesses, their aesthetic translations, and the realm of the ethical are of particular interest for understanding many of the positions I encountered during my fieldwork in Salento. I claim they are central in order to make sense of the affective and cognitive reactions that, on the one hand, representations of women-as-victims triggered in many of the feminists I met and that, on the other, performances such as the reading of *Ferite a Morte* elicited in their audiences. The ethical dimension, which I found to be so close to the aesthetic one in my research, also embraced the everyday performances and poetics of womanhood of my informants: they worked together in the construction of what I call "modern feminist womanhood." The importance that my informants gave to representations of women in images, in poetics, and in language relied on the fact that they had a central role in suggesting and imagining alternative possibilities for being women. These representative enterprises, laden with ethical and aesthetic connotations, embraced both the dimensions of the everyday and those of special occasions— a distinction that, as I pointed out above, I use only heuristically. These initiatives engaged different imagined publics and aesthetic dimensions.

While in this book I chose to present and describe on their own terms the activism of the Italian feminists with whom I worked, the discourses and practices around victims and victimization I address resonate with some of the issues that, *especially* since the 1990s, also characterize North American feminist debates.[25] To the activists that I met, women are not just victims or survivors; they are authoritative witnesses of sexed violence. This claim increases in significance if read in conversation with other feminist traditions, as in the following example. In her 2014 book *Knowing Victims: Feminism, Agency, and Victim Politics in Neoliberal Times*, Rebecca Stringer addresses the historical developments of the paradigm of victimization in North American feminism. She claims that:

> since the 1980s, across a wide array of discourses in media, academia, official politics and movement politics, there has been a concerted movement away from the language of victimhood, prompted by the emergence of a surprisingly widely shared critique of the very notion of "victim." This movement away from the language of victimhood has not meant talk of victimhood has ceased. Rather it has meant that talk of victimhood primarily assumes the form of negative critique of the notion of "victim": the proliferation of discourses in which the notion of victim arises in order to be critiqued, and is generally unseated by "agency" as the trope of legitimacy and preferred analytical choice. Our ways of thinking and talking about victims, victimization and victimhood have been reorganized around the dominance of anti-victim talk. (2)

According to Stringer, this happened in connection with "the rise and consolidation of neoliberism as a hegemonic political form." She asks herself: "Is it true that the language of victimhood stands immune to polysemy and resignification, and can only hold a single set of meanings—passivity, powerlessness, dependence and innocence?" (6). She argues that "feminism needs to act more strongly as a site of counter-hegemonic victim talk, instead of ceding ground to neoliberal values in the contemporary meaning of victimhood" (8). Ultimately, she claims that "contrary to their self-presentation, critiques of victim feminism do not move beyond victim politics, and do not affirm women's agency. Rather than move beyond victim politics, these critiques produce a revised version of victim politics that reflects the victim-blaming structure of neoliberalism's personal responsibility system. Creating new distinctions between genuine and false victims of gendered suffering, they influentially recast a spectrum of feminist issues—spanning victimization through violence, discrimination and inequality—as individual problems of personal responsibility, or as social problems to be dealt with by criminal law" (20). The only attempts to challenge these interpretations of victimhood, according to Stringer, come from postcolonial feminist critiques that present agency as "marking empowered feminine whiteness": "scholarly Western feminist critiques of the notion of 'victim' are characterized more strongly by the agency-affirming rhetoric and anti-victim motifs of neoliberal victim theory than by the task of interrogating the racialization (and other intersecting forms of identificatory particularization) of victimhood and agency within and beyond feminist discourse" (7). The Italian feminists with whom I worked at a first sight seemed to adhere to the victim-blaming discourse. For example, they strongly opposed the equation between women and victims, and criticized those who seemed to exploit that connection. In spite of these similarities, though, I claim that in the Italian context, especially among the Salentine activists, the disapproval of the victim status had other connotations. These activists understood victimhood as something beyond "passivity, powerlessness, dependence and innocence" (6). Specifically, they fostered a resignification of what agency could mean in relation to victimhood by considering the latter—in its relation with suffering, in particular—in a way that goes beyond issues of personal responsibility. Stringer suggests that in order to overcome the faults of victimization one reframe victims as survivors:[26] "The ethos of survivorship steps back from the exercise of judging good and bad victim behaviours and advances instead a non-expert approach that confers authority upon women's own (examinable, multiple and changing) perspectives on their experience of rape, giving rise to unique and subversive conceptualizations. Survivor discourse makes agency and vulnerability visible amidst the critique of victim-blame" (77). Yet, the figure of the survivor is not unambiguous, since it does not break with equating violence and trauma (see, e.g., Fassin 2008), nor with understanding victimhood as a matter of personal responsibility. Today, in fact, the ethos of survivorship can "operate on behalf of neoliberal victim theory. Where rape crisis feminists actively critique the social construction of victimhood and draw a distinction between self-blame (victim identity) and self-responsibility (survivorship), neoliberal victim theory collapses this distinction, situating the ideal would-be victim as already self-blaming—individually responsible for preventing, resisting, surviving and recovering from all manner of threats to personal safety, psychic stability and economic security" (Stringer 2014, 79).

The Italian case I am presenting here offers "a different view on the role of the language of victimhood in the politics of emancipation, providing alternatives to the confines, prejudices and contradictions of neoliberal victim theory" (Stringer 2014, 13). It does so in three ways: First, by embracing the "We Are Witnesses, Not Victims" trope, the Italian feminists with whom I worked did not erase the dimension of victimhood but incorporated it into the experience of the witness. This latter position is less prone to being associated with compulsory resilience, and therefore with the moral superiority inherent to the survivor trope. Being witnesses certainly had moral connotations, but these were associated with one's position before the law and not with discourses that "individualize, psychologize, and pathologize victimhood" (13), as Rina's words show.

Second, the feminists I met, by thinking about themselves as witnesses and not just as victims of violence, disarticulated (Pizza 2012, 2015) the relationships between victimhood, violence, and trauma. Their thinking about themselves as potentially violated did not imply that they considered themselves as victims—which, as Murgia pointed out, is just a *temporary* condition and needs to be acknowledged as such.

Finally, as I show in more detail in the rest of the book, the feminists recognized passivity as a form of agency and represented themselves as objects as a form of being agentive subjects: *S-oggette* (Subject-objects). As I show in the next chapter, such a condition encapsulates both meanings of "subject": that of being the agentive protagonist of one own's life, and that of being forced/acted upon (see also Agamben 1998; on action and passion, see Lambek 2010, 2007). They problematized the connections between passivity and victimhood by noting that victims could be active and passivity need not be synonymous with victimhood. This objectification of the body resonates, on the one hand, with Ziarek's readings of Agamben's *nuda vita*, namely with a position that stresses "both the political and ontological ambiguity of bare life, which escapes the very distinction between potentiality and actuality, presence and absence, life and death. Such political ambiguity means that bare life cannot function only as the target of sovereign decision, but that it can also be reclaimed for the sake of political transformation by oppositional democratic movements" (Ziarek 2012, 148; see also Agamben 1995 and Butler 2012, 122–123, on Agamben's notion of bare life).

On the other hand, it is in line with Butler's claims about the precarity of bodies in public protests (2012, 117–137). According to her, "Political claims are made by bodies as they appear and act, as they refuse and as they persist under conditions in which that fact alone is taken to be an act of delegitimation of the state" (2012, 124).[27] The material, precarious presence of bodies, in fact, can claim "the right to have rights, not as natural law or metaphysical stipulation, but as the persistence of the body against those forces that seek its debilitation or eradication" (Butler 2012, 124).

In sum, the representational objectification of potentially violated gendered bodies enacted by the activists I met can be read as being in line with the aforementioned perspectives: by putting oxymoronic performances onstage at the threshold of being subjects and objects, the activists suggested an understanding of victimhood, agency, and violence that could also offer interesting comparative elements to feminist debates going on elsewhere. As I explain in the next chapters, one of the most important features of the battle of representations engaged by the feminist activists with whom I worked revolved around their being "*S-oggette.*"

Notes

1. This friend told me that the last time she saw a *prefiche*-like performance during a funeral was in the early years of the twenty-first century in Sternatia, a town in the province of Lecce. This special type of crying was performed by some relatives of the dead.

2. See also Apolito 2007, 15.

3. This reception of the Mediterranean as an identity marker is widespread in contemporary Salento. See also Ben-Yehoyada 2011; Herzfeld 2005b; on *Meridianismi*, see Pizza 2015, 200–210.

4. Interestingly, this reception does not seem to include critiques and reinterpretations of this particular literature.

5. This episode is particularly interesting if read together with the issues around conscientious objection and abortion and the debates around the status of fetuses in the pro-life movement.

6. Today, young Salentinians migrate to study in the universities of northern Italy, but many choose to return to Salento, which has been developing in the past twenty years as a tourism destination (with a consequential development of the tertiary sector). Over the past two years, I have been witnessing a progressive increase in the numbers of agricultural cooperatives of young Salentinians who, animated by ecological and leftist ideals, decided to "return to the land" and to cultivate fields, reintroducing heirloom varieties of crops and more sustainable procedures.

7. The flyer continues: Let's meet without party labels (*sigle*), whoever wants to can bring flashlights and candles to testify against the most widespread crime against women. We from UDI Macare Salento will read some short messages that the women gave to Staffetta's amphora. If you want, you can also bring your messages, your words. We meet also to listen to each other.

8. The journey of the Staffetta caught the attention of the local newspapers, but, in general, not of the national press. The Staffetta, in my opinion, through the political choice of considering the amphora as a witness of violence against women and femminicidio, provided an understanding of violence beyond suffering and trauma. It did so by giving Italian women the possibility of thinking about themselves not just as victims but also as witnesses. Nonetheless, violence—including its traumatic implications—was indeed promoted by the Staffetta as an identity marker, and it was taken on in different ways by different individuals and women's group. Some of them, as I illustrate in this book, adopted a more radical understanding of the role of witnesses versus the role of victims. Others, instead, did not problematize it and took on the role of victims more uncritically.

9. It is worth noting that the word *testimone*, in Italian, refers to both the baton passed in an athletic relay race (also *staffetta*, in Italian) and to being a witness. Moreover, partisan women who fought against Fascism, are commonly referred to as "*staffette*." The choice of the Staffetta slogan, therefore, in association with the word *testimone*, has multiple resonances in Italian.

10. *Non vale* can also be translated as "it does not apply," or "it's unworthy" in other contexts. Although not literal, I chose to translate it as "it's unfair" because in this specific case it echoes its use in kids' disputes over games and rules, where something that does not apply is considered unfair. See also Gruppo Immagini Amiche (UDI), *Immagini amiche*. Email message sent on December 21, 2010.

11. It is worth noting that Webb Keane claims that the nature of representation includes its being both "action and objectification" (1997, xv). Moreover, he interestingly points out that the meaning of representation includes both the aspects of depiction and of delegation (7).

12. Following Herzfeld (see 2005b), I distinguish between the Mediterranean and Mediterraneanism—that is, a category developed in conversation with Said's well-known Orientalism, that shares with the latter its definitive feature of power asymmetries. In this respect, I follow Herzfeld's lead in arguing, with him, that "a critical study of the Mediterranean identities is not necessarily and should not be, an act of 'Mediterraneanism'" (2005b, 63). In reference to the Mediterranean, my ethnographic experience confirms that of Herzfeld (2005b) and others (see, e.g., Ben-Yehoyada 2011): I found that being Mediterranean (similar to the honor and shame complex) is a widespread—contextual, positional, and practical—self-stereotyping category in Salento.

13. On traditional literature on honor and shame in the Mediterranean and its criticisms, see, for example, Peristiany 1966; Goddard 1986, 1994; Gilmore 1987, 1990; Campbell 1964; Blok 1981, 2001; Herzfeld 1980, 1985, 2005b; Busatta 2006; Kirtsoglou 2004, 20–24; Plesset 2007; Galt 1985; among many others.

14. *Agedo* (Associazione di genitori, parenti e amici di persone LGBT*) is the association of "parents, relatives, and friends of LGBT* persons," www.agedo.it (accessed March 21, 2019).

15. I talked about this situation several times with both Carla and Renata, but since the economic aspect of this situation (which was quite unusual to me) was never broached, I did not dare ask about it directly. As far as I understood it, Renata was living with Carla and her mother after the death of Carla's dad and took care of some housecleaning chores, such as ironing, doing laundry, and so forth.

16. See, for example, Coundouriotis 2006; Collins 2012; Von Schnitzler 2014; Hermez 2011. For the debates on dignity and animal rights, see, for example, Cataldi 2002; Meyer 2001. See also Debes 2009, for a philosophic excursus on the history and uses of the notion of dignity, and Wainwright and Gallagher 2009, on the understandings of dignity in medicine. See Bostrom 2005 for dignity and the posthuman. See also Agamben 1998. On the relationship between honor and dignity from a Kantian perspective, see Kaufman 2011; La Vaque-Manty 2006; Bayefsky 2013.

17. On the link between aesthetics and value in relation to exhibitions in museums (but useful also beyond this particular setting), see Kratz 2011 on rhetorics of value.

18. Smiling is intuitively considered to be the opposite of weeping.

19. It is worth mentioning that there are multiple axiological reference points in the experiences of the women I worked with: for example, local, regional, national, European, and global.

20. On the binary distinction between victim and agent in the Italian context, see Giordano 2014, 9; Gribaldo 2014.

21. "Del femminismo necrofilo e la 'vittima' come modello sociale," *Al di là del Buco* (blog), http://abbattoimuri.wordpress.com/2014/06/04/del-femminismo-necrofilo-e-la-vittima-come-modello-sociale/ (accessed March 21, 2019)

22. Lucia, March 21, 2014.

23. Rina, March 20, 2014.

24. Notably, Foucault distinguished between morality and ethics, the former being a "system of codes and norms" and the latter the "practices and techniques that we perform on ourselves to *become* moral subjects" (Dave 2010a, 372). Some scholars adopted this distinction

on the basis of their particular analyses and ethnographic contexts (see Dave 2010a, 2012; Halperin 1995; Laidlaw 2002). While I tend to prefer to use the term *ethics* over *morality* for the Foucauldian resonances it brings to this book, I do not base my analyses on the aforementioned distinction. It is worth mentioning that Faubion contributed creatively to this debate on morality/ethics by distinguishing between the ethical and the "themitical" (in Lambek 2010; Faubion 2011).

25. The choice of not explicitly presenting the Italian situation in dialogue with the North American one is motivated by the need to avoid the possibility of understanding the former (more recent) within a narrative set by the developments of the latter. On the feminist debates around victims and victimization, see Stringer 2014; Wolf 1993; Roiphe 1994; van Dijk 1999; hooks 1986; Sommers 1994; McLeer 1998; Cole 1999; Faulkner and MacDonald 2009; Samet 2013; Kapur 2002.

26. In her reference to Lyotard's *differend*, she also mentions the figure of the plaintiff (2014, 67–73).

27. This also resonates with de Martino's observations on *presenza*, the construction of which goes through "the elementary being of the person" (1981 [1948], 189). See also Butler 2012.

5

PRODUCING WITNESSES

The Perlocutionary Effects of the Politics of Representation

IN THIS CHAPTER, AND THE NEXT, I CONTINUE to focus on the ethical dimensions of the representational struggle that I have described so far and that, in chapter 6, I more explicitly link to what Foucault called practices (i.e., labors and works) of ascesis. Through representation, my informants aimed to challenge the "patriarchal" constraints that associated women with (suffering) victims and to promote interpretations of women as empowered, socially relevant, and worthy/dignified (*degne*) witnesses. Moreover, it also aimed to *produce* witnesses: both among their publics and as a result of practices of autopoiesis. By engaging bodies, senses, and emotions and not only ideas and discourses, my informants wanted to promote dissensus: theirs was a form of "sensible politics" (McLagan and McKee 2012). One particular dimension of this representational enterprise was linked to the "perlocutionary" (Cavell and Goodman 2005; Munday 2009, 2010; Lambek 2010; Butler 1997) aspects of their "oxymoronic" representations of women.

Souls of the Earth and *Disanimate*: On the Affective Politics of Representation

Taurisano is a small town in the province of Lecce. A friend and I drove there late one November afternoon. The sky was brightly colored with the sunset, and the roads were wet, for it had been raining. We were heading toward the conference room where the first of three meetings organized on November 25, 2013, was to be held. Some women of the town had decided to organize Lost Love, the first edition of the Festival against Violence against Women (*Perduto Amore, Primo Festival Contro la Violenza sulle Donne*), and my friend had been invited by some of the organizers. It was the first time in Taurisano for the two of us, and we wanted to park the car in a central area, close to Via Roma, where the meeting was being held. We ended up in the *Corso* (main street) of Taurisano. While we were looking for a parking spot, we noticed that we were surrounded only by men. There was not a single woman in sight—walking, drinking coffee at the bar, shopping, or just passing by. We parked the car and walked through the *Corso*. Men regarded us with curiosity but without particular insistence. Yet, it was clear to both of us that the absence of women there was not just a coincidence.

While my friend and I were commenting on this awkward situation, she remembered that the women of Taurisano she had met some time before had told her about this particular custom of their town. They had also informed her that a woman they know, a new mom, got in trouble with her husband for strolling with her baby on the *Corso* in the daytime while talking on a cell phone. The men who were there at that time apparently informed her husband that she was talking on her mobile—who knows with whom—while she was alone with the baby and suggested he keep a closer eye on her.

My friend and I were trying to imagine what it must be like for a woman to live in Taurisano today when we ran into a poster for *Perduto Amore*. On the poster we saw the pictures of eight women from Taurisano (my friend's acquaintances) who chose this particular way to stand up against violence against women. Marta and I were astonished: given the local customs we had just bumped into, this choice seemed really brave. The courage of these women moved us for another reason, too; just a few months before the festival (July 2013), Taurisano had made the news for a case of femminicidio that ended with the suicide of the killer. The community was still divided, at the time of the festival, on the elaboration of their collective mourning. The families involved, apparently all well known in the small town, were still grieving their losses and formulating narratives that could explain, or maybe even justify, the deaths of their beloved members. Taking sides was a difficult task and promoting an initiative countering violence against women risked touching some sensitive spots, as one of the women who organized *Perduto Amore* told me. She mentioned that it had been tough talking about the festival to the families involved with the recent case of femminicidio. Yet, she added that their pain also needed to be accepted and listened to.

During the festival, Lucia Sabato, one of its organizers, presented her photographic exhibit called *Alma de Tierra* (Soul of the Earth, in Spanish), produced in collaboration with the local association *Flauto Magico*. In this exhibition, twenty-five black-and-white pictures of women from Taurisano were hung from two dark panels. Red gauze (that, according to the artist, symbolized death) and red roses decorated the black walls between the pictures.

Each woman in the photos was holding a white piece of paper that reported (silent) words against violence against women, mostly mementos for other women.

For an eye accustomed to Italian cemeteries, which are very different from North American ones, this installation clearly resonated with those images and imaginaries: the pictures of the women on dark walls, the antiqued photos, and the flowers around the pictures are ubiquitous characteristics of Italian graveyards. Clearly, the photographed bodies of the living women of Taurisano visually resonated with the ones of dead women. Since the latter do not usually hold messages for the living in the cemeteries, the exhibition conveyed an oxymoronic message.[1] It is precisely around the creative juxtaposition of two seemingly opposite conditions—being dead and speaking—that the exhibition was constructed.[2] It was an oxymoronic ambivalence that, I claim, was designed to catalyze affective resonances and to leave the observer cognitively and affectively disoriented. It was something that aimed to promote dissensus.[3]

Soul of the Earth, the title of the exhibition, can be understood in two different ways. Soul (*anima*, in Italian) can allude to an energetic, spiritual essence, and Earth (*Terra*, in Italian) can refer to our planet. In this sense, the installation aimed to remind viewers how women, by virtue of their reproductive bodies, are vital and fundamental for our planet and for life. Or, as one of the pictures of the installation states: "The woman is the soul of the world and gives life to life" (*La donna è l'anima del mondo dà vita alla vita*). In this sense the pictures were generative. Yet, "soul" could also be interpreted more technically and from a Catholic standpoint as an essential characteristic of the individual human being—one that outlives her deceased body that is often buried in the soil (*terra*, in Italian). This interpretation of *anima* is widespread in Italy. According to this reading, then, the title hinted at the presence of a living surplus that outlasts the bodies of the victims of femminicidio, in this case embodied by the living women in the pictures. This latter reading of the installation is consistent with the superimposition of living female bodies onto the ones of the victims of violence suggested and operated by the Staffetta and described previously. As I explained there, right from the beginning, the Staffetta associated the bodies and lives of the women who suffered sexed violence and femminicidio with all women on account of their female bodies. This association contributed to the establishment of a community of sense in which female bodies started to be portrayed and understood primarily as loci of potential violence.

Yet, in *Alma de Tierra* the (anonymous) bodies of the women who suffered violence, and who were considered as objects by the predatory script that according to feminists and to some scholars characterizes gender relations in Italy, were subsumed and transformed (and not mimicked or impersonated) through the activists' performances in the installation.[4] The predatory script is the cultural sexual script that portrays the ideal virile man as "asserting his masculinity in his homosocial environment by virtue of his sexual activity"[5] (Ferrero Camoletto and Bertone 2012, 434). According to Italian feminists, in this cultural script men are by nature (active and assertive) hunters and women are by nature (passive and vulnerable) prey. In the article *"Ecco come i media giustificano le violenze di genere"* (This Is How the Media Justify Gender Violence), for instance, published on the blog *Un altro genere di comunicazione* (another gender/genre of communication), "Mary," the author, deconstructs some articles published in local and national newspapers. (S)he shows how the language used to narrate the killings of women and the images associated with the news contribute to creating both "sentiments of empathy with the persecutor" and a debasement of the victims who are eroticized or implicitly blamed for having shown ambivalent behaviors and for having asked for it.[6] Articles such as this one travel extensively on the online feminist circuits; even when they are not the authors of the articles, my informants post, repost, like, and share them, tagging friends and acquaintances, who in turn feel compelled to do the same.[7] In Lucia Sabato's exhibition, however, the objectification of the bodies of the activists at the same time was taken to an extreme and overturned the "patriarchal" imagery; the women from Taurisano portrayed in the installation made themselves *objects* in order to be witnesses of the *objectification* of women's bodies in Italian society.[8] They testified in front of the court of their local (imagined and actual) publics by mobilizing affects and emotions precisely by means of their (oxymoronic) objectified bodies. In this artistic exhibition, the pictures of the living women were located at a threshold, participating while at the same time *transcending* seemingly opposite conditions: being subjects and objects, being active and passive, being alive and dead, and, I claim, being witnesses and victims.[9] As a matter of fact, they were *all* this at the same time.

The women of Taurisano did not indulge in a kind of self-representation that easily fit with the expectations of the observer, accustomed to campaigns and performances against sexed violence that represented women in the position of victims—with black eyes, visible scars, and traces of blood. Instead, *Alma de Tierra*'s iconography explicitly challenged these expectations: it presented and represented Taurisano's citizens, the same ones the spectators could meet at the grocery store, or at their kids' schools, or at the gym. By entrusting local people to talk as proxies for the (mostly distant) victims of femminicidio that inhabited everyday newspapers, Lucia Sabato was aiming to unsettle the affective and cognitive parameters of perception of the viewer and to frame violence against women as something not alien to the community of Taurisano.[10] These allusive images therefore occupied a liminal place. In Nuzzo's terms, the women of Taurisano did not want to allow the gaze of the other to define them. Consistent with the slogan of Staffetta, the women of the installation were not (only) victims but witnesses.

Lucia Sabato explained her intentions, as the creator of the pictures and the installation, to me in different terms over a *caffè in ghiaccio con latte di mandorla*, a typical Salentine summery alternative to espresso coffee, on a very hot afternoon a few months later. She believes that, as an artist, she cannot explain with words who women are or should be, nor the violence they go through. The persons of the public, provoked by the artistic production, should "make this effort by themselves, so that they can remember" their conclusions. When I asked her what types of reactions she saw and what type of feedback she had received from her audience in Taurisano, she replied, with disappointment, that "the only thing they saw was that their neighbors and acquaintances were the protagonists of the pictures." Yet, to me, that seemed like a good starting point. The next year, in fact, on the occasion of the second edition of *Perduto Amore*, Lucia presented another installation against violence toward women. Its title was OMADA, "On women's side (I commit) [*ci metto la faccia*, lit., I put my face]." As a poster in the exhibition hall explained:

> The exhibition OMADA stems from the idea to get the male subjects of the town involved in the campaign against violence against women. The title of the exhibition is simply the reflection of the name Adamo [Adam]. By reading the letters backward, in fact, you get the name Omada that gives the sense of being a feminine word and metaphorically alludes to the most sensitive part of each and every man. The protagonists of the exhibition were chosen randomly, thanks to some research conducted on the territory, and each one of them expressed his opinion freely. Faithfully, Lucia Sabato.

In the Omada exhibition, pictures of men of Taurisano were placed on a dark panel. Under each picture appeared quoted statements with the first name and surname of the photographed person. If there are clear analogies between the installations of the first and of the second editions of *Perduto Amore*, there are also remarkable differences. The pictures from the first edition showed women of Taurisano in antiqued photos. Their first names and surnames did not appear, since they were impersonating a generalized feminine subject, and they held papers with phrases against violence toward women that they had not written. In the second edition, by contrast, Taurisano men appeared in colored photos. Their names were indicated at the end of the quoted sentence that accompanied each photo. These were personal and signed statements against violence against women. If *Alma de Tierra* was visually quoting Italian graveyards, Omada focused instead on contemporary Taurisano people. In both installations, men and women from the town were framed as witnesses of violence against women. Yet, the ways in which the representation and the interpretation of being witnesses was accomplished differed considerably. In the first installation the women were witnesses by proxy, and the power of their being witnesses came from their objectified bodies and from their oxymoronic performance. In the second, by contrast, men became witnesses of violence against women. Not surprisingly, given their different status within Italian society and its "patriarchal" framework, men interpreted and performed their being witnesses in a different way. They appeared as they were, and their words were personal statements. In Lucia Sabato's words, this was the result of the fact that "they made the efforts by themselves" to see and sense violence against women as something embedded in the worlds they inhabited and in the relations between sexes. In this respect, the choice of placing an open microphone in one of the rooms of the building where the festival took place was consistent with the moral and ethical exhortation to "becoming witnesses," which was part of the subtext of these initiatives, and, more generally, of the battle of representations that I am describing in this book.

An open microphone was placed in the middle of the room: visitors to the *Perduto Amore* festival could freely use it to "declare" wrongdoings and injustices linked to violence against women. Following the quoted words of Malala Yousafzai, one of the winners of the 2014 Nobel Prize for Peace—"I am here to give words also to those who have no voice"—visitors were exhorted to "give their voice" (lit., the poster said "give your voice"), to become witnesses. *Metterci la faccia* (to commit), then, appeared not to be enough; men (and women) also needed to enlist their voices to denounce violence against women and to support women's causes. Images and words were, therefore, equally important here and elsewhere during my fieldwork as a battlefield for political action against violence against women.

* * *

A poster advertised a public debate promoted by the public library of Galatina for the 2013 International Day of Women (March 8, 2013).[11] The theme of the meeting, organized in collaboration with other local associations, including DNA Donna, was "the body of women in advertising and in the media." The title of this event, interestingly, was *Disanimate*: a neologism created by assembling the privative prefix *dis* and the adjective (feminine, plural) *animate* (animated), understood in the senses of being both alive and bearers of a soul. In English, I would translate this title as "deprived of soul/life." The poster of this event showed a picture of a mannequin, naked and divested of individualized traits. While it was evident that it was a dressmaker's dummy (a plastic reproduction of a human body), its position was highly unconventional. It was sitting with its legs bent in order to hide its pubic area, its head was turned away from the observer, and its left hand did not hang parallel to the bust but was anchored to the floor, as if it were supporting the weight of its whole body.

The designer of this poster was Sara, a member of DNA Donna. I contacted her immediately after a common friend had told me about the initiative and shown me the poster. Sara is a professional graphic designer based in Salento, where she was born. She had worked for many feminist campaigns, including the three national campaigns of the UDI. She was very sensitive to women's issues although verbally and behaviorally, on more than one occasion, she manifested to me a clear uneasiness in recognizing herself as part the Italian feminist panorama. She did not feel as if she was an insider, since she claimed she did not fully understand feminist language, she did not like to attend feminist gatherings, and she did not fully comprehend the way issues were framed among the groups of feminists she had met. These and other remarks on similar matters were one of the main topics of a four-hour long road trip we took together and that emerged periodically in our conversations. I had indicated to Sara, via email, that I was interested in knowing a bit more about the poster, and I began our subsequent Skype conversation telling her that, while I really liked the poster of *Disanimate*, I was curious to know the story behind it: why she chose that title, and that image, for the Galatina debate. After a bit of embarrassment (she wondered whether I thought that the poster was inappropriate for the topic of the meeting), she patiently retraced with me the steps that led her to this particular design. She told me that there were some key ideas behind it; like all her works, the design was the result first of "emotional work" and only second the result of a *labor limae*—that is, a process of fine-tuning her ideas. Her creations always arise from a particular "emotional place," she noted, which is followed by a "rational phase." Sara noted that *Disanimate/* "Taking the soul away" meant for her "depriving someone of the relationship between her body and the world." This idea, she claimed, resulted from her engagement with a talk by the philosopher Galimberti that she had listened to some time ago. In her opinion, this "deprivation" was what sexist advertisements did with the bodies of women. The mannequin in the poster, while not individualized, counterintuitively did not give the observer the idea that she was a passive object: this was precisely the reason why Sara chose this image. She wanted to be at one and the same time "evocative" and "ambiguous" and constructed the poster by starting from the feelings and emotions that the image of the mannequin triggered in her. These were connected to the feeling of not wanting to be seen as passive, as a victim. While she believed that the problems of violence against women and the oppressive power of "patriarchy" were real for many women, she did not feel these issues were part of her own story, language, and education. On more than one occasion she mentioned that her father, who had passed away prematurely, had pushed both his sons and his daughters to be able to support themselves, both economically and emotionally, and not have to rely on others for their material and spiritual sustenance. As a consequence of her education, she developed a sort of uneasiness in relation to representations and self-representations of women as passive and dependent on men. Sara's attempt to challenge these commonsensical ideas of women was remarkable; the picture of the mannequin seemed to mesh powerfully with this goal. The ambiguity of the image of the poster, an ambiguity that Sara had expressly sought, revolved (again) around the fusion of activity and passivity, and around the affective and intellectual confusion that this oxymoronic image could generate in the observer. By the word "confusion," as its etymology indicates, I mean a mingling that provokes disorientation and lack of understanding. This is what Sara experienced when she chose the image, and this is what she wanted to trigger by using that particular photo to promote the event in Galatina.

As I noted of the photographic exhibition in Taurisano, which was using this same stylistic feature, although differently, the affective and cognitive confusion was meant to be produced by means of an oxymoronic representation— that is, the juxtaposition of seemingly opposite factors. Interestingly, in both these cases, the oxymoronic representations revolved around elements that, semiotically, referred to a status of both activity and passivity, to being both persons and objects, to being both victims and witnesses. In other words, the ambiguity sought by Sara was shaped around what I refer to as the two apparently opposite meanings of the term "subject" (from the Latin *subicio*, meaning to be thrown under): that of being the agentive protagonist of one own's life, and that of being forced/acted upon (see also Agamben 1998; on action and passion, see Lambek 2000a, 2010, 2007). These two aspects of being subjects resonate with the aforementioned fusion of activity and passivity and, thus, in my ethnographic field, with the issue of being (represented as) both victims and witnesses. The mannequin, similar to the pictures of the women from Taurisano, was meant to be a bearer of affective resonances and dissensus. While the picture of the mannequin, at a first glance, alluded to the objectification of women's bodies in sexist advertisements, Sara did not intend it to mimic, replicate, or identify with those bodies. The mannequin spoke for women without language, by subsuming and transforming the overexposed bodies of women. The dressmaker's dummy, similar to the aforementioned representations, was presented as an agentive object. In this case, it was an object that did not offer itself to the gaze of the observer, one that covered its pubic area, and one that bore the weight of its own body. Once again, a personified object performed the role of witness in the attempt to challenge—affectively as well, in Rancièrian terms—the widespread cultural representations of women-as-victims. The mannequin "spoke" as a witness from a liminal place (see Turner 1969; Lambek 2007), at the threshold between being either subject or object, since it was both. This place was liminal inasmuch it went beyond this distinction and held together both meanings of being subjects.[12]

Although inflected differently, then, *Alma de Tierra* and *Disanimate* shared a common grammar that offered an alternative and ambiguous representation of what being a woman was or should be, in contrast to common representations. In doing so, much like the performances of dignity I described above, they promoted dissensus. While the illocutionary effect of these images emerged in the oxymoronic representations of women around the two meanings of being subject, their perlocutionary qualities, at least indirectly (in the intentions of their producers), generated a "perceptive perturbation" (see Christine Ross 2008, 12)—what I called a sense of ambivalence, of confusion in the observers/audience.[13] In other words, much like the poetics of feminist womanhood that I described in the previous chapter, on the basis of Sara's words, the subject/object ambiguity functioned to question affectively and cognitively the commonsensical understandings of the status of women in society. This is why these representations had the perlocutionary effect of promoting dissensus (on precarious visualities and Rancière, see also Christine Ross 2008) around women and their role in contemporary Italian society.

Representation as Political Praxis

As I showed above, my informants were not just spectators of dominant discourses and representations of women and violence. Their political activity had a lot to do with fighting a war of representations. Criticizing Italian society and its "patriarchal" biases was indeed important, but alone it was not enough: alternative perspectives needed to be produced and offered beyond the commonsensical ones. Carla's words were very clear on this point as well, and her Facebook activity was consistent with her ideas: the web was a locus of political activism for her as well. Besides cultivating her feminist online persona by, for example, having a blog, posting and reposting articles on women's matters, sponsoring email bombings, and promoting petitions, she had also been concentrating on the issue of promoting different types of womanhood. In order to do so, she produced quantities of Facebook notes that navigated the web by virtue of the hundreds of friends and acquaintances tagged in them. Published on her social networks of choice, she collected biographies of "women who made history"—women whose "queer" subjectivities could be a model for all of us.

Carla was not alone in her project. Luisa was Apulian but not from Salento: her different Italian accent was one of the first of her features I noticed when we met. Having spent a lot of time in Lecce and in Salento, I had evidently internalized the sort of skepticism that most of the people I encountered have for those who come from the northern part of the region (and especially from Bari, the regional administrative center). My internal reaction sounded weird to me, since my own accent—northern Italian—has been one of the reasons for which I had experienced (friendly) mocking, by my informants, since I first arrived there.

I first met Luisa, a middle-aged woman, on a hot summer day in an anti-violence center in a town in the southern province of Lecce. I had joined some activists of DNA Donna, at that time in its start-up phase and without a head-quarters, in a formal meeting with the personnel of a women's shelter. Luisa was giving a class for volunteers, and we had the chance to spend the lunch break with her in a private room and to discuss some of the issues and procedures that DNA Donna had to follow in order to formally to become an association.

After this very interesting meeting, at which I received detailed information on the juridical status of women's shelters in Apulia and in Italy, a smaller group of us remained with Luisa, who immediately started talking, informally, about something important to her. She explained to us that she and others at the regional administrative offices in Bari, where she worked as a consultant, were writing a legal proposal for the regional women's shelters. One of the most important points that she stressed in talking about this law (approved in 2014) was that the philosophy behind the choices that were directing their conception of the bill was completely rooted in women's activism. She had been working in the local women's associations for years before tackling this law and made clear that these grassroots experiences were what was really giving form to the law. Since "we all know the importance of language in the struggle against patriarchy," she explained to us, her team was working toward the elimination in the bill of the word *abuse*—a term that is widely used in Italian jurisprudence and in other national and regional laws. The reason for this choice was as simple as it was important. The presence of abuse implies, indirectly, the presence, acceptance, and legitimization of the use of women by men: something she and the other writers of the law strongly wanted to avoid. The law was approved in 2014, with the title "Norms for Preventing and Opposing Gendered Violence, for Supporting the Victims, for Promoting Women's Freedom, and Self-determination."[14]

Luisa's quasi-Agambenian observations on the inclusive exclusions of Italian legal terminology (see Agamben 1995) can be seen as an attempt to devictimize the status of women in the (mostly regional) public opinion. Similar to what had happened to the predatory script (see above), the commonsensical interpretation of women as weak subjects in need of protection or as passive victims of violence had seeped into the Italian juridical system—in this case through the language of abuse. Interestingly, the word *victim* appears in the title of Luisa's law; its inclusion was mainly meant to direct the actions of women's shelters in the Apulia region. Victimhood is cited in connection with women's freedom and self-determination—an important detail to acknowledge. Women do suffer. They are considered to be passive objects. They are the recipients of men's violence. Yet, the Apulian law through the excision of the word *abuse* from its text seemed to suggest a way to go beyond the status of victim and to imagine different and more empowering possibilities. The message that this bill conveyed differed considerably from the ones women received from other welfare agents: the *Regione Puglia* supported women not as victims, but as free and self-determined subjects. If this does not seem like much of an achievement, it is worth noting that I was told by an informant who works for a counseling center for women that she received a phone call in April 2014 from a woman who asked for help, since she was witnessing a man beating a woman unknown to her. Interestingly, the woman who called the center did not consider calling the police instead, as would have been intuitive in other regional contexts. While I do not want to make a case on the basis of this single episode, her decision and action were nonetheless consistent with a certain diffused lack of trust in Italian institutions actually promoting women's well-being. Thanks to the linguistic representational battle of Luisa (and others), from being objects of tutelage women started to become and to be acknowledged and recognized as self-determined subjects.

This attention to language as a dimension of representation, of which the Apulian law is just an example, was pivotal in my informants' political goals and experiences. Images, too, as I showed above, were central in the political activities of many of the women with whom I worked. The same applies to "social performances."

* * *

Luca gently greeted me and accompanied me into the conference room. I sensed in his attitude a certain degree of skepticism mixed with curiosity. It was the first time I had met him, and I soon realized that our common acquaintance had not told him much about me, except that I was a friend and an anthropologist who lived in North America and studied the Salento area. My friend came with us into the conference room of the women's shelter and remained silent most of the time, only occasionally engaged in the conversation by Luca, who at the beginning turned to her to make himself more comfortable. Pretty early on in our meeting, in an attempt to make all of us feel at ease with the situation, Luca told me how my friend, the one who was sitting with us at the table, was a "woman with balls/testicles" (*una donna con le palle*). My friend looked at me. I looked at her, and, subsequently, we both looked at Luca. He immediately realized what happened and added that since we "were feminists" he had "to pay attention to how" he spoke. He, an employee of the women's shelter, immediately tried to explain that he "takes balls to be not just a masculine attribute but also a feminine one" and that "in this sense, there are many more women with balls than men." I smiled and added that I understood what he meant and that this was why I could safely say that, as far as I had gathered from our brief exchange, he was a "man with a vagina—which, of course, is a compliment."

My friend looked at me with astonishment and amusement: she could not believe I had really said this to an employee of the women's shelter, and moreover at our first meeting. Luca smiled and gently blushed: he said it was the first time he had ever been told he was a man with a vagina. Moreover, he muttered that, of course, vagina could be used as balls/testicles, but he quickly changed the topic of the conversation to overcome his embarrassment. Apparently, through my slightly cheeky remarks, I had gained his respect and trust. From then on, he also considered me as a woman with balls/testicles (although he subsequently used other expressions to make his point). His skeptical attitude disappeared, and he gave me freedom of action at the shelter. He answered my many questions patiently, and he allowed me to interview people and attend initiatives at that women's shelter and at the others at which he worked. He actually arranged interviews on my behalf, informed me about initiatives that might be relevant to my research, and let me attend some of their meetings with women they were following from behind a wall fitted with a two-way mirror. Being a woman with balls was still (see Blok 1981; Gilmore 1987) currently used in Italy as a way to express capability, strength, and courage—a woman's exceptional status amid common representations of women-as-victims (for a comparison, see Blok 1981, 429). The connections between male genitalia and inner qualities and virtues did not seem to be problematic to Luca, at least not until I inverted the factors of that equation.

I cannot assess the role that our conversation had in the development of this initiative, but six months after my first meeting with Luca, one of the Salentine women's shelters I followed for this research promoted a photo contest called "Woman is. 101 shots to narrate a woman—Campaign for the awareness and prevention of gendered violence." The aim of the contest was "to give a positive message: exalting, through the evocative and immediate language typical of photography, a new figure of woman: reactive, and willing to take her internal potential back in its entirety." The contest, the press release continued, wanted to represent "the woman in her everyday life, willing to take back her interior potential, a new woman and REACTIVE. A POSITIVE message, which breaks with the habitual images of violence that we are used to [seeing] in the campaigns against gendered violence" (emphasis in the original).[15]

The visual aspects of women's representations, which included spectacles, performances, and images, grew to have particular importance in my field-work. As I explained before, my focus on the visual is not intended to erase all the other senses from my ethnography. Instead, the examples that follow, and the ones I have already narrated, aim to stress precisely the affective and cognitive dimensions of visual representations. With Grasseni, I claim that "vision, both as theoretically dense metaphor (as worldview), and as part of a phenomenology of the senses (as visions), is relevant to anthropological practice, and is not necessarily visualist" (2007, xv; see also Herzfeld 2011, for a comparison).

Producing Witnesses: The Perlocutionary Effects of Representational Ambiguity

One of the most common performances of feminist womanhood by the activists I met had to do with the consistent, and at times provocative, challenge of the Italian grammar rule that prescribes the use of the masculine form for addressing mixed groups. For example, when in front of a public group of men and women, it is grammatically correct to address the audience by saying "*buonasera a tutti*" (good evening to everybody), where *tutti* is the masculine plural form for "all," even if there is a majority of women. The Salentine feminists I met, who strongly believe in the importance of deconstructing the sexism embedded in the Italian language, often challenge this rule by addressing the public, during events and performances, by saying "*buonasera a tutti* (masculine plural) *e buonasera a tutte* (feminine plural)" or, when they feel particularly provocative, by just saying "*buonasera a tutte*" (feminine plural). Typically, men and some women of the public react to the latter with surprise because my feminist friends' greeting sounds like a grammatical error. According to Italian grammar, in fact, the presence of just one man among a group of women demands that one use the masculine plural. After a "*buonasera a tutte*" greeting, normally I would see persons in the audience turning around validating the presence of men in the room and puzzled by the seeming grammatical incompetence of the speaker. While women are always in the majority at such events, there is generally at least one man in the room, who then finds himself unwillingly the focus of unwanted attention. Clearly, my informants, by using the "*buonasera a tutte*" greeting, expected these types of reactions among their audiences. Yet, the affective confusion caused by the unanticipated disregard for an Italian grammar rule presented them with an opportunity to comment briefly on how they do not feel addressed by the words *"buonasera a tutti,"* given the fact that they are women, and, furthermore, it is an opportunity to make a point on the naturalization of sexist practices. On more than one occasion, I witnessed these types of performances and I observed the reactions of the public dazed by the choice, amused by the performance, or simply irritated. During a book presentation, I saw a member of the town council, who was sitting in the first row of the audience, reacting to my informant's greeting by almost jumping in his seat, frowning, and looking around in the hope of intercepting other equally irritated gazes of fellow politicians. After the event, this *assessore* told my friend that "her presentation had been good in spite of the bad start." I could read pride on her face. Indeed, her attempts to promote dissensus somehow sank in: even if, apparently, they did not convince the *assessore*, they had reached him, and clearly they had been received well by the women in the audience who had clapped during her presentation. Her public remarks had "disarticulated" (Pizza 2015, 125) a dimension of sexism "naturalized" in the Italian language and had, so to speak, produced new witnesses.[16] Diana Taylor, in her interesting ethnography *Disappearing Acts: Spectacles of Gender and Nationalism in Argentina's "Dirty War"* (1997), claims that witnesses are a special type of spectator, since they want to "impress upon" an audience (Felman and Laub 1992, 204).[17]

In my ethnographic findings, this intention to "impress upon" the observers was obtained by using the various oxymoronic devices I described above and it included affective resonances. It was this space of uncertainty and oxymoronic confusion—or of "precarious visuality" (Christine Ross 2008)—in reference to the representations engaged by the feminists I met, that opened the way for novel and unconventional understandings of sexed violence and of what being a women meant, or could mean, in contemporary Italy.[18] The attempt at changing one's perceptions of the world and of genders' relations through aesthetic engagement, which I witnessed in Salento, resonates well with Mazzarella's statement that "any social project that is not imposed through force alone must be affective in order to be effective" (2009, 99). The senses of confusion, ambivalence, bewilderment, and puzzlement that the oxymoronic representations triggered in their audiences were meant to be forms of political activism, pursued by means of particular representational, sensory, and artistic engagements. The latter aimed at widening the common sensorium, and at challenging commonsensical representations of women, by expanding the range of affective, sensory, and cognitive possibilities around what being women should and could be. Moreover, as I claim in the next chapter, the aforementioned representations were, first of all, ways for the performing activists themselves to imagine new subjectivities, alternatives to those that the status quo promoted and acknowledged. In this respect, the spectator of the representations who experienced this confusion, this dissensus, could herself become a witness. This happened not only by virtue of the "palpable connections" that the "very body of the perceiver and the perceived" share in mimetic performances (which, to a certain extent, define, even if contrastively, every representation; see Taussig 1992, 250). It also occurred as a consequence of the special connections between the act of witnessing and that of being a spectator addressed by Taylor, like in the "*buonasera a tutte*" example. In a reading of the relationship between spectator and witness inspired by Felman and Laub's work on the Shoah (1992), the ethnographer points out that "though neither the perpetrator nor the victim of events, the witness is part of the conflict and has a responsibility in reporting and remembering of events" (Taylor 1997, 25). The spectator/witness, by virtue of her listening to others' testimonies, becomes a "participant and co-owner of the traumatic event" and is "at the same time a witness to the trauma witness and a witness to himself" (Taylor quoting Laub and Felman 1997, 27; for a comparison see Fassin 2008; Fassin and Rechtman 2009).

In sum, following these lines of thought, I claim that the oxymoronic representations that I have ethnographically described so far, by virtue of the perceptive, affective, and cognitive puzzlement they conveyed, allowed for the possibility of sensing and making sense of women according to parameters that differed from the commonsensical ones, constructed around the association between women and victims (and between violence and suffering). These alternative representations conveyed and prompted affective resonances that rested upon a performance of ambiguity. This confusion or blending together that brings to mind the one described by Felman in relation to the viewers of the film *Shoah* (Felman and Laub 1992, 202–281), triggered by aesthetic (i.e., sensory and artistic) representations, opened up particular possibilities of practices and performances: that of the witness. These representations constructed new audiences (or counterpublics) of witnesses of women-as-witnesses (and not as victims). The bewildered public of the spectacles could become witness itself of violence against women and femminicidio, as well as of different ways to understand women's roles in society. The latter element, in particular, allowed for a redefinition of common sense in Rancièrian terms, and, consistent with Panagia's claims, occurred in relation to the presence of unqualified affects around the representations.

Notes

1. By "oxymoron," I mean a "figure of speech in which apparently contradictory terms appear in conjunction." See "oxymoron," http://www.oxforddictionaries.com/us/definition/american_english/oxymoron (accessed March 21, 2019).

2. Clearly, the personified amphora of the Staffetta was bearing an oxymoronic message, too.

3. It is worth mentioning that the concept of intercorporeality traces back to Merleau-Ponty and has been variously employed in performance studies (and beyond). See, for example, Dufrenne 1973; Tamisari 2006; Palmer and Jankowiak 1996; Crossley 1995; Al-Mohammad 2012; Csordas 2008.

4. In his well-known book on mimesis, Taussig argues that every representational act is achieved "through the intervention of the mimetic faculty" (1992, 250). I agree with him, while noticing that, in this case, the mimetic element is subsumed, transcended, and transformed into something that is meant to challenge commonsensical perceptions of what being a woman is or should be. On performances of death and feminist artistic perspectives, see, for example, Simard 2015.

5. See Ferrero Camoletto and Bertone 2012, 2010; Bertone and Ferrero Camoletto 2009; Gilmore 1987.

6. "Ecco come i media giustificano le violenze di genere," *Generazione* (blog), http://comunicazionedigenere.wordpress.com/2012/05/02/analisi-di-come-i-media-giustificano-le-violenze-di-genere/ (accessed March 21, 2019).

7. In this respect, they differ from the *Pupazza* (see chap. 3). Instead, they function more like the amphora of the Staffetta. In the Staffetta, this physical and artistic *personified* object was the witness of/for dead women—that is, the element that talked for them by proxy and without language and that mediated relations. Here *objectified* subjects—that is, pictures of living women—are considered to be witnesses for/of those who died or suffer as a result of sexed violence.

8. For a comparison, see Agamben 1998 on shame.

9. Regarding this particular attribute of photography, Edwards also stresses in writing that "photographs, especially in their global consumption, are often of people, thus blurring the distinction between subject and object, photograph and referent in significant ways" (2012, 222).

10. Clearly, this was aimed at giving new instruments to the community of Taurisano in order to process the grieving associated with the deaths of the two fellow citizens that had occurred some months before.

11. "Incontro-dibattito presso la Biblioteca Comunale 'Pietro Siciliani' il giorno 8 marzo alle ore 10.00," Città di Galatina, http://www.comune.galatina.le.it/item/disanimate-il-corpo-delle-donne-nella-pubblicita-sessista-e-nei-media (accessed March 21, 2019).

12. In this book, I use representations in a wider sense as a general term to refer to performances and practices engaged to show something through something else. In that light, for heuristic reasons, I distinguish between spectacles and practices, the former being related to special events and the latter to ordinary life. Loosely following Lowell Lewis (2013), I adopt performance as a transversal term in this heuristic division of time, with the intention of stressing the performative aspects of performing. In this respect, performance-as-something-performative can be applied to special and ordinary circumstances (31–32)—including the ones related to *Alma de Tierra* and *Disanimate*. The images used in these initiatives had a perlocutionary dimension: they performed womanhood in a way that challenged commonsensical representations of women-as-victims.

13. The attention given by the philosopher Cavell (see Cavell and Goodman 2005; Munday 2009, 2010; Lambek 2010) to the work of Austin (1962) concentrated on the perlocutionary elements of speech. In his analyses of the latter, passionate utterances and the realm of the everyday play central roles. Cavell notably defines the illocutionary and perlocutionary

statements as follows: the former refers to what is done with words, and the latter to what is done by words. Perlocutionary utterances affect interlocutors and are bearers of moral dimensions. Cavell's observations on perlocutionary utterances can be relevant to illuminate the dynamics of what I call the oxymoronic representations of my informants (see also Butler 1997, who notably addresses the role of perlocutionary utterances in the politics of the performative, especially in relation to the analysis of the linguistic dimensions—in particular, of hate speech). I claim that just as passionate utterances influence the interlocutor, so too do the particular representations that I called oxymoronic. The effectiveness of these perlocutionary devices is consistent with Cavell's analyses, context-dependent, and negotiated with the spectators. On the general claim that performances affect both actors and audiences, see Kratz 1994; Livingstone 2005. On *performance*, see, for example, Turner 1979, 1986; Kolankiewicz 2008; Korom 2013; Phelan 1993; Schechner 2003; Schieffelin 1985.

14. Regione Puglia, http://www.regione.puglia.it (accessed April 23, 2018).

15. "Scade l'8 Agosto 2014 il termine per partecipare al Contest Fotografico 'Donna E': 101 Scatti per Raccontare una Donna.' Ecco il bando e le indicazioni per partecipare," *Musicaos Editore* (blog), http://musicaos.org/2014/08/01/scade-l8-agosto-2014-il-termine-per-partecipare-al-contest-fotografico-donna-e-101-scatti-per-raccontare-una-donna-ecco-il-bando-e-le-indicazioni-per-partecipare/ (accessed March 21, 2019).

16. This practice is translated, in written Italian language, in the recent introduction and use of the asterisk (*) as a gender-inclusive feature. Placed at the end of words, the asterisk is used to refer to both masculine and feminine endings. Therefore, in written Italian, my informants would write "*buonasera a tutt*.*"

17. "To bear witness is to take responsibility for truth . . . to testify—before a court of law or before the court of history and of the future; to testify before an audience of readers or of spectators—is more than simply to report a fact or an event or to relate what has been lived, recorded, and remembered. Memory is conjured here essentially in order to address another, to impress upon a listener, to appeal to a community. To testify is always, metaphorically, to take the witness stand, or to take the position of the witness insofar as the narrative account of the witness is at once engaged in an appeal and bounded by an oath" (Felman and Laub 1992, 199, 204). On the act of witnessing, understood as a disciplined presence that opens up new ways of being, see Dave 2014.

18. The issue of failing to decipher visual signs is a topic that Felman also addresses in her analysis of the film *Shoah* by Claude Lanzmann (1985) (Felman and Laub 1992, 204–283). She claims that in the film, the victims, the bystanders, and the perpetrators are defined by different performances of the act of seeing, all of them characterized by their failure to decipher visual signs. The victims do not understand, the bystanders overlook, and the perpetrators do not want to see. The Shoah is, according to her, an event without a witness, since it precludes both seeing and a "community of seeing" (211): something that the movie extends to its audience. The film is constructed around the collection of many testimonies in different languages and translated into French. This "places us in the position of the witness who sees and hears, but cannot understand the significance of what is going on" until the intervention of an—often inaccurate—translation (212). As Taylor points out, in this process the viewer/listener is created as an active see-er, who becomes a witness by virtue of participating in the traumatic event: she becomes a co-owner of that event.

6

FARE-COME-SE (DOING-AS-IF) AND ARTISTIC ENGAGEMENTS

Ethics, Aesthetics, and the Politics of Becoming

IN THIS CHAPTER, IN LIGHT OF WHAT I have discussed so far, I trace another explicit connection between the aesthetic (sensory and artistic) enterprises and the ethical dimension of Salentine activists. I argue that performing modern feminist womanhood, in the various representational ways that I have discussed so far and in ways I discuss in this chapter, is a form of autopoiesis, or of ascesis (in Foucauldian terms). In particular, in dialogue with the so-called anthropology of ethics, I present the political, ethical, and aesthetic practice of fare-come-se (doing-as-if) that I have encountered during my ethnography. In doing so, I reframe and expand one of the most successful ethnographic tropes used for understanding Italian culture(s): the bella figura (making a good impression). If the latter, a meaningful but not central aspect in the lives of the feminists I met, implies acting upon oneself in order to be compliant with others' expectations and with the shared criteria that help in assessing one's performances, doing-as-if does not. Doing-as-if, which I understand as an ethos of becoming (Ziarek 2001; Ibrahim 2014), is not teleologically oriented and aims at imagining (Andriolo 2006) new practices and the criteria to judge and understand them. Similarly, political engagement with the arts, adopted by some of the feminists I met, locates their imaginations of alternative ways of being women in an ethical horizon of becoming. This process is a form of dissensus and yet another example of how the ethical and aesthetic realms are intermingled in my ethnographic field (and beyond).

Facebook Politics

"Whoever does not sign will be unfriended."

This peremptory statement was posted by Rina as a comment to a link on Facebook in which, together with some two hundred other women, she had tagged me. Rina had posted on her Facebook page one of the many petitions in support of women's causes that she shared there on a regular basis. Rina was in her fifties and very active on Facebook and on the internet in general. Everything there—from sharing articles and petitions to posting pictures and statuses—revolved around her feminist persona. Her comments were witty and full of puns. She wrote daily about (national and local) news relevant for feminist issues and publicly praised or criticized other women activists (mostly, her Facebook friends), in so doing demonstrating variations on the theme of "conflict between women" (see chap. 2). She commented on the posts of other friends in the same spirit, with words and emoticons showing satisfaction and gratitude when she was praised, and *centratura* and *senso di sé* (see chap. 2) when criticized. She wrote notes, proffering reflections on particular feminist themes and, especially, situating her personal positions within those. She participated virtually in events organized and published on Facebook by other feminist friends by clicking on the "I will attend" button, even when it was physically impossible for her to do so. The latter aspect of participation seemed secondary; what really mattered was giving visibility on the web both to her friends' political activities and to her personal *political choice* of attending them. Rina, when sharing the events organized by some of her *preferred* friends on her personal page, always tagged other "worthy" friends—judged so according to complicated and somehow *performative* criteria. Having an event (or post) shared by her on Facebook, and appearing (or not) in her tags, was a measure of one's positioning within Rina's range of interests, a judgment of one's worthiness and of one's political relevance. For those women who considered Rina's gaze to be an authoritative one, being seen and approved by her and being (or not being) included in these "sharings" or tags made a big difference. I have often received face-to-face comments from other feminists about who appears in Rina's tags and, especially, on who does *not* appear (but perhaps once did). Rina herself was very opinionated about these issues, as well, and about who was and who was not "worthy" of being tagged.

Rina shared images, too. Often, they were photos taken with her smartphone in her everyday life. The suggested reading of these pictures was normally alluded to in the words she used to comment on them: almost always the images were linked to her feminist identity. She posted (and tagged her "worthy" friends in), for example, pictures of women's sociality, vagina-like images of nature (vaginas were celebrated as a form of beauty, and she saw them in such things as open figs, in the logs of old olive trees, or in particular shapes of cliffs), and pictures of special women she encountered. She posted videos of songs with a feminist message, accompanied by some of their lyrics (obviously those she considered particularly meaningful). Rina also created and published her own videos on Facebook: YouTube links to video blogs addressing her political (feminist) opponents, ironic (political) reinterpretations of songs, montages of images from particularly meaningful political meetings, and so on. In all her online activity, she widely employed the instrument of tagging as a way to give visibility to her political activities. Tagging friends allowed her to reach the Facebook walls of friends of friends (who often were not actually *her* friends) and to be seen beyond her known audience. In sum, by looking at Rina's Facebook profile, an image emerged of a smart, convinced, authoritative, and passionate feminist with many strong opinions—that is, of a woman whose life revolved completely around women's issues and activism.[1] This is something the rest of us, in our off-line lives, cannot live up to. Yet, I had the chance to witness not only the online performances of modern feminist womanhood of Rina (and of other informants) but also the contexts and the material aspects surrounding her practices of "Facebooking." I was physically present when, with her notebook or smartphone in her hands, she wrote or commented on, tagged, and edited her Facebook page. On those occasions, I observed her practices, listened to her comments, and asked questions about her choices: I was a spectator of her acts of creating and molding her online feminist persona. For example, I observed Rina counting the "likes" acquired on her (and others') posts, addressing these numbers, and discussing the varied success of her different posts. I saw her assess who liked what and when and who did not like something, as well as monitor who accepted her tags and who did not (and, possibly, whether those who did not accept her tags accepted someone else's). Moreover, I witnessed her check someone's online status and Facebook activities in order to assess, for example, whether these persons deliberately or unintentionally ignored her tags or posts, or whether they commented or liked other posts before hers. She controlled who shared her links, and, if shared, ensured their origin was referenced (something that might not pertain to Facebook's netiquette but that she insists is a necessary political acknowledgment of disparity; on *disparità* as a political praxis, see chap. 2). Her friends (myself included) were controlled, judged, evaluated, and measured according to all these (and more) parameters that provided various types of information to Rina. These parameters concerned not just how much those others cared about the struggle against patriarchy but also whether they were "worthy" activists, or whether they belonged to her faction in off-line life—that is, whether they sympathized or not, and how much, with Nuzzo's faction within the UDI, and whether they sympathized or not with SNOQ. In such a context, the simple action of liking a picture or a post might have important political and personal consequences—for the ethnographer as well.[2] These activities were part of Rina's everyday life and took up much of her time. Yet, I have reason to believe that these practices were not limited to the aforementioned examples. I remember that on one occasion when I returned to Salento for the summer after months spent in North America, I sent her a text message asking if I could come to her house for a visit, since I was in the area. I remember I mentioned to her that I would be coming with my friend Carmela, whom she did not know. She agreed eagerly and, when I saw Rina, I suspected that she had checked the Facebook profile of Carmela (whom Rina would be able to identify from my own Facebook friends list) before our meeting in order to gather information on her, for Rina mentioned some of Carmela's musical passions and details about her life as if they were matters of public knowledge.[3]

While Rina's online feminist persona appeared immaculate and impeccable, her off-line feminist persona was far more complicated and multifaceted than her online performance. Nonetheless, the former was considered, in a way, the "true" Rina: her online persona was more important and accurate since it spoke about the woman she wanted to become, about the woman that she *was*—only, not *yet* (for a comparison, see Miller 2011, 40–52).

The relationship between the public and the personal was a sensitive field for my informants: in many respects, they explicitly contested the conflation between personal and private and, less explicitly, between public and political—but not in consistent ways (see Michael Warner 2002, in particular 44–63; Cody 2011).[4] In light of this, it is not surprising that Facebook was a political platform they particularly used. Since the personal was political in a radical way for my informants, this social medium, which engages with the (construction and performances of the) personal in a public way, translated into an ideal *locale* for their political activities.[5] These revolved around (online as well as off-line) performances of modern feminist womanhood that aimed at challenging commonsensical ways of seeing and sensing womanhood in their (online and off-line, actual or imagined) audiences and publics. In this respect, what I have witnessed on Facebook in relation to the cultivation and performance of womanhood was not so dissimilar from what I have witnessed off-line and described in chapter 4. The attention and labor that Rina and other activists with whom I worked put into constructing their online personae paralleled the attention and labor that informed their representations in the physical world. These performances had ethical connotations, both off-line and online. In the latter space, for example, the more one was active in posting, reposting, sharing, and so on, the more one demonstrated one's concern about women's causes. Concern was not something that had to do only with making information circulate, it also revolved around being witnesses and conveying alternative representations of women. These were framed as ways to challenge and fight "patriarchy."

Fare-come-se—Doing-as-If

One of the elements that I noticed, right from the beginning of my ethnography, was the *inconsistency* of the performances of feminist womanhood, as ethical and aesthetic enterprises, in the lives of my informants. While I do not consider consistency as a completely attainable project—and, even less, as a *necessary* or even *desirable* one in relation to ethics—I was nonetheless very interested in the ambivalences they had toward their self-representations as feminists. The variations occurred not just from one audience to another (actual or imagined) but also in relation to the same ones.

In the struggle of representations that I have described so far, performing modern feminist womanhood was a central political practice for the Salentine women with whom I worked. Carone, when talking about political practices, distinguished between pretending (in Italian, *fare finta*) and doing-as-if (in Italian, *fare-come-se*). While pretending shares some traits with doing-as-if, the big distinction between the two, according to her, lies in the fact that the former expression does not aim to "change reality," while the latter, according to her, is a specific feature of her understanding of political action. According to Carone, then, doing-as-if entails a discontent with "reality as it is" and is geared toward political change. She claims that when a woman does-as-if, she does not always know exactly how to name or how to enact what she feels. Nonetheless, she puts those feelings at the center of her political experience:

> Doing as if has something to do with hope, utopia and why not? With lunacy, if by "lunacy" we understand something not expected by "normality." . . . It is something that resembles what I think I understood about the writing of a woman named Teresa [De Lauretis] when she writes about queer subjects [*soggetti eccentrici*]. [Doing as if] is the queer invention that manages to remain down to earth while remaining at the threshold between reality and what will be. For this reason, it succeeds in practicing in reality a part of what the future will bring. Politics always needs to arrive before the law . . . politics needs to imagine what does not exist yet . . . women managed to really change something when they had the capability and the will to dream, to imagine, and at the same time to practice . . . doing as if brings you to do things that otherwise you wouldn't do, you wouldn't think, and you wouldn't practice. Because only if you intensively think of something as possible, only if you think of this as the only possible thing, will you make it real. (Carone 2011)

Carone's remarks seem illuminating to me—the connections between doing-as-if and De Lauretis's *Soggetti Eccentrici* (1999) place the ethical and aesthetic experiences of the feminists with whom I worked in the realms of performances and of everyday life, at the threshold between the construction of subjectivities, their fitting (or not) into the dominant common sense, and political activism.[6]

If doing-as-if could certainly be part of a political campaign (Carone associates it with, for example, UDI's 50e50), it was in the ordinary lives of my informants that I found it more explicitly practiced.[7] Doing-as-if represented a clear connection in their political activism between the sensory and aesthetic realms and the ethical one, as it emerged from my fieldwork—one that was not based on the woman one was but rather on the woman one wanted to become. It also set their political and existential experiences within different temporalities, by inserting the future (including its unknowability) into the present. There are many examples in this book that can exemplify Carone's doing-as-if in my informants' ordinary lives. I can mention, for example, Eugenia's adoption of being feminist as an identity marker in relation to the hardness and disillusionment of her personal, emotional, and work experiences. Carmen's pride in offering her narrative of coming back to her birth town as the result of an achieved psychological maturity (in reference to her fleeing attitude), while hardly being able to make a living and to get out of her parents' house, is another example (she is currently living in another city). Elder UDI members who, in narrating the 1982 congress, claim that their brave choice left them free and wholesome . . . and without a salary, economically dependent on their partners, is yet another. On the basis of my current ethnography, I cannot assess whether this doing-as-if is, in the long run, really an effective political strategy, as Carone claims that it is: one that changes reality and the ways in which their (actual or imagined) audiences see and sense. Surely, though, doing-as-if was something that changed my informants' perception of their role in the world and their visualities and feelings about it. It also helped others (including myself) imagine new possibilities of being women (the possible "dissonances" in the lives of my informants that I described are not accessible to all the persons they encounter). It also told me, the ethnographer, of the importance that the gazes of the others had for the women I met. In sum, doing-as-if put the individual and collective sensory, emotional, and affective experiences of being women at the center of my informants' political activism. It represented modern feminist womanhood as something not yet attained but still meaningful to imagine and actualize new possibilities of being. In this sense, it was a transformative enterprise: performing, performative, and perlocutionary. Imagination, understood in Andriolo's sense as something rooted in bodies, was an ethical and aesthetic project since it entrenched political activism and autopoiesis in the realm of representations. It was a political activity, since it aimed at changing their own and others' visualities and ways of experiencing and sensing womanhood.

The connections between performances and social life have been variously explored by anthropologists. As I showed in chapter 4, the literature on honor and shame has extensively done so. Following the lead of Herzfeld (1985), for example, Dubisch analyzed the poetics of womanhood in Greece (1995), arguing that "to perform . . . is to present the socially constructed self before others . . . and thus to convince and to draw recognition from others of one's place and one's satisfactory performance of that role. I would add . . . that these performances are transformative and not simply expressive. . . . In other words, they are creative endeavors" (Dubisch 1995, 204–205).[8] This latter point is analogous to what is claimed by scholars of performances and, in particular, in the Italian context, by those who deal with performances of bella figura (good impression; see, e.g., Plesset 2006; Del Negro 2004; Nardini 1999). In this respect, and inspired by their work, I maintain that the performances and practices of modern feminist womanhood that I found in Salento, online and off-line, seemed to be at the same time *performing* and *performative* of gender and status (Guano 2007, 52; on performativity, see Butler 2006, 1997, 2014; on the relations between gender and bella figura, see, in particular, Plesset 2006; Nardini 1999; Pipyrou 2014a). Nonetheless, in my ethnographic case study, this aesthetics was performed, practiced, and displayed as an embodied ethics, in the Foucauldian sense, since it might be framed as an ascetic work that both showed and renegotiated one's position in society's (moral) worlds. Indeed, what my ethnographic material and analyses add to these debates is to show how the transformative aspect of performances does not always occur in foreseen and foreseeable directions. If bella figura implies complying with acknowledged and shared social aesthetic norms, what I describe below as doing-as-if does not and gestures toward something that *is not yet* and that, in a certain way, is even obscure for the performer herself. In other words, the results of the transformation brought about by the performances, and their perlocutionary effects, in the political experience of the Salentine feminists were not always known in advance. Interestingly, though, often the principal publics of these performances were the performers themselves.

Anthropology of Ethics

As becomes clear at this point in the book, some of the women activists I met embodied quite straightforwardly the connections between aesthetic practices, ethical labor, art (understood as something that offers weapons to fight patriarchy), and political activism. They attempted to create new publics able to acknowledge them and to change the performances and practices of seeing and sensing of their audiences.[9] My informants' peculiar ways of linking aesthetic work (and labor) and the construction of (new) subjectivities in their political activism, in the practices of doing-as-if as well as in the other practices described in the previous chapters, could be read in relation to recent works of anthropologists who are interested in the ethical realm.[10] In particular, I am referring to anthropologists who adopt a so-called "Aristotelian" perspective.[11] Within this trend, Foucault's work on ascesis informs some.[12] Following the lead of the French philosopher, who, in his late work defined ethics as a work of art (see also Faubion 2001), Halperin, for example, proposes that queer identities in Foucault's work epitomize the human condition in general.[13] If one follows this argument, then what Foucault wrote in relation to homosexuals could be valid for everybody: "It's up to us to advance into a homosexual ascesis that would make us work on ourselves and invent (I don't say discover) a manner of being that is still improbable" (Foucault 1997, 137).[14] Ascesis—understood as both a poiesis and a practice—is a political, ethical, and aesthetic enterprise.[15] In my ethnographic field of study, it is embedded in my informants' poetics of modern feminist womanhood, which are enacted through such things as artistic engagements, performances of dignity, oxymoronic representations, and the cultivation of doing-as-if. In other words, ascesis took the contours of engaging with representations of (modern) feminist womanhood and of portraying women as witnesses rather than as victims in relation to common or dominant understandings of the relationships between women and violence. By doing so, my informants set their political activism within the realm of *becoming* rather than being (see also Dave 2011, 2014; and Lambek 2014). They built their ethical/aesthetic/political enterprises around the representations of the women *they wanted to be* rather than the women they *actually were.*

In sum, the ethical dimension of performing (modern) feminist womanhood permeated the everyday lives of the women I met. We saw this, for example, in their attempts to represent themselves as *degne* (worthy, dignified) in their specific local communities, or as worthy within feminist circles. Their performance of feminist womanhood changed according to their (imagined or actual) publics, and it was informed by what I see as a missionary intent. As a part of the representational struggle discussed above, many of my informants explicitly aimed to show other contemporary Italian women new possibilities of being, outside "patriarchal" constraints, and to possibly convince them to do the same. In this respect, they seemed to parallel the features of renovated humanity—by presenting themselves as out-and-out exempla—that emerged as significant elements in conversion narratives in the anthropological literature on Christianity.[16] Moreover, by focusing through autopoietic practices on the women they wanted to become rather than on the women they actually were, the activists with whom I worked were deeply teleological: they set their political action in the realm of what was not yet or in an *alternative* time.

S/oggett/E: On Becoming Who You Are (Only, Not *Yet*)

It was Sunday morning. Loredana and I woke up early: we had enjoyed a "girls' night" together in Lecce the night before, with a lot of talking about life and love and a fair amount of beer. My friend Loredana De Vitis is a journalist, writer, and artist who lives in the Salento area. On this morning, other members of the association Io Sono Bellissima ("I am wonderful"; ISB from now on) were waiting for us for the first meeting of S/oggett/E. We could not be late. Reluctantly, we got up from the queen-sized bed we had been sharing with her cat, Julia, and we headed toward the coffee machine. Loredana's phone rang. "Hello! Yes. I understand. Are you sure? I can come. Forty minutes. Sure, no problem. Bye." "Giovanna, let's go. We are going to pick Diana up. We are late. Hurry up!" Unenthusiastically, I left the espresso I was sipping in the kitchen sink and moved toward the bathroom.

My friend and I got into the car: "Lore, are you sure that wasn't an excuse? Are you sure that she REALLY messed up last night with her friend who was supposed to drive her to Lecce?" With her eyes on me, Loredana did not reply as she picked up the phone and dialed a number: "Hi, Diana. I am coming. You ARE coming, right?" She smiled, and added, looking directly into my eyes: "You know, my friend Giovanna thinks this might be an excuse. . . . OK, see you in a while." She hung up the phone without taking her eyes off mine and without commenting. She was grinning with satisfaction. First, I rolled my eyes. Then I smiled and told her I was sure that it would have been a tough morning for me. We laughed.

Forty minutes later we got there—finally. My stomach was upset. The meeting was in a square of a town in the province of Lecce. Diana got into the car. She muttered a "Ciao" and took her seat in the rear, just behind me. I greeted her and introduced myself briefly, informally. She remained silent. Loredana did all the initial talking: it was the first time they had met in person, and my friend has the gift of being able to fill the silences with *nonchalance*— something I always really appreciate when I am with her, especially in new situations. I peeked at Diana from the car's side-view mirror. I did not want her to see me staring at her. She was looking out the window, while Loredana was doing all the talking. Her haircut was asymmetrical and multicolored. Her eyes were swollen. Her dark piercings stood out on her pale face. "How old are you, Diana?" I asked, exploiting one of Loredana's pauses.

"What do you think?" she replied.

I smiled. "Twenty-three?" I asked with a soft, unchallenging voice. I looked into the mirror and saw Diana's body almost jumping on her seat.

"Nineteen. But everybody thinks that I am sixteen," she replied. Her voice was mildly hoarse and twangy. She looked puzzled but gratified.

"What do you sing?" I asked.

"I am a 'screamo' singer," she replied.

"Can you explain your technique to me?" I added, without emphasis. I peeked into the mirror, again, and saw her smiling. Her eyes were glowing.

During that car ride, in addition to a detailed description of the world of Italian "screamo" singers and of some of the techniques she uses, I learned that Diana lived with her mom and had just finished school. She was looking for a job and cultivating her passion for music in spite of her family and friends' questions. She did not define herself as a feminist: in fact, I doubt she had spent much time thinking about it.

* * *

ISB was an association based in Lecce.[17] It was created as a result of an initiative by Loredana. Her engagement with women's politics started in the UDI but developed independently, outside the restricted feminist circuits that were often rather self-referential. ISB's audience was wider, and the language it used was meant also to be accessible to those who were not into women's politics, like Diana. Just a couple of persons on the staff of the association were feminist activists, and not all of the women of its governing board would have defined themselves as feminists—those who did certainly did not define themselves in the same ways. ISB's primary concern was the struggle against stereotypes: it took representations very seriously. One of the initiatives promoted by ISB was called S/oggett/E: *Rassegna d'armi di artiste* (S/oggett/E, exposition of weapons of women artists). The title forced the linguistic element into a graphic sign by using slashes in the middle of a word: *soggette* (meaning subjects, a substantive inflected in the feminine plural; *soggette* exists in Italian not as a noun but as an adjective meaning subjected). The slashes highlighted the core of the word, which is *oggett(e)* (a substantive meaning objects, inflected in the feminine plural; *oggette* does not exist in the feminine version either, in Italian). The fusion between being subjects and objects evoked by the title of the initiative paralleled its graphic nature: for the Italian reader, S/oggett/E was a word and a graphic sign at the same time. It was more allusive than descriptive and was meant to provoke a sense and affect of estrangement into whoever bumped into it. As Loredana explained to me, the idea of this title came to her mind from the acknowledgment that "we would never free ourselves from the role of objects in our society" and that we need to exchange "knowledge" and "praxis" (*saperi e prassi*) in order to be empowered by this condition, which we cannot excise. Being objects, for her, resonated with the fact that we are recipients of others' (especially men's) gazes and that the latter engage chains of comparisons if not of competitions among women. Those gazes are interiorized by all of us, but they are not *ours*. According to ISB, using the liberating and empowering language of art to push ourselves out of our comfort zones allows us to "transform our gaze on ourselves, and to discover new ways of looking, notwithstanding the ones in which our ('patriarchal') society cages us (*ci ingabbia*)." In other words, according to De Vitis, by engaging their bodies and their senses artistically, women are able to change their practices and performances of seeing: first, by transforming their own personal gaze, and, second, by transforming the gazes of the spectators.

These "expositions of weapons of women artists" were composed by three series of workshops led, respectively, by a musician, a photographer, and a poet. On Sundays, the teachers and the (small) groups of women met at the Casello. This was a former rail tollhouse that fell into disuse and that a group of young Salentines renovated and transformed into an event space. I have attended many meetings organized there by Loredana, at one of which I had made a presentation.

Diana attended two of the three workshops (the ones on music and photography), and, in spite of her difficult economic and existential situation, the organizers of the initiative told me she was one of the persons who profited the most from S/oggett/E. Loredana told me that the workshops helped Diana find a better "center" (*centratura*) in reference to her personal and emotional lives. My friend argues that this was a result of the fact that, by "going out of her comfort zones," she learned that it is OK to be different and to embrace alternative possibilities of being a woman. The latter element had been evident, according to the organizers of the workshops, when another member of the S/oggett/e group had apparently called her names, picking on Diana's "nonconformity." Loredana claimed that this episode marked a turning point for Diana who, "by virtue of the experience of S/oggett/E," found herself questioning her own affective reactions to what, until shortly before that, she would have considered to be an insult, a judgment, and an appraisal of her "not fitting in" society. Instead, she found the courage to embrace her actual or supposed "queerness" in front of others as well as in front of herself and to transform the gaze of the other into something harmless. This happened, according to De Vitis, "without engaging with anything feminist." As I mentioned, Diana probably completely ignores the meaning and the history of the word *feminism*.

The arts in S/oggett/E were framed as weapons, and the artists as she-warriors, evidencing a theoretical move that associated what I have described as the role of the witness with artistic creations.[18] In other words, it connected being "witnesses" with a form of poiesis as well as with the ethics and aesthetics of (feminist) womanhood. The aim of these workshops was "expressing, exchanging, and building forms of beauty," and they were presented as "an itinerary leading to the discovery of ways and forms where subjectivity expresses itself, establishes itself, and produces political acts. If the world is constantly trying to make us objects, we have means, strategies, and instruments in order to affirm that we are subjects. Rather, *soggette*. With word, sound and image—these are some of our 'weapons'—we can resist and attack the ugly things of the world."[19]

Many dimensions of S/oggett/E offered interesting elements for my work. This initiative exemplified the link between art and politics, aesthetics and ethics, it resonated with the issues around visibility and being sensible she-warriors that I considered above, and it helped substantiate Carla's claims of the necessity to assert women's agency and to show leadership in politics. Moreover, for my informants it exemplified the difference between being victims and witnesses, and it confirmed an element that emerged in this book also in connection with *Alma de Tierra* and *Disanimate* (chap. 5) in relation to representations of the two dimensions of being subjects: the fact that they spoke as *testimoni*, witnesses, from a liminal, oxymoronic place. S/oggett/E quite literally comprised the two meanings of being subject: S/oggett/E were not only and mainly women who were objects/victims, as the society wanted them to be. They were witnesses—Soggette—through the materiality of their bodies, emotions, and affects: they became agentive objects through actions of poiesis, through the practice of poiesis, through a labor of art. S/oggett/e explicitly underscored an important dimension that was also present, though less plainly, in Immagini Amiche: the link between the artistic dimensions and the construction of (renovated) subjectivities. ISB emphasized an aspect of aesthetics known as autopoiesis (see, e.g., Foucault 2005; Faubion 2001; Dave 2012), understood as intrinsic to artistic creations. Interestingly, it made a political statement and a specific and explicit battlefield against "patriarchy" of this element.

This latter aspect was not idiosyncratic, and I also found it on other occasions during my fieldwork. Pina Nuzzo, for example, who is a painter as well as an activist in feminist politics, always told me that every campaign she promotes is for her like a "work of art." By using this expression, she did not mean to gesture (only) toward the large amount of work and skill that the organization and promotion of such initiatives requires but mainly to the communicative aspects of material artistic productions and to their ability to convey meanings and feelings, for both the artist and the public. In this sense, they are political activities, since they allowed for the emergence of elements of novelty and of new insights and representations of the world. S/oggett/E explored these connections in a thorough way: in the performances fostered by the initiative, the participants were experiencing the two dimensions of being subjects that were believed to be intrinsic to the artistic dimension. The latter put the actors/artists in the position of being at the same time agents and objects of the performance, from the points of view of both the audience and the performers. S/oggett/e were both *recipients* of others' gazes and judgments (on the Lacanian gaze, see Taylor 1997, 30) and *agentive subjects*—that is, creators of the artistic spectacles.

What is more interesting, though, for the purpose of my analysis of the Italian feminist political activism that I encountered in Salento, is that S/oggett/E, while aiming to move its audience affectively, did not focus exclusively on its (actual or imagined) publics by means of the artistic weapons it used. What this initiative was meant to do, primarily, was change the *ways actors/artists/performers thought and felt about themselves*, as the example of Diana shows. S/oggett/E's main concern was not to create artistic performances in order to enlighten the public, or to express the specific individualities, ways of being, or essences of the performers. Rather, it was to provide the protagonists chances to create themselves according to unforeseen dimensions and directions—beyond passive victimhood, and beyond the objectification of women's bodies—in order to become who they are (only, not *yet*).[20] In my Foucauldian reading of this initiative, creative/artistic acts were not perceived as simply voicing a given subjectivity that preexisted the artistic creation, but the latter was understood to be creating the former. In this respect, S/oggett/E epitomized Mahmood's claim that "the importance of . . . practices does not reside in the meanings they signify to their practitioners, but in the work they do in constituting the individual" (2005, 29). Constituting the individual, here meaning a representational struggle against "patriarchy," was a political enterprise; as I have mentioned often in this book, the personal and the political were tightly linked in the lives of my informants.

The dynamics of reciprocal creation between the artist and her artistic performances expressed by ISB were central to Loredana's life and projects. *Col Corpo Capisco* (With the Body I Know), besides being the Italian title of a novel that I introduced to her in one of our conversations (Grossman 2009), was one of the tropes that we used often in our exchanges on these topics. In her holistic vision of the world, the intelligence of the body, enhanced in artistic representations, was able to guide and not just complement that of the mind. Through the artistic journeys promoted by the ISB initiative, then, the women who participated could learn more about themselves, discover themselves differently, and become alternatives to the widespread representations of women as passive victims of physical, symbolic, or structural violence. They could challenge the commonsensical understandings of the roles and status of women in Italian society that informed how others see and sense them as women. Moreover, those artistic journeys could prompt new possibilities, ones that were different from those that have often been internalized and that defined, sometimes subconsciously, how women looked at themselves and at other women.[21]

S/oggett/E, in other words, promoted imagination in the construction of subjectivities in a way that resonated with Andriolo's reading of Coetzee, and complemented some of Murgia's observations (see chap. 4). In her article on protest suicide, Andriolo (2006) offers an interesting reading of the novel *Elizabeth Costello* by Coetzee. She claims that the novelist's understanding of imagination may shed some light on suicide as a form of political protest. For Andriolo, "imagining" is an "embodied minding" (100), where the latter term preserves both the meaning of caring and of mental reasoning. "Imagining can penetrate into territories that are impossible for abstract thought" (101) and "engages the body as an experiential and metaphorical site" (100). S/oggett/E endorsed experiences of imagination in this sense: starting from the bodies of women in artistic representations in order to give directionality to the process, this initiative framed imagination as both an embodied experience and the result of a labor—that is, of an ongoing practice.

In other words, while the project of ISB could be read as promoting practices of autopoiesis (see Faubion 2001), or of ascesis, it also suggested further developments. I believe that the contribution of my ethnographic material to the current anthropological debates on these topics resides in the consequences of the quite explicit link between practice and autopoiesis, the work of art and political activism that animated the lives of some of the women activists I met in Salento.[22] In this respect, it represents a point of conjunction between the aforementioned literature on the anthropology of ethics and the work of Rancière.

What I believe S/oggett/E and the other representations I have described so far suggest is a possible conciliation between the Aristotelian perspective on the anthropological study of ethics, on the one hand, and politics understood as a reconfiguration of the sensible in Rancièrian terms, on the other. By transforming their subjectivities, the Salentine activists I worked with hoped to challenge the current Italian "patriarchal" understandings of womanhood. This particular gloss on the "personal is political" adage puts the realm of sensations and artistic work and labor at the center of their feminist being in the world, epitomizing the close relations between ethics and aesthetics mentioned above. The ethical enterprises with which the women I met engaged in order to imagine new subjectivities were political enterprises; they challenged commonsensical understandings—understood both as what makes sense and what can be sensed (see Panagia 2009, 3)—of women-as-victims and the power structures that determined what being a woman is or should be in contemporary Italy. In sum, using a Rancièrian terminology, within a framework that adopts an understanding of politics as (specific) partition(s) of the sensible, I claim that S/oggett/E epitomized an element of dissensus.[23] By engaging the bodies of women (understood as she-warriors) in aesthetic (sensory and artistic) performances, ISB aimed to include in the political distribution of the sensible their own experiences, which the women previously felt had no part in it. In doing so, S/oggett/E represented ways in which "sensation interrupts common sense" (Panagia 2009, 2), allowing for an expansion of the terms in which the world was perceived and sensed. This political enterprise also aimed at changing one's own gaze and the ones of her (actual or imagined) publics.

Dignity, Shame, and Doing-as-If

In his account of the intellectual history of the term *dignity*, Agamben writes that *degna* (worthy/dignified), today, "is the person who, while lacking public dignity, *does as if* she possesses it" (1998, 62, emphasis mine). The resonances between the Italian philosopher's definition of dignity and the experiences of Carone and the other feminists, in relation to the "phenomenology of dignity" that I have described in this book, are compelling and important. I have extensively explained how Italian feminists have been denouncing the lack of recognition of women's dignity in Italian society. Femminicidio and violence against women represented the extremes of a continuum of violence that undermined women's dignity in the first place. In this panorama, I argued, being (or being represented as) witnesses was a feminist marker in a context where women were often associated with (or spontaneously adhere to) the role of victims.

In the representational struggle in which my informants were engaging, as a feature of their political activism, dignity was something they wanted to attain in order to be considered relevant, significant, and worthy—all things they felt women were generally *not* in "patriarchal" environments.[24] In order to "make it real," as Carone would say, they did-as-if they were *degne*—that is, they did-as-if they were recognized as socially worthy/dignified. It is precisely here that Agamben's words, Carone's experience, and the political praxis of Salentine activists coincide. Feeling worthy/dignified was an emotion and being *degne* was something that engaged the senses with sensory and artistic practices. In my ethnographic field of Salento, being witnesses through representing oneself as a witness, I argue, was a way both to *show* dignity and to *feel degne*. Doing-(aesthetically)-as-if one were worthy/dignified (which I frame as an emotion) was a way to cultivate dignity (see Agamben 1998; Carone 2011) and, eventually, to be recognized as *degne*. In other words, it was both performative and perlocutionary, a "sensible politics" and a "politics of becoming." Dignity was not something necessarily already given but was framed as a practice, as something that needed to be cultivated and recognized—setting the political activism of my informants, again, in the realm of becoming, rather than in the realm of being.

Notes

1. On Facebook as well, my informants do-as-if. See chapter 6.
2. While I tended not to intervene directly on Facebook, by openly commenting on the posts, statuses, and images of Rina and of the other feminists with whom I worked online, I realized I could not avoid giving signs of participation in their online activities. I used to accept every tag (even the ones I did not agree with) and to use the "like" instrument as a way of communicating my support for their cause. Occasionally, I shared some links or posts (mostly, as a way to give audience to their initiatives). Of course, knowing that my Facebook activity could be scrutinized by Rina and some others, I behaved consistently in reference to my other friends (nonfeminist, and not linked with my ethnography). This lack of intervention also helped me protect my informants from the possible gazes of my other Facebook friends. I have considered opening a specific Facebook account for the purposes of my ethnography, but, given the peculiarities of my informants, I am pretty sure it would have been understood as a way of putting distance between my own life and theirs—something that would have been detrimental to my ethnography. I preferred to use the privacy settings on Facebook, by dividing my friends into groups, and to allow certain people, and not others, to see my activities online. Sometimes, for example, I had to put Rina and others in my acquaintances group in order to remove myself from their gaze.
3. Carmela is not a public figure and does not share common acquaintances with Rina aside from myself.
4. Nuzzo, for example, writes that "very often, in women's political spaces, an excess of words exposes a difference between how a woman represents herself, and her real experience [*sic*]. The risk is not being able to distinguish between what is personal, and therefore political, and what is private and should remain so" (Nuzzo 2011b). This is a clear stance against some opponents within UDI and against the traditions of the practice of self-awareness, and, in Carla's words, it becomes a critique that can be ascribed to pretending and not doing-as-if. These remarks are nonetheless interesting since they pose a clear distinction between the private and the personal. Nuzzo explained this distinction to me (email, October 15, 2014) by referring to an example. She writes: "I never found it necessary to ask individual women to tell their stories or experiences of violence, since this would not have added anything to what we already know about violence. What we already know is enough to make it the object of political actions." Moreover, Marta, who participated in the preparation of the Fifteenth Congress, told me that in the aftermath of Berlusconi's sexual scandal some UDI women claimed that, being inheritors and witnesses of the political thought that states that the personal is political, they knew how to distinguish and demonstrate that bringing the attention

to the private realm functions as a way to dissimulate personal responsibilities, whereas *partire da sé* (starting from oneself) is a pivotal element of Italian feminist political activism. For the relations between public and private, personal and political, see Michael Warner 2002; Cody 2011; G. Linke 2011; Landes 1998. It is worth noting that Michael Warner's attention to counterpublics and to their role in redefining the terms by which we understand the public and the private (see 2002, 61) parallel the attention to representations and to their perlocutionary function in my informants' activism: the attention to visibility and the awareness of some gazes and not others can be framed within such an understanding of public opinion (i.e., as formed by different publics).

5. On Facebook as a locus for ethnography, see Miller 2011; Gershon 2011; Boellstorff et al. 2012; Uimonen 2013; Elisabetta Costa 2016, 2018; Nicolescu 2016; on Twitter, see Bonilla and Rosa 2015 on #Ferguson; Ince, Rojas and Davis 2017 on #BlackLivesMatter; Portwood-Stacer and Berridge 2015.

6. The origin of the expression "fare-come-se" does not lie in my informants' engagement in the "as if" in Western philosophy (e.g., in the work of Kant, Pascal, and Derrida), but it is a reflection on the lyrics of a song by the Italian singer Elisa, entitled "*Qualcosa che non c'è.*"

7. In her ethnographic study of the Egyptian Islamic Revival and of the Women's Mosque Movement, Mahmood (2005) makes a similar point. She inquires into the cultivation and performance of two emotions—fear (2001a) and *istihya*/shyness (2001b)—suggesting that, in her ethnographic context, the practice of specific emotions, "rather than formal behavior[s]," were "a condition for the emergence of the self as such and integral to its realization" (2001b, 845). She problematizes the connection between emotions, authenticity, and spontaneity, arguing for the possibility of conceiving the cultivation and performance of emotions as a form of ethical practice. The emotion that I believe, on the basis of my ethnographic research, my informants are cultivating when performing (and practicing) modern feminist womanhood is that of being worthy/dignified.

8. On this point, see also Del Negro and Berger on the performative elements of performance (2001).

9. It is worth noting that, if creating new audiences can trigger new performances of seeing and sensing in the public, it can also be the other way around. Kapchan (2008) and Muñoz (2000), for example, seem to offer examples of the reverse dynamics: in the first case, audiences are constructed on the basis of a shared literacy of listening, and, in the second, according to certain ways of feeling (a community of affect). See also McLagan 2012.

10. See, for example, Mahmood 2005; Lambek 2010; Dave 2011, 2012.

11. On the different approaches to the anthropological study of ethics, see, for example, Lambek 2000b, 2010; Faubion 2011; Zigon 2007, 2008.

12. See, for example, Foucault 1997; Halperin 1995; Faubion 2001; Dave 2011; Mahmood 2005.

13. Lambek claims that the Foucauldian autopoiesis could be combined with Arendt's understanding of action through the adoption of Nehamas's understanding of ethics as the "art of living" (2010, 16).

14. Halperin's comments on Foucault's words are consistent with how some of my informants think about representation—an approach epitomized, in particular, by those who gravitate around the experience of S/oggett/E (see chap. 6): "Hence, to cultivate oneself . . . is not to explore or experience some given self, conceived as a determinate private realm, a space of personal interiority, but instead to use one's relation to oneself as a potential resource with

which to construct new modalities of subjective agency and new styles of personal life that may enable one to resist or even to escape one's social and psychological determinations" (Halperin 1995, 76).

15. Interestingly, according to some of the anthropologists that choose an Aristotelian approach for the study of ethics, the creative potential of ascesis stems from its being at the same time poiesis and praxis. Michael Lambek, in particular, stressed the connections between ethics and practice by referring to an Aristotelian distinction of the forms of human activity (poiesis, praxis, and theoria) emended through the work of Arendt ([1958] 1998). Within the realm of poiesis (making), Arendt distinguishes work from labor. *Work* refers to the production of finished products, *labor* to that of continuous life-reproducing activities (Lambek 2010). The consequences of this intellectual move are paramount: as Lambek points out: "The Arendtian category of labor both undermines any clear distinction between pro-duction and action (aesthetics and ethics) and locates itself firmly in the sphere of the ordi-nary" (15).

16. By the term *exempla*, plural of *exemplum*, I refer explicitly to a literary genre that was popular in the Middle Ages, especially in relation to the lives of saints, and that was used in sermons and predication with a moralizing intent. It offered examples of behavior that the audience was expected to emulate. The reference to the Christian religious tradition is not accidental.

17. The adjective is feminine singular. Io Sono Bellissima, http://www.iosonobellissima.it/ (accessed April 23, 2018). The translation of *bellissima* with "wonderful" is a choice of Lore-dana De Vitis. It appears in the English version of their website.

18. ISB does not distinguish between visual arts and performances since it considers all forms of art to be performative.

19. "Soggette. Rassegna d'Armi d' Artiste," Io Sono Bellissima, http://www .iosonobellissima.it/soggette-rassegna-darmi-dartiste/ (accessed April 23, 2018).

20. This element obviously resonates with Carone's doing-as-if.

21. On art and activism in an "open ended" and nonconformist perspective, see, for example, Uzwiak 2016; Raunig 2014; Vidal-Ortiz, Viteri Burbano, and Serrano Amaya 2014.

22. On the connections between ethics, aesthetics, and political activism, see also Dave 2011; on performance and politics, see Tamisari 2006; on the role of practice in the ethical realm, see Lambek 2000a, 2014.

23. This element is present also in the examples of representations I analyzed previously in this chapter and in those I examine in the rest of the chapter.

24. In this respect, it is worth mentioning the importance that terms like *senso di sé, cen-tatura*, and *disparità* have in Italian feminist jargon (see chap. 2).

CONCLUSION

SINCE 2011, THE EMERGENCE OF AN "INCOMMENSURABLE" (POVINELLI 2006; Dave 2011), brought forward by the introduction of the word *femminicidio* and the world vision it conveys, has created a new women's question in Italy. The renegotiation of (some) feminist positions within such a framework was defined by the attempt to disrupt the commonsensical perception of what violence against women was and of who were the perpetrators, the witnesses, and the victims of that violence. This often happened in contrast to the dominant interpretations that tended to neutralize the relationships between women and victims. In other words, the discursive and affective construction of femminicidio provided a new understanding of the world—that is, creating what I called a "community of sense" of women who reinterpreted (see Lambek 2014) their lives within a continuum of violence of which femminicidio was its extreme manifestation.

The women with whom I worked saw potentialities and possible faults in this new framework. In order to challenge the latter, they engaged representational struggles by organizing disagreement and by generating and promoting dissensus, in Rancièrian terms. They did so through the reconfiguration of representations of women conceived not (only) as victims but as witnesses, through various performances of ambiguity that were meant to have the perlocutionary effect of changing the practices and performances of seeing and sensing around "being women" in contemporary Italy.

This latter dimension was particularly relevant in both the lives and the political practices of the Salentine feminist women I met. My informants considered pivotal to their being feminist women what Rancière might call the "reconfiguration of the sensible," a project that they pursued mainly through the representational struggle that I have presented in this book. This form of "sensible politics" (McLagan and McKee 2012) involved not only artistic objects, and the language and the images used to portray women, but also particular poetics of (modern and feminist) womanhood, inspired by performances and practices of dignity. These performances and practices, in their relationships with being witnesses, worked as multivalent symbols in this framework: dignity was not, merely, something given to every single person by virtue of being human. Dignity, especially in its emotional implications (see, for a comparison

Mahmood 2001a on fear and 2001b on ishtiya/shyness), was something that needed to be cultivated, performed, and, eventually, acknowledged by others. It was something that happened in between the sensory and the aesthetic, the personal and the social. In Salento, women adopted dignity in a way that resonated with certain dimensions of the local traditional notion of honor as a measure of social worth, and, at the same time, as a reference point to the wider discourse on human rights. In my ethnographic field, it was a way to practice and perform modern feminist womanhood.

Performing modern feminist womanhood was central in the feminist political activism that I encountered, which relied on doing-as-if (fare-come-se) as a political praxis. In this book, in contrast with bella figura, I framed this doing-as-if as an ethical/aesthetic enterprise rooted in a politics of becoming. It was performed both off-line and online, and it could be understood as a Foucauldian work of ascesis. The same could be said for the engagement with the arts. I showed how some of my informants theorized the arts as weapons in the struggle against "patriarchy" and promoted the performance of arts for constructing new types of womanhood.

All these dimensions, I have argued, set the political activism of the women I worked with in the realm of becoming rather than in the realm of being—that is, they were teleologically oriented toward a version of themselves that was not *yet* and that they *represented in order to make it happen*. My informants' alternative representations of women, in other words, corresponded to what they considered to be modern feminist womanhood: something that they wanted to both embrace *and* promote. By affecting the spectators, the activists I met hoped to challenge commonsensical representations of women-as-victims and to create, affirm, and imagine new ways of being women. The activists considered these practices of (Foucauldian) ascesis to be generative of new subjectivities (not yet attained but sought for), which developed in unforeseen directions. In these political representations, the language of aesthetics met the language of ethics, contributing to the imagination of new possibilities of being in the world. In Braidotti's words, being women, for the women I met, was being "a subject-in-process, a mutant, the other of the Other, a post-Woman embodied subject cast in female morphology who has already undergone an essential metamorphosis" (2002, 12).

Describing and assessing the mid- to long-term effects and configurations of this metamorphosis can be a further development of this research. Are the political struggles of the women I met resulting in a broad and long-term societal change in the Italian public opinion around women and violence against women? Is their opening toward an intersectional feminism with *Non-UnaDiMeno* introducing further dimensions of "witnessing" and "producing witnesses" in the Italian context? Can these intersectional perspectives inaugurate the emergence of a new shared dimension of political struggles with and around migrants and non-Italian women in Italy? The latter, largely silent in the context I described in this book, are an important component of contemporary Italian society, which is currently struggling around migrants' rights for the widespread presence of anti-immigration discourses. Will the community of sense that emerged in reference to violence against women and femminicidio and that I described in this book be able to develop into a more inclusive community? Will it be able to include different dimensions of violence, in the future, and new experiences of victimhood and witnessing in its political activism? These are important questions for contemporary Italy and central challenges for contemporary feminisms, in Italy and beyond. The recent development and international impact of the #metoo (in Italy, #quellavoltache) movement gestures toward an internationalization of the protests, although it is too early to assess its long-term effects and efficacy. How does the activism of the women I met and described in this book fit into this wider perspective? What can their attention to "representational activism" add to these global protests?

Mirzoeff (2014), in the afterword of *How to See the World*, asks, with the South African photographer and artist Zanele Muholi, "What does it mean to be seen to be a citizen in a global era? Who represents us at local and national levels in a globalized society?" This book is just one example, among many, showing how those who should "represent" us often fail to do so and how change can be brought forward by explicitly embracing a representational struggle, by being "representational activists" and not only "visual" ones. If anything, the story of my informants is a story of women who embraced the challenge of representing themselves according to different dimensions and who used their imaginations and skills to try to *produce* change. While their battles, histories, and political theories can be understood as context-specific, and rooted in a pensiero della differenza sessuale that might be perceived as deeply "other" by some North American readers, I claim that the Salentine activists' lives, stories, and experiences might speak to a broader context. Their activism can be read in conversation with that of those who, in today's globalized and media-saturated world, are engaging in their own "representational struggle." In other words, while in narrating the stories of the women I met in Salento I resisted the urge of presenting their political experience within a framework molded on the nature and issues of current North American debates, I do believe that their experience could be read and discussed within a broader, "global," context and I see in this a further direction of research. How can their experience stimulate or provoke other activists elsewhere? How are "representational activists" worldwide interacting and how are they imagining their political activism? How are "representational struggles" connected, or disconnected, worldwide? Pushing this research further in these directions is not (only) a comparative matter but a political (representational) enterprise per se: it can "build bridges" among marginalized communities worldwide, disarticulating current "regimes of perception" and fostering new dimensions of dissensus.

SELECTED BIBLIOGRAPHY

A A.VV. 2007. "Comitato scientifico per la valorizzazione delle tradizioni italiane." *Antropologia Museale* 17: 18–22.

Abis, Stefania, and Paolo Orrù. 2016. "Il femminicidio nella stampa italiana: Un'indagine linguistica." *Gender/Sexuality/Italy* 3: 18–33.

Agamben, Giorgio. 1995. *Homo Sacer*. Turin: G. Einaudi.

———. 1998. *Quel che resta di Auschwitz: L'archivio e il testimone*. Turin: Bollati Boringhieri.

Ahmed, Sarah. 2004. *The Cultural Politics of Emotion*. Edinburgh: Edinburgh University Press.

Alcaro, Mario. 1999. *Sull'identità meridionale: Forme di una cultura Mediterranea*. Turin: Bollati Boringhieri.

Allen, Lori. 2008. "Getting by the Occupation: How Violence Became Normal during the Second Palestinian Intifada." *Cultural Anthropology* 23(3): 453–487.

———. 2013. *The Rise and Fall of Human Rights: Cynicism and Politics in Occupied Palestine*. Stanford, CA: Stanford University Press.

Al-Mohammad, Hayder. 2012. "A Kidnapping in Basra: The Struggles and Precariousness of Life in Postinvasion Iraq." *Cultural Anthropology* 27: 597–614.

Ambrosini, Maurizio. 2013. "Immigration in Italy: Between Economic Acceptance and Political Rejection." *Journal of International Migration and Integration* 14(1): 175–194.

Ammirati, Angela, Monia Andreani, Lucia Cardone, Denise Celentano, Loredana De Vitis, Alessandra Pigliaru, Ivana Pintadu, Doriana Righini, Federica Timeto, and Giovanna Vingelli. 2013. *Contro Versa*. Reggio Calabria, Italy: Sabbiarossa.

Anderson, Benedict R. O. 1991. *Imagined Communities: Reflections on the Origin and Spread of Nationalism*. London: Verso.

Andriolo, Karin. 2006. "The Twice-Killed: Imagining Protest Suicide." *American Anthropologist* 108(1): 100–113.

Angel-Ajani, Asale. 2000. "Italy's Racial Cauldron: Immigration, Criminalization and the Cultural Politics of Race." *Cultural Dynamics* 12: 331–352.

Apolito, Paolo. 2000. "Tarantismo, identità locale, postmanernità." In *Quarant' anni dopo De Martino: Atti del convegno internazionale di studi sul tarantismo*, edited by Gino L. Di Mitri, 137–146. Nardò, Italy: Besa.

———. 2007. "I Beni DEA e il 'fare' le tradizioni." *Antrolopogia Museale* 17: 12–17.

Arendt, Hannah. (1958) 1998. *The Human Condition*. Chicago: University of Chicago Press.

Aretxaga, Begona. 1997. *Shattering Silence: Women, Nationalism, and Political Subjectivity in Northern Ireland*. Princeton, NJ: Princeton University Press.

———. 2003. "Maddening States." *Annual Review of Anthropology* 32: 393–410.

Aretxaga, Begona, and Joseba Zulaika. 2005. *States of Terror: Begoña Aretxaga's Essays*. Reno: Center for Basque Studies, University of Nevada.

Arin, Canan. 2001. "Femicide in the Name of Honor in Turkey." *Violence against Women* 7(7): 821–825.

Asselin, Olivier, Johanne Lamoureux, and Christine Ross. 2008. *Precarious Visualities: New Perspectives on Identification in Contemporary Art and Visual Culture.* Montreal: McGill-Queen's University Press.

Austin, John L. 1962. *How to Do Things with Words.* Oxford: Clarendon.

Baba, Loredana. 2010. "Ernesto De Martino a European Perspective in Italy at the Mid of the XXth Century. (Essay)." *Studia Europaea* 55(1): 129.

Badii, Michela. 2012. *Processi di patrimonializzazione e politiche del cibo.* Segrate, Italy: Morlacchi.

Ballacchino, Katia. 2013. "Per un'antropologia del patrimonio immateriale. Dalle Convenzioni Unesco alle pratiche di comunità." *Glocale* 6–7: 17–22.

Bandelli, Daniela. 2017. *Femicide, Gender and Violence: Discourses and Counterdiscourses in Italy.* Cham, Switzerland: Palgrave Macmillan.

Bandelli, Daniela, and Giorgio Porcelli. 2016. "'Femminicidio' in Italy: A Critique of Feminist Gender Discourse and Constructivist Reading of the Human Identity." *Current Sociology* 64(7): 1071–1089.

Barberis, Eduardo, and Paolo Boccagni. 2014. "Blurred Rights, Local Practices: Social Work and Immigration in Italy." *British Journal of Social Work* 44(1): 70–87.

Barletta, Rosella. 1994. *Tabacco Tabaccari e Tabacchine nel Salento: Vicende storiche, economiche e sociali.* Fasano di Brindisi, Italy: Schena.

Bayefsky, Rachel. 2013. "Dignity, Honour, and Human Rights: Kant's Perspective." *Political Theory* 41(6): 809–837.

Bellassai, Sandro. 2005. "The Masculine Mystique: Antimodernism and Virility in Fascist Italy." *Journal of Modern Italian Studies* 10(3): 314–335.

Ben-Yehoyada, Naor. 2011. "The Moral Perils of Mediterraneanism: Second-Generation Immigrants Practicing Personhood between Sicily and Tunisia." *Journal of Modern Italian Studies* 16(3): 386–403.

Berger, John. 1972. *Ways of Seeing.* London: British Broadcasting.

Bertone, Chiara, and Raffaella Ferrero Camoletto. 2009. "Beyond the Sex Machine? Sexual Practices and Masculinity in Adult Men's Heterosexual Accounts." *Journal of Gender Studies* 18(4): 369–386.

Blackstone, Lee Robert. 2009. "The Spider Is Alive: Reassessing Becker's Theory of Artistic Conventions through Southern Italian Music." *Symbolic Interaction* 32(3): 184–206.

Bloch, Maurice. 1986. *From Blessing to Violence: History and Ideology in the Circumcision Ritual of the Merina of Madagascar.* Cambridge: Cambridge University Press.

———. 1992. *Prey into Hunter: The Politics of Religious Experience.* Cambridge: Cambridge University Press.

Blok, Anton. 1981. "Rams and Billy-goats: A Key to the Mediterranean Code of Honour." *Man* 16(3): 427–440.

———. 2001. *Honour and Violence.* Cambridge: Polity.

Boellstorff, Tom, Bonnie Nardi, Celia Pearce, and T. L. Taylor. 2012. *Ethnography and Virtual Worlds: A Handbook of Methods.* Princeton, NJ: Princeton University Press.

Bohrer, Ashley. 2015. "Fanon and Feminism: The Discourse of Colonization in Italian Feminism." *Interventions: International Journal of Postcolonial Studies* 17(3): 378–393.

Bonilla, Yarimar, and Jonathan Rosa. 2015. "#Ferguson: Digital Protest, Hashtag Ethnography, and the Racial Politics of Social Media in the United States." *American Ethnologist* 42(1): 4–17.

Bono, Paola, and Sandra Kemp. 1991. *Italian Feminist Thought: A Reader.* Oxford: B. Blackwell.

Bonomi Romagnoli, Barbara. 2014. *Irriverenti e libere: Femminismi nel nuovo millennio.* Rome: Riuniti.

Bosio, Gianni, and Clara Longhini. 2007. *1968 Una ricerca in Salento: suoni grida canti rumori Storie Immagini.* Calimera-Lecce, Italy: Kurumuni.

Bostrom, Nick. 2005. "In Defense of Post-human Dignity." *Bioethics* 19(3): 202–214.

Bourdieu, Pierre, and Loic Wacquant. 2004. "Symbolic Violence." In *Violence in War and Peace,* edited by Nancy Scheper-Hughes and Philippe Bourgois, 272–275. Malden, MA: Blackwell.

Bracke, Maud. 2013. "Between the Transnational and the Local: Mapping the Trajectories and Contexts of the Wages for Housework Campaign in 1970s Italian Feminism." *Women's History Review* 22(4): 625–642.

———. 2014. *Women and the Reinvention of the Political: Feminism in Italy, 1968–1983.* New York: Routledge.

Braidotti, Rosi. 1996. "Nomadism with a Difference: Deleuze's Legacy in a Feminist Perspective." *Man and World* 29: 305–314.

———. 2002. *Metamorphoses: Towards a Materialist Theory of Becoming.* Cambridge: Polity, in association with Blackwell.

———. 2003. "Becoming Women: Or Sexual Difference Revisited." *Theory, Culture and Society* 20(3): 43–64.

———. 2005. "A Critical Cartography of Feminist Post-postmodernism." *Australian Feminist Studies* 20(47): 169–180.

Brennan, Teresa. 2004. *The Transmission of Affect.* Ithaca, NY: Cornell University Press.

Burke, Carolyn. 1994. *Engaging with Irigaray.* New York: Columbia University Press.

Busatta, Sandra. 2006. "Honour and Shame in the Mediterranean." *Anthrocom* 2(2): 75–78.

Butler, Judith. 1997. *Excitable Speech: A Politics of the Performative.* New York: Routledge.

———. 2004. *Precarious Life: The Powers of Mourning and Violence.* London: Verso.

———. (1990) 2006. *Gender Trouble.* New York: Routledge.

———. 2012. "Bodies in Alliance and the Politics of the Street." In *Sensible Politics: The Visual Culture of Nongovernmental Activism,* edited by Meg McLagan and Yates McKee, 117–138. New York: Zone Books.

———. (1993) 2014. *Bodies That Matter: On the Discursive Limits of "Sex."* New York: Routledge.

———. 2015. *Senses of the Subject.* New York: Fordham University Press.

Campbell, John Kennedy. 1964. *Honour, Family, and Patronage. A Study of Institutions and Moral Values in a Greek Mountain Community.* Oxford: Clarendon.

Cancellieri, Adriano, and Elena Ostanel. 2015. "The Struggle for Public Space." *City* 19(4): 499–509.

Capussotti, Enrica. 2010. "Nordisti contro Sudisti: Internal Migration and Racism in Turin, Italy: 1950s–1960s." *Italian Culture* 27(2): 121–138.

Carone, Milena A. 2011. *A Carte Scoperte.* Rome: O.GRA.RO.

Carr, Summerson. 2009. "Anticipating and Inhabiting Institutional Identities." *American Ethnologist* 36(2): 317–336.

Cassano, Franco. 1996. *Pensiero meridiano.* Rome: Laterza.

Castelli, Federica. 2013. "Questo corpo è politica. Toccarsi, scontrarsi, creare, occupare: La piazza come luogo di radicalità." *DWF* 97(1).

Cataldi, Suzanne L. 2002. "Animals and the Concept of Dignity: Critical Reflections on a Circus Performance." *Ethics and the Environment* 7(2): 104–126.

Cavarero, Adriana. 1987. *Diotima: Il pensiero della differenza sessuale*. Milan: La Tartaruga.

———. 2007. *Orrorismo, ovvero della violenza sull'inerme*. Milan: Feltrinelli.

Cavell, Stanley, and Russell B. Goodman. 2005. *Contending with Stanley Cavell*. New York: Oxford University Press.

Ciciliot, Valentina. 2010. "Le beatificazioni e le canonizzazioni di Giovanni Paolo II come strumenti di governo della Chiesa." *Humanitas* 65(1): 118–142.

Cicioni, Mirna. 1989. "'Love and Respect, Together': The Theory and Practice of Affidamento in Italian Feminism." *Australian Feminist Studies* 4(10): 71–83.

Clough, Patricia T., and Jean O'Malley Halley, eds. 2007. *The Affective Turn: Theorizing the Social*. Durham, NC: Duke University Press. Kindle Edition.

Codacci-Pisanelli, Carlo. 2009. *Streghe. Macàre, maghi e guaritori del Salento*. Tricase, Italy: Libellula.

Cody, Francis. 2011. "Publics and Politics." *Annual Review of Anthropology* 40: 37–52.

Coetzee, J. M. 2003. *Elizabeth Costello: Eight Lessons*. London: Secker & Warburg.

Cole, Alyson M. 1999. "'There Are No Victims in This Class': On Female Suffering and Anti-'Victim Feminism.'" *NWSA Journal* 11(1): 72–96.

Collins, Diana. 2012. "Performing Location and Dignity in a Transnational Feminist and Queer Study of Manila's Gay Life." *Feminist Formations* 24(1): 49–72.

Coronil, Fernando, and Julie Skurski, eds. 2006. *States of Violence*. Ann Arbor: University of Michigan Press.

Costa, Diana. 2011. "I Passiuna tu Christù—Rito e teatro di una cantica popolare della Grecìa Salentina." *Antropologia e teatro* 2: 140–169.

Costa, Elisabetta. 2016. *Social Media in Southeast Turkey: Love, Kinship and Politics*. London: UCL Press.

———. 2018. "Affordances-in-Practice: An Ethnographic Critique of Social Media Logic and Context Collapse." *New Media and Society* 20(10): 3641–3656.

Coundouriotis, Eleni. 2006. "The Dignity of the 'Unfittest:' Victims's Stories in South Africa." *Human Rights Quarterly* 28(4): 842–867.

Cozzi, Leslie. 2011. "Spaces of Self-consciousness: Carla Accardi's Environments and the Rise of Italian Feminism." *Women and Performance: A Journal of Feminist Theory* 21(1): 67–88.

Crossley, Nick. 1995. "Body Techniques, Agency, and Intercorporeality: On Goffman's Relations in Public." *Sociology* 29(1): 133–149.

Crowhurst, Isabel, and Chiara Bertone. 2012. "Introduction: The Politics of Sexuality in Contemporary Italy." *Modern Italy* 17(4): 413–418.

Csordas, Thomas J. 2008. "Intersubjectivity and Intercorporeality." *Subjectivity* 22(1): 110–120.

Cvetkovich, Ann. 1992. *Mixed Feelings: Feminism, Mass Culture, and Victorian Sensationalism*. New Brunswick, NJ: Rutgers University Press.

———. 2007. "Public Feelings." *South Atlantic Quarterly* 106(3): 459–468.

———. 2010. Introduction. In *Political Emotions*, edited by Janet Staiger, Ann Cvetkovich, and Ann Reynolds, 1–17. New York: Routledge.

Daboo, Jerri. 2010. *Ritual, Rapture and Remorse: A Study of Tarantism and Pizzica in Salento*. Bern: Peter Lang.

Dalla Torre, Elena. 2014. "The Clitoris Diaries: La Donna Clitoridea, Feminine Authenticity, and the Phallic Allegory of Carla Lonzi's Radical Feminism." *European Journal of Women's Studies* 21(3): 219–232.

Dandini, Serena, and Maura Misiti. 2013. *Ferite a Morte*. Milan: Rizzoli.

D'Arcais, Paolo Flores. 2011. "Berlusconismo." *New Left Review* 68: 121–140.

Das, Veena, ed. 1990. *Mirrors of Violence: Communities, Riots, and Survivors in South Asia*. Delhi: Oxford University Press.

———. 2007. *Life and Words Violence and the Descent into the Ordinary*. Berkeley: University of California Press.

———. 2008. "Violence, Gender, and Subjectivity." *Annual Review of Anthropology* 37: 283–299.

Das, Veena, Arthur Kleinman, and Margaret Lock, eds. 1997. *Social Suffering*. Berkeley: University of California Press.

Das, Veena, Arthur Kleinman, Mamphela Ramphele, and Pamela Reynolds, eds. 2000. *Violence and Subjectivity*. Berkeley: University of California Press.

———. 2001. *Remaking a World: Violence, Social Suffering, and Recovery*. Berkeley: University of California Press.

Dave, Naisargi. 2010a. "Between Queer Ethics and Sexual Morality." In *Ordinary Ethics*, edited by Michael Lambek, 368–375. New York: Fordham University Press.

———. 2010b. "To Render Real the Imagined: An Ethnographic History of Lesbian Community in India." *Signs* 35(3): 595–619.

———. 2011. "Indian and Lesbian and What Came Next: Affect, Commensuration, and Queer Emergences." *American Ethnologist* 38(4): 650–665.

———. 2012. *Queer Activism in India: A Story in the Anthropology of Ethics*. Durham, NC: Duke University Press.

———. 2014. "Witness: Humans, Animals, and the Politics of Becoming." *Cultural Anthropology* 29(3): 433–456.

Debes, Remy. 2009. "Dignity's Gauntlet." *Philosophical Perspectives* 23: 45–78.

De Giorgi, Pierpaolo. 1999. *Tarantismo e rinascita: I riti musicali e coreutici della pizzica-pizzica e della tarantella*. Lecce, Italy: Argo.

———. 2008. *Il mito del tarantismo: dalla terra del rimorso alla terra della rinascita*. Galatina, Italy: Congedo.

Dei, Fabio. 2011. "Pop-politica: Le basi culturali del Berlusconismo." *Studi Culturali* 3: 471–490.

De Lame, Danielle. 2005. "Re-Imagining Rwanda: Conflict, Survival and Disinformation in the Late Twentieth Century." *American Anthropologist* 107(1): 161–162.

De Lauretis, Teresa. 1990. "Feminism and Its Differences." *Pacific Coast Philology* 25(1–2): 24–30.

———. 1999. *Soggetti Eccentrici*. Milan: Feltrinelli.

Del Giudice, Luisa. 2005. "The Folk Music Revival and the Culture of Tarantismo in the Salento." In *Performing Ecstasies: Music, Dance, and Ritual in the Mediterranean*, edited by Luisa del Giudice and Nancy E. Van Deusen, 217–272. Ottawa: Institute of Mediaeval Music.

Dell'Abate-Çelebi, Barbara. 2016. "The Challenge of the Thought of Sexual Difference within Gender Mainstreaming." *Beykent Üniversitesi Sosyal Bilimler Dergisi* 9(1): 61–71.

Del Negro, Giovanna. 2004. *The Passeggiata and Popular Culture in an Italian Town: Folklore and the Performance of Modernity*. Montreal: McGill-Queen's University Press.

Del Negro, Giovanna, and M. Harris Berger. 2001. "Character Divination and Kinetic Sculpture in the Central Italian Passeggiata (Ritual Promenade): Interpretive Frameworks and Expressive Practices from a Body-Centered Perspective." *Journal of American Folklore* 114(451): 5–19.

De Luna, Giovanni. 2011. *La Repubblica del dolore: Le memorie di un'Italia divisa*. Milan: Feltrinelli.

de Martino, Ernesto. (1958) 1975. *Morte e pianto rituale: Dal lamento funebre antico al pianto di Maria*. Milan: Feltrinelli.

———. (1961) 1976. *La terra del rimorso: Contributo a una storia religiosa del Sud*. Milan: Il Saggiatore.

———. (1959) 1980. *Sud e Magia*. Milan: Feltrinelli.

———. (1948) 1981. *Il mondo magico: Prolegomeni a una storia del magismo*. Turin: Bollati Boringhieri.

De Sousa, Ronald. 2001. "Moral Emotions." *Ethical Theory and Moral Practice* 4(2): 109–126.

Dicker, Rory C. 2003. *Catching a Wave: Reclaiming Feminism for the 21st Century*. Boston: Northeastern University Press.

Di Nola, Annalisa. 1998. "How Critical Was De Martino's 'Critical Ethnocentrism' in Southern Italy?" In *Italy's 'Southern Question': Orientalism in One Country*, edited by Jane Schneider, 157–176. Oxford: Berg.

Diotallevi, Luca. 1999. "The Territorial Articulation of Secularization in Italy: Social Modernization, Religious Modernization." *Archives des Sciences Sociales des Religions* 107: 77–108.

Domínguez Ruvalcaba, Héctor, and Ignacio Corona. 2010. *Gender Violence at the U.S.–Mexico Border: Media Representation and Public Response*. Tucson: University of Arizona Press.

Dominijanni, Ida. 2005. "Rethinking Change: Italian Feminism between Crisis and Critique of Politics." *Cultural Studies Review* 11(2): 25–35.

Dubisch, Jill. 1995. *In a Different Place*. Princeton, NJ: Princeton University Press.

Dufrenne, Mikel. 1973. *The Phenomenology of Aesthetic Experience*. Evanston: Northwestern University Press.

Edwards, Elizabeth. 2012. "Objects of Affect: Photography beyond the Image." *Annual Review of Anthropology* 41: 221–234.

El-Kholy, Heba Aziz. 2002. *Defiance and Compliance: Negotiating Gender in Low-Income Cairo*. New York: Berghahn Books.

Eltringham, Nigel. 2004. *Accounting for Horror: Post-genocide Debates in Rwanda*. London: Pluto.

Evans-Pritchard, Edward E. (1937) 1965. *Witchcraft, Oracles and Magic among the Azande*. Oxford: Clarendon.

Faeta, Francesco. 2011. *Le ragioni dello sguardo: pratiche dell'osservazione, della rappresentazione, e della memoria*. Turin: Bollati Boringhieri.

Faggioli, Massimo. 2012. "The New Elites of Italian Catholicism: 1968 and the New Catholic Movements." *Catholic Historical Review* 98(1): 18–40.

Fantoni, Laura. 2007. "Precarious Changes: Gender and Generational Politics in Contemporary Italy Sources." *Feminist Review* 87: 5–20.

Farmer, Paul. 2003. *Pathologies of Power: Health, Human Rights, and the New War on the Poor*. Berkeley: University of California Press.

Farmer, Paul, and Haun Saussy. 2010. *Partner to the Poor: A Paul Farmer Reader*. Berkeley: University of California Press.

Fassin, Didier. 2008. "The Humanitarian Politics of Testimony: Subjectification through Trauma in the Israeli-Palestinian Conflict." *Cultural Anthropology* 23(3): 531–558.

Fassin, Didier, and Richard Rechtman. 2009. *The Empire of Trauma*. Princeton, NJ: Princeton University Press.

Faubion, James D. 2001. "Toward an Anthropology of Ethics: Foucault and the Pedagogies of Autopoiesis." *Representations* 74(1): 83–104.

———. 2011. *An Anthropology of Ethics*. Cambridge: Cambridge University Press.

Faulkner, Ellen, and Gayle Michelle MacDonald. 2009. *Victim No More: Women's Resistance to Law, Culture and Power*. Halifax: Fernwood.

Favret-Saada, Jeanne. 1981. *Deadly Words: Witchcraft in the Bocage*. Cambridge: Cambridge University Press.

Federici, Silvia. 2004. *Caliban and the Witch*. New York: Autonomedia.

———. 2008. "Witch-Hunting, Globalization, and Feminist Solidarity in Africa Today." http://www.commoner.org.uk/?p=60 (accessed March 21, 2019).

Feldman, Allen. 1991. *Formations of Violence the Narrative of the Body and Political Terror in Northern Ireland*. Chicago: University of Chicago Press.

Felman, Shoshana, and Dori Laub. 1992. *Testimony: Crises of Witnessing in Literature, Psychoanalysis, and History*. New York: Routledge.

Ferrari, Fabrizio M. 2012. *Ernesto de Martino on Religion*. Sheffield: Equinox.

Ferrero Camoletto, Raffaella, and Chiara Bertone. 2010. "Coming to Be a Man: Pleasure in the Construction of Italian Men's (Hetero)Sexuality." *Italian Studies* 65(2): 235–250.

———. 2012. "Italians (Should) Do It Better? Medicalisation and the Disempowering of Intimacy." *Modern Italy* 17(4): 433–448.

Fleetwood, Nicole R. 2011. *Troubling Vision: Performance, Visuality, and Blackness*. Chicago: University of Chicago Press.

Foucault, Michel. 1997. "The Ethics of the Care of the Self as a Practice of Freedom." In *Essential Works of Michel Foucault, Volume I: Ethics, Subjectivity, and Truth*, edited by Paul Rabinow, 281–301. New York: New Press.

———. 2005. *The Hermeneutics of the Subject: Lectures at the College de France, 1981–1982*. New York: Picador.

———. (1972) 2010. *The Archeology of Knowledge and the Discourse on Language*. New York: Pantheon Books.

Foucault, Michel. 1997. *Ethics: Subjectivity and Truth*. Edited by Paul Rabinow. New York: New Press.

Fregoso, Rosa Linda, and Cynthia L. Bejarano, eds. 2010. *Terrorizing Women: Feminicide in the Américas*. Durham, NC: Duke University Press.

Funahashi, Daena Aki. 2013. "Wrapped in Plastic: Transformation and Alienation in the New Finnish Economy." *Cultural Anthropology* 28(1): 1–21.

Gallini, Clara, and Marcello Massenzio. 1997. *Ernesto De Martino Nella Cultura Europea*. Naples: Liguori.

Galt, Anthony. 1985. "Does the Mediterranean Dilemma Have Straw Horns?" *American Ethnologist* 12(2): 369–371.

Gamberi, Cristina. 2015. "L'alfabeto della violenza. Lo spettacolo Doppio Taglio e le rappresentazioni del femminicidio nei media italiani." *Gender/Sexuality/Italy* 2: 149–165.

Garelli, Franco. 2007a. "The Church and Catholicism in Contemporary Italy." *Journal of Modern Italian Studies* 12(1): 2–7.

———. 2007b. "The Public Relevance of the Church and Catholicism in Italy." *Journal of Modern Italian Studies* 12(1): 8–36.

———. 2013. "Flexible Catholicism, Religion and the Church: The Italian Case." *Religions* 4: 1–13.

Gaspar de Alba, Alicia, and Georgina Guzmán. 2010. *Making a Killing: Femicide, Free Trade, and La Frontera*. Austin: University of Texas Press.

Gershon, Ilana. 2011. "Un-Friend My Heart: Facebook, Promiscuity, and Heartbreak in a Neoliberal Age." *Anthropological Quarterly* 84(4): 865–894.

Giardini, Federica. 2011. *Sensibili guerriere: Sulla forza femminile*. Rome: Iacobelli.

Gilmore, David D., ed. 1987. *Honor and Shame and the Unity of the Mediterranean*. Washington, DC: American Anthropological Association.

———. 1990. "Men and Women in Southern Spain—Domestic Power Revisited." *American Anthropologist* 92(4): 953–970.

Ginsborg, Paul. 2004. *Silvio Berlusconi: Television, Power and Patrimony*. London: Verso.

Ginsborg, Paul, and Enrica Asquer. 2011. *Berlusconismo: Analisi di un sistema di potere*. Rome: Laterza.

Giordano, Cristiana. 2005. "The Past in the Present: Actualized History in the Social Construction of the Present." In *Critical Junctions: Anthropology and History beyond the Cultural Turn*, edited by D. Kalb and H. Tak, 53–71. Oxford: Berghahn.

———. 2014. *Migrants in Translation: Caring and the Logics of Difference in Contemporary Italy*. Berkeley: University of California Press.

Gluckman, Max. 1955. *Custom and Conflict in Africa*. Oxford: Blackwell.

Goddard, Victoria. 1986. "Honour and Shame: The Control of Women's Sexuality and Group Identity in Naples." In *The Cultural Construction of Sexuality*, edited by Pat Caplan, 166–192. London: Routledge.

———. 1994. "From the Mediterranean to Europe: Honour, Kinship and Gender." In *The Anthropology of Europe*, edited by Victoria Goddard, Joseph R. Llobera, and Chris Shore, 57–91. Oxford: Bloomsbury Academic.

Gorton, Kristyn. 2007. "Theorizing Emotions and Affects: Feminist Engagements." *Feminist Theory* 8(3): 333–348.

Gould, Deborah. 2010. "On Affect and Protest." In *Political Emotions*, edited by Janet Staiger, Ann Cvetkovich, and Ann Reynolds, 18–39. New York: Routledge.

Grasseni, Cristina. 2007. *Skilled Visions: Between Apprenticeship and Standards*. New York: Berghahn Books.

———. 2011. "Skilled Visions: Toward and Ecology of Visual Inscriptions." In *Made to Be Seen: Perspectives on the History of Visual Anthropology*, edited by Marcus Banks and Jay Ruby, 19–43. Chicago: University of Chicago Press.

Gregg, Melissa, and Gregory J. Seigworth. 2010. *The Affect Theory Reader*. Durham, NC: Duke University Press.

Gribaldo, Alessandra. 2014. "The Paradoxical Victim: Intimate Violence Narratives on Trial in Italy." *American Ethnologist* 41(4): 743–756.

Gribaldo, Alessandra, and Giovanna Zapperi. 2010. "Che cosa vogliono quelle immagini da me? Genere, desiderio eiImmaginario nell'Italia berlusconiana." *Studi Culturali* 1: 71–78.

———. 2012. *Lo schermo del potere: Femminismo e regime della visibilità*. Verona, Italy: Ombre Corte.

Grossman, David. (2003) 2009. *Col Corpo Capisco*. Milan: Mondadori.

Guano, Emanuela. 2007. "Respectable Ladies and Uncouth Men: The Performative Politics of Class and Gender in the Public Realm of an Italian City." *Journal of American Folklore* 120(475): 48–72.

Halperin, David. 1995. *Saint Foucault: Towards a Gay Hagiography*. New York: Oxford University Press.

Harding, Susan. 1987. "Convicted by the Holy Spirit: The Rhetoric of Fundamental Baptist Conversion." *American Ethnologist* 14(1): 167–181.

Harper, Douglas. 2002. "Talking about Pictures: A Case for Photo Elicitation." *Visual Studies* 17: 13–26.

Hartman, Saidiya V. 1997. *Scenes of Subjection: Terror, Slavery, and Self-making in Nineteenth-Century America*. New York: Oxford University Press.

Hajek, Andrea. 2018. *"Je ne suis pas Catherine Deneuve*. Reflections on contemporary debates about sexual self-determination in Italy." *Modern Italy*, 23(2): 139–143.

Hermez, Sami. 2011. "On Dignity and Clientelism: Lebanon in the Context of the 2011 Arab Revolution." *Studies in Ethnicity and Nationalism* 11(3): 527–538.

———. 2012. "The War Is Going to Ignite: On the Anticipation of Violence in Lebanon." *PoLAR* 35(2): 327–344.

Herzfeld, Michael. 1980. "Honour and Shame: Problems in the Comparative Analysis of Moral Systems." *Man* 15(2): 339–351.

———. 1985. *The Poetics of Manhood: Contest and Identity in a Cretan Mountain Village*. Princeton, NJ: Princeton University Press.

———. 1998. "Factual Fissures: Claims and Contexts." *Annals of the American Academy of Political and Social Sciences* 560(1): 69–82.

———. 2004. *The Body Impolitic: Artisans and Artifice in the Global Hierarchy of Value*. Chicago: University of Chicago Press.

———. (1997) 2005a. *Cultural Intimacy: Social Poetics in the Nation-State*. New York: Routledge.

———. 2005b. "Practical Mediterraneanism: Excuses for Everything, from Epistemology to Eating." In *Rethinking the Mediterranean*, edited by William V. Harris, 45–63. Oxford: Oxford University Press.

———. 2008. "Mere Symbols." *Anthropologica* 50: 141–155.

———. 2011. "Ethical and Epistemic Reflections on/of Anthropological Vision." In *Made to Be Seen*, edited by Marcus Banks and Jay Ruby, 313–333. Chicago: Chicago University Press.

Hinderliter, Beth, William Kaizen, Vered Maimon, Jaleh Mansoor, and Seth McCormick, eds. 2009. *Communities of Sense: Rethinking Aesthetics and Politics*. Durham, NC: Duke University Press.

Hinton, Alexander Laban. 1998. "Head for an Eye: Revenge in the Cambodian Genocide." *American Ethnologist* 25(3): 352–377.

———. 2012. "Violence." In *A Companion to Moral Anthropology*, edited by Didier Fassin, 500–517. Chichester, West Sussex, UK: Wiley-Blackwell.

Hinton, Alexander Laban, and Kevin Lewis O'Neill. 2009. *Genocide: Truth, Memory, and Representation*. Durham, NC: Duke University Press.

Hipkins, Danielle. 2011. "'Whore-ocracy': Show Girls, the Beauty Trade-Off, and Mainstream Oppositional Discourse in Contemporary Italy." *Italian Studies* 66(3): 413–430.

Hobson, Barbara, ed. 2003. *Recognition Struggles and Social Movements: Contested Identities, Agency and Power*. New York: Cambridge University Press.

hooks, bell. 1986. "Sisterhood: Political Solidarity between Women." *Feminist Review* 23: 125–138.

Iacona, Riccardo, and Sabrina Carreras. 2012. *Se Questi Sono Gli Uomini*. Milan: Chiarelettere.

Ibrahim, Awad. 2014. *The Rhizome of Blackness: A Critical Ethnography of Hip-Hop Culture, Language, Identity and the Politics of Becoming*. New York: Peter Lang.

Ince, Jelani, Fabio Rojas, and Clayton A. Davis. 2017. "The Social Media Response to Black Lives Matter: How Twitter Users Interact with Black Lives Matter through Hashtag Use." *Ethnic and Racial Studies* 40(11): 1814–1830.

Inserra, Incoronata Nadia. 2017. *Global Tarantella: Reinventing Southern Italian Folk Music and Dances.* Urbana: University of Illinois Press.

Irigaray, Luce. 1985a. *Speculum of the Other Woman.* Ithaca, NY: Cornell University Press.

———. 1985b. *This Sex which Is Not One.* Ithaca, NY: Cornell University Press.

Jeffreys, Sheila. 1997. "Transgender Activism: A Lesbian Feminist Perspective." *Journal of Lesbian Studies* 1(3–4): 55–74.

Jeganathan, Pradeep Krishnakumar. 1997. "After a Riot: Anthropological Locations of Violence in an Urban Sri Lankan Community." PhD diss., University of Chicago.

Kapchan, Deborah A. 2008. "The Promise of Sonic Translation: Performing the Festive Sacred in Morocco." *American Anthropologist* 110(4): 467–483.

Kapur, Ratna. 2002. "The Tragedy of Victimization Rhetoric: Resurrecting the 'Native' Subject in International/Post-Colonial Feminist Legal Politics." *Harvard Human Rights Journal* 15(1): 1–48.

Kaufman, Whitley. 2011. "Understanding Honor: Beyond the Shame/Guilt Dichotomy." *Social Theory and Practice* 37(4): 557–574.

Keane, Webb. 1997. *Signs of Recognition: Powers and Hazards of Representation in an Indonesian Society.* Berkeley: University of California Press.

King, Russell, and Nicola Mai. 2004. "Albanian Immigrants in Lecce and Modena: Narratives of Rejection, Survival and Integration." *Population, Space, and Place* 10: 455–477.

Kirtsoglou, Elisabeth. 2004. *For the Love of Women. Gender, Identity and Same-Sex Relations in a Greek Provincial Town.* New York: Routledge.

Kolankiewicz, Leszek. 2008. "Towards an Anthropology of Performance(s)." *Performance Research* 13(2): 8–24.

Korom, Frank J. 2013. *The Anthropology of Performance: A Reader.* Chichester, West Sussex, UK: Wiley-Blackwell.

Koyama, Emi. 2003 "Transfeminist Manifesto." In *Catching a Wave: Reclaiming Feminism for the 21st Century,* edited by Rory C. Dicker and Alison Piepmeier, 244–259. Boston: Northeastern University Press.

Kral, Françoise. 2014. *Social Invisibility and Diasporas in Anglophone Literature and Culture: The Fractal Gaze.* Houndmills, Basingstoke, Hampshire, UK: Palgrave Macmillan.

Kratz, Corinne Ann. 1994. *Affecting Performance: Meaning, Movement, and Experience in Okiek Women's Initiation.* Washington, DC: Smithsonian Institution.

———. 2011. "Rhetorics of Value: Constituting Worth and Meaning through Cultural Display." *Visual Anthropology Review* 27(1): 21–48.

Laidlaw, James 2002. "For an Anthropology of Ethics and Freedom." *Journal of the Royal Anthropological Institute* 8(2): 311–332.

Lambek, Michael. 2000a. "Nuriaty, the Saint and the Sultan: Virtuous Subject and Subjective Virtuoso of the Post-Modern Colony." *Anthropology Today* 16(2): 7–12.

———. 2000b. "Between Poetry and Philosophy." *Current Anthropology* 41(3): 133–157.

———. 2007. "Sacrifice and the Problem of Beginning: Meditations from Sakalava Mythopraxis." *Journal of the Royal Anthropological Institute* 13(1): 19–38.

———, ed. 2010. *Ordinary Ethics.* New York: Fordham University Press.

———. 2014. "The Interpretation of Lives or Life as Interpretation: Cohabiting with Spirits in the Malagasy World." *American Ethnologist* 41(3): 491–503.

Landes, Joan B. 1998. *Feminism, the Public and the Private*. Oxford: Oxford University Press.

Lanternari, Vittorio. 1995. "Tarantismo: Dal medico neopositivista all'antropologo, alla etnopsichiatria di oggi." *Storia, antropologia, e scienze del linguaggio* 3: 67–92.

———. 1997. *La mia alleanza con Ernesto de Martino e altri saggi post-demartiniani*. Naples: Liguori.

———. 2000. "Tarantismo: Vecchie teorie, saperi nuovi." In *Quarant'anni dopo De Martino*, edited by Gino Di Mitri, 119–134. Nardò, Italy: Besa.

Lapassade, Georges. 1994. *Intervista sul tarantismo*. Maglie, Italy: Madona Oriente.

La Vaque-Manty, Mika. 2006. "Dueling for Equality: Masculine Honor and the Modern Politics of Dignity." *Political Theory* 34(6): 715–740.

Laviosa, Flavia. 2010. "The Frontier Apulia and Its Filmmakers after 1989." *California Italian Studies Journal* 1(1): 1–9.

———. 2011. "Tarantula Myths and Music: Popular Culture and Ancient Rituals in Italian Cinema." In *Popular Italian Cinema: Culture and Politics in a Postwar Society*, edited by Flavia Brizio-Skov, 153–188. London: I. B. Tauris.

———. 2015. "Killing in the Name of Love. Violence against Women in Italy." *JOMEC Journal* 8: 1–14.

Lever, Alison. 1986. "Honour as a Red Herring." *Critique of Anthropology* 6(3): 83–106.

Linke, Gabriele. 2011. "The Public, the Private, and the Intimate. Richard Sennett's and Laurel Berlant's Cultural Criticism in Dialogue." *Biography* 34(1): 11–24.

Linke, Uli. 2006. "Contact Zones. Rethinking the Sensual Life of the State." *Anthropological Theory* 6(2): 205–225.

Lipperini, Loredana, and Michela Murgia. 2013. *L'ho Uccisa Perchè L'amavo (falso!)*. Rome: Laterza.

Livingstone, Sonia. 2005. "On the Relation between Audiences and Publics." In *Audiences and Publics: When Cultural Engagement Matters for the Public Sphere*, edited by Sonia Livingstone, 17–41. Bristol, UK: Intellect Books.

Lonzi, Carla. 1974. *Sputiamo su Hegel: La Donna Clitoridea e la Donna Vaginale*. Milan: Rivolta Femminile.

Lowell Lewis, John. 2013. *The Anthropology of Cultural Performance*. New York: Palgrave Macmillan.

Lüdtke, Karen. 2008. *Dances with Spiders: Crisis, Celebrity and Celebration in Southern Italy*. New York: Berghahn Books.

Lumley, Robert, and Jonathan Morris. 1997. *The New History of the Italian South: The Mezzogiorno Revisited*. Devon, UK: University of Exeter Press.

Mackenzie, C. 2014. *Vulnerability: New Essays in Ethics and Feminist Philosophy*, Studies in Feminist Philosophy. New York: Oxford University Press.

Magaraggia, Sveva, and Mariagrazia Leone. 2010. "Gender and Women's Studies in Italy: Looking Back to Look Forward." *European Journal of Women's Studies* 17(4): 425–429.

Mahmood, Saba. 2001a. "Feminist Theory, Embodiment, and the Docile Agent: Some Reflections on the Egyptian Islamic Revival." *Cultural Anthropology* 16(2): 202–236.

———. 2001b. "Rehearsed Spontaneity and the Conventionality of Ritual: Disciplines of 'Salat.'" *American Ethnologist* 28(4): 827–853.

———. 2005. *Politics of Piety: The Islamic Revival and the Feminist Subject*. Princeton, NJ: Princeton University Press.

Malagreca, Miguel. 2006. "Lottiamo Ancora: Reviewing One Hundred and Fifty Years of Italian Feminism." *Journal of International Women's Studies* 7(4): 69–89.

Mankekar, Purnima. 1999. *Screening Culture, Viewing Politics: An Ethnography of Television, Womanhood, and Nation in Postcolonial India.* Durham, NC: Duke University Press.

Marinaro, Isabella. 2003. "Integration or Marginalization? The Failures of Social Policy for the Roma in Rome." *Modern Italy* 8(2): 203–218.

Massenzio, Marcello. 2005. "The Italian School of 'History of Religions.'" *Religion* 35(4): 209–222.

Massumi, Brian. 2002. "The Autonomy of Affect." In *Parables for the Virtual: Movement, Affect, Sensation*, edited by Brian Massumi, 23–45. Durham, NC: Duke University Press.

———. 2015. *Politics of Affect.* Cambridge: Polity.

Mazzarella, William. 2003. *Shoveling Smoke: Advertising and Globalization in Contemporary India.* Durham, NC: Duke University Press.

———. 2004. "Culture, Globalization, Mediation." *Annual Review of Anthropology* 33: 345–367.

———. 2009. "Affect: What Is It Good For?" In *Enchantments of Modernity: Empire, Nation, Globalization*, edited by Saurabh Dube, 291–309. New Delhi: Routledge.

McLagan, Meg. 2012. "Imagining Impact: Documentary Film and the Production of Political Effects." In *Sensible Politics: The Visual Culture of Nongovernmental Activism*, edited by Meg McLagan and Yates McKee, 305–319. New York: Zone Books.

McLagan, Meg, and Yates McKee. 2012. *Sensible Politics: The Visual Culture of Nongovernmental Activism.* New York: Zone Books.

McLeer, Anne. 1998. "Saving the Victim: Recuperating the Language of the Victim and Reassessing Global Feminism." *Hypatia* 13(Winter): 41–55.

McNay, Lois. 1992. *Foucault and Feminism: Power, Gender and Self.* Cambridge: Polity.

Meyer, Michael. 2001. "The Simple Dignity of Sentient Life: Speciesism and Human Dignity." *Journal of Social Philosophy* 32(2): 115–126.

Michetti, Maria, Margherita Repetto, and Luciana Viviani. 1998 [1985]. *Udi: Un laboratorio di politica delle donne—Idee e materiali per una storia.* Rome: Rubettino.

Milan Women's Bookstore Collective. 1990. *Sexual Difference: A Theory of Social-Symbolic Practice.* Bloomington: Indiana University Press.

Miller, David. 2011. *Tales from Facebook.* Cambridge: Polity.

Mina, Gabriele, and Sergio Torsello. 2006. *La Tela Infinita.Bibliografia degli Studi sul Trantismo Mediterraneo 1945–2006.* Nardò, Italy: Besa.

Minghelli, Giuliana. 2016. "Icons of Remorse: Photography, Anthropology and the Erasure of History in 1950s Italy." *Modern Italy* 21(4): 383–407.

Mingozzi, Gianfranco, dir. 1961. *La taranta.* Documentary film. 19 min., 16 mm. Produced by Franco Finzi de Barbora.

Mirzoeff, Nicholas. 2006. "On Visuality." *Journal of Visual Culture* 5(1): 53–79.

———. 2014. *How to See the World.* Basic Books.

Molé, Noelle J. 2008. "Living It on the Skin: Italian States, Working Illness." *American Ethnologist* 35(2): 189–210.

———. 2010. "Precarious Subjects: Anticipating Neoliberalism in Northern Italy's Workplace." *American Anthropologist* 112(1): 38–53.

———. 2012. *Labor Disorders in Neoliberal Italy: Mobbing, Well-Being, and the Workplace.* Bloomington: Indiana University Press.

———. 2013a. "Existential Damages: The Injury of Precarity Goes to Court." *Cultural Anthropology* 28(1): 22–43.

———. 2013b. "Trusted Puppets, Tarnished Politicians: Humor and Cynicism in Berlusconi's Italy." *American Ethnologist* 40(2): 288–299.

Morgan, Karen, and Suruchi Thapar Bjorkert. 2006. "'I'd Rather You'd Lay Me on the Floor and Start Kicking Me': Understanding Symbolic Violence in Everyday Life." *Women's Studies International Forum* 29: 441–452.

Morris, Penelope. 2006. *Women in Italy, 1945–1960: An Interdisciplinary Study*. Italian and Italian American Studies. New York: Palgrave Macmillan.

Mowatt, Rasul, Bryana French, and Dominique Malebranche. 2013. "Black/Female/Body Hypervisibility and Invisibility: A Black Feminist Augmentation of Feminist Leisure Research." *Journal of Leisure Research* 45(5): 644–660.

Muehlebach, Andrea. 2009. "Complexio Oppositorum: Notes on the Left in Neoliberal Italy." *Public Culture* 21(3): 495–515.

———. 2011. "On Affective Labor in Post-Fordist Italy." *Cultural Anthropology* 26(1): 59–82.

———. 2012. *The Moral Neoliberal: Welfare and Citizenship in Italy*. Chicago: University of Chicago Press.

———. 2013. "The Catholicization of Neoliberalism: On Love and Welfare in Lombardy, Italy." *American Anthropologist* 115(3): 452–465.

Munday, Ian. 2009. "Passionate Utterance and Moral Education." *Journal of Philosophy of Education* 43(1): 57–74.

———. 2010. "Improvisation in the Disorders of Desire: Performativity, Passion and Moral Education." *Ethics and Education* 5(3): 281–297.

Muñoz, José Esteban. 2000. "Feeling Brown: Ethnicity and Affect in Ricardo Bracho's 'The Sweetest Hangover (and Other STDs).'" *Theatre Journal* 52(1): 67–79.

Muraro, Luisa. 1988. *Il concetto di genealogia femminile*. Rome: Centro Culturale Virginia Woolf.

———. 1991. *L'Ordine Simbolico Della Madre*. Rome: Riuniti.

———. 1994. "Aurtoridad sin Monumentos." *Duoda: Revista d'Estudis Feministes* 7: 86–100.

———. 2012. *L'Autorità*. Turin: Gemme.

Murgia, Michela. 2011. *Ave Mary: E la Chiesa inventò la donna*. Turin: Einaudi.

Nacci, Anna. 2001. *Tarantismo e neotarantismo: Musica, danza, transe: bisogni di oggi, bisogni di sempre*. Nardò, Italy: Besa.

———. 2004. *Neotarantismo: Pizzica, transe e riti dalle campagne alle metropoli*. Viterbo, Italy: Stampa Alternativa/Nuovi Equilibri.

Nagengast, Carole. 1994. "Violence, Terror, and the Crisis of the State." *Annual Review of Anthropology* 23: 109–136.

Napolitano, Valentina. 2009. "The Virgin of Guadalupe: A Nexus of Affect." *Journal of the Royal Anthropological Institute* 15(1): 96–112.

———. 2016. *Migrant Hearts and the Atlantic Return*. New York: Fordham University Press.

Napolitano, Valentina, and Kristin Norget. 2011. "Economies of Sanctity." *Postscripts: Journal of Sacred Texts and Contemporary Worlds* 5(3): 251–264.

Nardini, Gloria. 1999. *Che Bella Figura! The Power of Performance in an Italian Ladies' Club in Chicago*. Albany: State University of New York Press.

Navaro-Yashin, Yael. 2007. "Fantasy and the Real in the Work of Begona Aretxaga." *Anthropological Theory* 7(1): 5–8.

———. 2009. "Affective Spaces, Melancholic Objects: Ruination and the Production of Anthropological Knowledge." *Journal of the Royal Anthropological Institute* 15(1): 1–18.

——. 2012. *The Make-Believe Space: Affective Geography in a Postwar Polity*. Durham, NC: Duke University Press.

Nicolescu, Razvan. 2016. *Social Media in Southeast Italy: Crafting Ideals*. London: UCL Press.

Nuzzo, Pina. 2008a. *Comunicato UDI Nazionale* (Presentazione della Staffetta UDI). Unpublished document.

——. 2008b. *Comunicato UDI Nazionale (Staffetta: Comunicato)*. Unpublished document.

——. 2010. *Perciò Se Ci Offendi Non Vale*. Unpublished document.

——. 2011a. *Noi.dell'Udi, noi con le donne*. Unpublished document.

——. 2011b. *Lettera per 13 Febbraio*. Unpublished document.

Nuzzo, Pina, and Clara Albani. 2010. *Invito al Cafè-Débat*. Email sent to UDI women, November 3.

Ottonelli, Valeria. 2011. *La libertà delle donne*. Genoa: Il Melangolo.

Pace, Enzo. 2013. "Achilles and the Tortoise. A Society Monopolized by Catholicism Faced with an Unexpected Religious Pluralism." *Social Compass* 60(3): 315–331.

Palmer, Gary B., and William R. Jankowiak. 1996. "Performance and Imagination: Toward an Anthropology of the Spectacular and the Mundane." *Cultural Anthropology* 11(2): 225–258.

Palmisano, Stefania. 2010. "Spirituality and Catholicism: The Italian Experience." *Journal of Contemporary Religion* 25(2): 221–241.

Palumbo, Berardino. 2003. *L'Unesco e il campanile*. Rome: Meltemi.

——. 2006. "Iperluogo." *Antropologia Museale* 14: 45–47.

——. 2009. *Politiche dell'inquietudine*. Florence: Le Lettere.

Panagia, Davide. 2009. *The Political Life of Sensation*. Durham, NC: Duke University Press.

Pandolfi, Mariella. 1990. "Boundaries inside the Body: Women's Sufferings in Southern Peasant Italy." *Culture, Medicine and Psychiatry* 14(2): 255–273.

Panther, Natalie. 2008. *Violence against Women and Femicide in Mexico: The Case of Ciudad Juarez*. Saarbrücken: VDM.

Parati, Graziella, and Rebecca West, eds. 2002. *Italian Feminist Theory and Practice: Equality and Sexual Difference*. Madison, NJ: Fairleigh Dickinson University Press.

Parmigiani, Giovanna. 2018. "Femminicidio and the Emergence of a 'Community of Sense' in Contemporary Italy." *Modern Italy* 23(1): 19–34.

Passerini, Luisa. 1996. "Gender Relations." In *Italian Cultural Studies: An Introduction*, edited by David Forgacs and Robert Lumley, 144–159. Oxford: Oxford University Press.

Payan, Tony Z., Anthony Kruszewskim, and Kathleen A. Staudt, eds. 2009. *Human Rights along the U.S.–Mexico Border: Gendered Violence and Insecurity*. Tucson: University of Arizona Press.

Pearce, Cathie, Debora Kidd, Rebecca Patterson, and Una Hanley. 2012. "The Politics of Becoming." *Qualitative Inquiry* 18(5): 418–426.

Pellegrino, Manuela. 2013. "'Dying Language' or 'Living Monument.' Language Ideologies, Policies and Practices in the Case of Griko." PhD diss., University College London.

——.2015. "I Glossa Grika: Itte C'è Avri—La Lingua GrecoSalentina tra Passato e Futuro." In *Raccontare la Grecìa*, edited by Giovanni Azzaroni and Matteo Casari. Martano, Italy: Kurumuni.

——. 2016. "Performing Griko beyond Death." *Palaver* 5(1): 137–172.

Peristiany, John G. 1966. *Honour and Shame: The Values of Mediterranean Society*. Chicago: Midway Reprint.

Però, Davide. 2007. *Inclusionary Rhetoric/Exclusionary Practices: Left-Wing Politics and Migrants in Italy.* New York: Berghahn Books.

Pesmen, Dale. 2000. *Russia and Soul: An Exploration.* Ithaca, NY: Cornell University Press.

Petryna, Adriana. 2002. *Life Exposed: Biological Citizens after Chernobyl.* Princeton, NJ: Princeton University Press.

Phelan, Peggy. 1993. *Unmarked: The Politics of Performance.* London: Routledge.

Pipyrou, Stavroula. 2012. "Commensurable Language and Incommensurable Claims among the Greek Linguistic Minority of South Italy." *Journal of Modern Italian Studies* 17(1): 70–91.

———. 2014a. "Cutting Bella Figura: Irony, Crisis and Secondhand Clothes in South Italy." *American Ethnologist* 41(3): 532–546.

———. 2014b. "Colonialism and Southernisation: The Case of the Grecanici in Calabria." *Etnografia e Ricerca Qualitativa* 2: 245–263.

———. 2016. *The Grecanici of Southern Italy.* Philadelphia: University of Pennsylvania Press.

Pizza, Giovanni. 1999. "Tarantismi oggi: Un panorama critico sulle letture contemporanee del tarantismo (1994–1998)." *Panorami* (7–8): 253–273.

———. 2004. "Tarantism and the Politics of Tradition in Contemporary Salento." In *Memory, Politics and Religion: The Past Meets the Present in Europe,* edited by H. Haukanes, 199–223. Münster, Germany: LIT.

———. 2012. *La Vergine e il Ragno.* Montesilvano, Italy: Rivista Abruzzese.

———. 2013. "Gramsci e de Martino: Appunti per una riflessione." *Quaderni di Teoria Sociale* 13: 75–120.

———. 2015. *Il Tarantismo Oggi.* Alessano, Italy: Carocci.

———. 2016. "Margini." *AM* 13(37–39): 105–109.

Plesset, Sonja. 2006. *Sheltering Women: Negotiating Gender and Violence in Northern Italy.* Stanford, CA: Stanford University Press.

———. 2007. "Beyond Honor: A New Approach to the Many Sides of Shame." *Journal of Modern Italian Studies* 12(4): 430–439.

Pojmann, Wendy. 2006. *Immigrant Women and Feminism in Italy.* Aldershot, UK: Ashgate.

———. 2013. *Italian Women and International Cold War Politics, 1944–1968.* 1st ed. New York: Fordham University Press.

Portwood-Stacer, Laura, and Susan Berridge. 2015. "Introduction." *Feminist Media Studies* 15(1): 154.

Postil, John, and Sarah Pink. 2012. "Social Media Ethnography: The Digital Researcher in a Messy Web." *Media International Australia* 145: 123–134.

Povinelli, Elizabeth A. 2001. "Radical Worlds: The Anthropology of Incommensurability and Inconceivability." *Annual Review of Anthropology* 30(3): 319–334.

———. 2006. *The Empire of Love: Toward a Theory of Intimacy, Genealogy, and Carnality.* Durham, NC: Duke University Press.

Pramstrahler, Anna. 2015. "Il femminicidio in Italia: Tra mancanza di statistiche ufficiali e impatto mediatico." *Gender/Sexuality/Italy* 2: 144–148.

Putino, Angela. 1987. "Arte di polemizzare tra donne." *Sottosopra.* http://www.libreriadelledonne.it/_oldsite/news/articoli/sottosopra87.htm (accessed March 21, 2019).

Radford, Jill, and Diana E. H. Russell, eds. 1992. *Femicide: The Politics of Woman Killing.* Buckingham, UK: Open University Press.

Rancière, Jacques. 1992. "Politics, Identification, and Subjectivization." *October* 61: 58–64.

———. 1995. *On the Shores of Politics*. New York: Verso.

———. 1999. *Disagreement: Politics and Philosophy*. Minneapolis: University of Minnesota Press.

———. 2000. "Dissenting Words: A Conversation with Jacques Rancière conducted and translated by Davide Panagia." *Diacritics* 30(2): 113–126.

———. 2004a. *The Politics of Aesthetics*. New York: Continuum.

———. 2004b. "The Politics of Literature." *SubStance* 33(1): 10–24.

———. 2006. "Thinking between Disciplines: An Aesthetics of Knowledge." *Parrhesia* 1: 1–12.

———. 2010. *The Aesthetic Unconscious*. Cambridge: Polity.

Raunig, Gerald. 2014. "Singers, Cynics, Molecular Mice: The Political Aesthetics of Contemporary Activism." *Theory, Culture and Society* 31(7–8): 67–80.

Repetto, Federico. 2015. *Cultura Pubblicitaria E Berlusconismo: Le Origini Dell'egemonia Della TV Commerciale E Il Suo Declino All'epoca Dei Social Media*. Ariccia, Italy: Aracne.

Riches, David. 1986. *The Anthropology of Violence*. Oxford: Blackwell.

Righi, Andrea. 2013. "Origin and Dismeasure: The Thought of Sexual Difference in Luisa Muraro and Ida Dominijanni, and the Rise of Post-Fordist Psychopathology." *Res Publica: Revista de Filosofía Política* 29: 35–56.

Rodano, Marisa. 2010. *Memorie di una che c'era: Una storia dell'Udi*. Milan: Il Saggiatore.

Roiphe, Katie. 1994. *The Morning After: Sex, Fear, and Feminism*. Boston: Little, Brown.

Ronchetti, Alessia. 2011. "Pensare la differenza, tra filosofia e politica: Intervista ad Adriana Cavarero." *Italian Studies* 66(1): 128–136.

Ronzon, Francesco. 2011. "Icons and Transvestites: Notes on Irony, Cognition, and Visual Skill." In *Skilled Visions*, edited by Cristina Grasseni, 45–66. New York: Berghahn Books.

Rose, Gillian. 2012. *Visual Methodologies: An Introduction to Researching with Visual Materials*. Los Angeles: Sage.

Ross, Charlotte. 2010. "Critical Approaches to Gender and Sexuality in Italian Culture and Society." *Italian Studies* 65(2): 164–177.

Ross, Christine. 2008. "Introduction." In *Precarious Visualities: New Perspectives on Identification in Contemporary Art and Visual Culture*, edited by Johanne Lamoureux, Christine Ross, and Olivier Asselin, 3–16. Montreal: McGill-Queen's University Press.

Rossi, Annabella. 2000. *Lettere da una tarantata: Con uno nota di Tullio De Mauro*. Lecce, Italy: Argo.

Rovetto, Florencia Laura. 2015. "Violencia contra las mujeres: Comunicación visual y acción política en 'Ni Una Menos' y 'Vivas Nos Queremos.'" *Contratexto* 24: 13–34.

Russell, Diana E. H., and Roberta A. Harmes. eds. 2001. *Femicide in Global Perspective*. New York: Teachers College Press.

Rutherford, Danilyn. 2012. "Commentary: What Affect Produces." *American Ethnologist* 39(4): 688–691.

Salazár Parreñas, Rheana J. 2012. "Producing Affect: Transnational Volunteerism in a Malaysian Orangutan Rehabilitation Center." *American Ethnologist* 39(4): 673–687.

Samet, Robert. 2013. "The Photographer's Body: Populism, Polarization, and the Uses of Victimhood in Venezuela." *American Ethnologist* 40(3): 525–539.

Santoro, Vincenzo. 2010. *Memorie della Terra: Racconti e canti di lavoro e di lotta del Salento*. Rome: Squilibri.

Santoro, Vincenzo, and Sergio Torsello. 2002. *Tabacco e Tabacchine nella Memoria Storica: Una Ricerca di Storia Orale a Tricase nel Salento*. Lecce, Italy: Manni.

——. 2005. *Il Salento Levantino: Memoria e Racconto del Tabacco a Tricase e in Terra d'Otranto*. Lecce, Italy: Aramiré.

Saunders, George R. 1995. "The Crisis of Presence in Italian Pentecostal Conversion." *American Ethnologist* 22(2): 324–340.

Scarparo, Susanna. 2005. "In the Name of the Mother. Sexual Difference and the Practice of Entrustment." *Cultural Studies Review* 11(2): 36–48.

Schechner, Richard. 2003. *Performance Theory*. London: Routledge.

Scheper-Hughes, Nancy. 1993. *Death without Weeping: The Violence of Everyday Life in Brazil*. Berkeley: University of California Press.

Scheper-Hughes, Nancy, and Philippe Bourgois. 2004. *Violence in War and Peace*. Malden, MA: Blackwell.

Schieffelin, Edward L. (1985) 2013. "Performance and the Cultural Construction of Reality." In *The Anthropology of Performance: A Reader*, edited by Frank Korom, 107–123. Chichester, West Sussex, UK: Wiley-Blackwell.

Schmidt, Bettina E. 2001. *Anthropology of Violence and Conflict*. London: Routledge.

Schneider, Jane. 1998. *Italy's "Southern Question": Orientalism in One Country*. Oxford: Berg.

Sega, Maria Teresa. 2005. "Passaggi di memoria. Le donne, la Resistenza, la storia." *Venetica: Rivista di storia contemporanea* 3: 11.

Sempruch, Justyna. 2004. "Feminist Constructions of the 'Witch' as a Fantasmatic Other." *Body and Society* 10(4): 113–133.

——. 2008. *Fantasies of Gender and the Witch in Feminist Theory and Literature*. West Lafayette, IN: Purdue University Press.

Se Non Ora Quando. 2011. Manifesto.

Seppilli, Tullio. 1995. "Ernesto de Martino e la nascita dell'etnopsichiatria italiana." *Storia, Antropologia e Scienze del Linguaggio* 10(3): 147–156.

Seymour, Mark. 2005. "Keystone of the Patriarchal Family? Indissoluble Marriage, Masculinity and Divorce in Liberal Italy." *Journal of Modern Italian Studies* 10(3): 297–313.

Signorelli, Amalia. 1996. "Il tarantismo . . . che purtroppo non c'è più." *Studi e Materiali di Storia delle Religioni* 62(20): 591–598.

Sigona, Nando. 2005. "Locating 'The Gypsy Problem.' The Roma in Italy: Stereotyping, Labelling and 'Nomad Camps.'" *Journal of Ethnic and Migration Studies* 31(4): 741–756.

Simard, Mélissa. 2015. "Mort et sacrifice dans la performance féministe ibéro-américaine: Œuvres d'Ana Mendieta et de Rocío Boliver." *Amerika* 12.

Sluka, Jeffrey A., ed. 2000. *Death Squad: The Anthropology of State Terror*. Philadelphia: University of Pennsylvania Press.

Sommers, Christina Hoff. 1994. *Who Stole Feminism? How Women Betrayed Women*. New York: Simon and Schuster.

Sorge, Antonio. 2015. *Legacies of Violence: History, Society, and the State in Sardinia*. Toronto: University of Toronto Press.

Sorge, Antonio, Jonathan Padwe, and Sara Shneiderman. 2015. "The Past Sits in Places: Locality, Violence, and Memory in Sardinia." *Critique of Anthropology* 35(3): 263–279.

Spinelli, Barbara. 2008. *Femminicidio: Dalla denuncia sociale al riconoscimento giuridico internazionale*. Milan: F. Angeli.

——. 2011. "Il riconoscimento giuridico dei concetti di femmicidio e femminicidio." In *Femicidio: dati e riflessioni intorno ai delitti per violenza di genere*, edited by Cristina Karadole and Anna Pramstrahler, 125–142. Regione Emilia Romagna, Italy: Assessorato Promozione Politiche Sociali.

———. 2013. "Femminicidio e riforme legislative." *Questione Giustizia* 6: 50–61.

———. 2014. "Perché si chiama femminicidio." In A.A.VV. "FEMMINICIDIO: Il femminile impossibile da sopportare." E-book. http://www.istitutofreudiano.it/sites/default/files /femminicidio.pdf (accessed March 21, 2019).

Staiger, Janet, Ann Cvetkovich, and Ann Reynolds. 2010. *Political Emotions*. New York: Routledge.

Stewart, Kathleen. 2007. *Ordinary Affects*. Durham, NC: Duke University Press.

Stoller Paul. 1989. *Taste of Ethnographic Things: The Senses in Anthropology*. Philadelphia: University of Pennsylvania Press.

———. 1997. *Sensuous Scholarship*. Philadelphia: University of Pennsylvania Press.

Strazzeri, Irene. 2014. *Post-patriarcato: L'agonia di un ordine simbolico—Sintomi, Passaggi, Discontinuità, Sfide*. Rome: Aracne.

Stringer, Rebecca. 2013. "Vulnerability after Wounding: Feminism, Rape Law, and the Differend." *SubStance* 42(3): 148–168.

———. 2014. *Knowing Victims: Feminism, Agency and Victim Politics in Neoliberal Times*. New York: Routledge.

Stromberg, Peter G. 1993. *Language and Self-transformation: A Study of the Christian Conversion Narrative*. Cambridge: Cambridge University Press.

Sturken, Marita, and Lisa Cartwright. 2009. *Practices of Looking: An Introduction to Visual Culture*. New York: Oxford University Press.

Sweeney, Belinda. 2004. "Trans-ending Women's Rights: The Politics of Trans-inclusion in the Age of Gender." *Women's Studies International Forum* 27: 75–88.

Tambar, Kabir. 2011. "Iterations of Lament: Anachronism and Affect in a Shi'i Islamic Revival in Turkey." *American Ethnologist* 38(3): 484–500.

Tambor, Molly. 2014. *The Lost Wave: Women and Democracy in Postwar Italy*. Oxford: Oxford University Press.

Tamisari, Franca. 2006. "The Responsibility of Performance: The Interweaving of Politics and Aesthetics in Intercultural Contexts." *Visual Anthropology Review* 21(1–2): 47–62.

Taussig, Michael. 1986. *Shamanism, Colonialism, and the Wild Man: A Study in Terror and Healing*. Chicago: University of Chicago Press.

———. 1992. *Mimesis and Alterity: A Particular History of the Senses*. New York: Routledge.

———. 1997. *The Magic of the State*. New York: Routledge.

———. 1999. *Defacement: Public Secrecy and the Labor of the Negative*. Stanford, CA: Stanford University Press.

Taylor, Diana. 1997. *Disappearing Acts: Spectacles of Gender and Nationalism in Argentina's "Dirty War."* Durham, NC: Duke University Press.

Thrift, Nigel. 2004. "Intensities of Feeling: Towards a Spatial Politics of Affect." *Geografiska Annaler, Series B: Human Geography* 86(1): 57–78.

———. 2008. *Non-representational Theory Space, Politics, Affect*. London: Routledge.

Tóibín, Colm. 2012. *The Testament of Mary*. Toronto: McClelland and Stewart.

Trono, Anna, and Fabiola Pesare. 2013. "La donna nella realtà produttiva salentina: Tabacchi e Tabacchine nel Salento Leccese." In *Dentro e fuori la fabbrica: Il tabacco in Italia tra memoria e prospettive*, edited by Rossella Del Prete, 145–149. Milan: Franco Angeli.

Tuccari, Francesco, and Bruno Bongiovanni. 2004. *L'opposizione al governo Berlusconi*. Roma-Bari: GLF Laterza.

Tuckett, Anna. 2018. *Rules, Paper, Status: Migrants and Precarious Bureaucracy in Contemporary Italy*. Stanford, CA: Stanford University Press.

Turina, Isacco. 2011. "Consecrated Virgins in Italy: A Case Study in the Renovation of Catholic Religious Life." *Journal of Contemporary Religion* 26(1): 43–55.

———. 2013. *Chiesa e biopolitica: Il discorso cattolico su famiglia, sessualità e vita umana da Pio XI a Benedetto XVI*. Milan: Mimesis.

Turner, Victor W. 1967. *The Forest of Symbols: Aspects of Ndembu Ritual*. Ithaca, NY: Cornell University Press.

———. 1969. *The Ritual Process*. London: Routledge and Kegan Paul.

———. 1979. *Process, Performance, and Pilgrimage: A Study in Comparative Symbology*. New Delhi: Concept.

———. 1986. *The Anthropology of Performance*. New York: PAJ.

Ufficio Statistico della Regione Puglia, 2013. *Focus Novembre 2013. Recenti dinamiche del mercato del lavoro femminile in Puglia*.

Uimonen, Paula. 2013. "Visual Identity in Facebook." *Visual Studies* 28(2): 122–135.

United Nations Entity for Gender Equality and the Empowerment of Women. 1992. Committee on the Elimination of Discrimination against Women (CEDAW), General Recommendation 19, https://www.un.org/womenwatch/daw/cedaw/recommendations/recomm.htm (accessed April 7, 2019)

United Nations Human Rights Council. 2012. "Report of the Special Rapporteur on Violence against Women, Its Causes and Consequences, Rashida Manjoo." Mission to Italy. https://www.ohchr.org/Documents/HRBodies/HRCouncil/RegularSession/Session20/A-HRC-20-16-Add2_en.pdf (accessed April 8, 2019).

Uzwiak, Beth A. 2016. "Community Engagement in Precarious Times: When Ethnography Meets Socially Engaged Art." *Anthropology Now* 8(2): 44–56.

van Dijk, J. J. M. 1999. "Introducing Victimology." In *Caring for Crime Victims: Selected Proceedings of the Ninth International Symposium on Victimology, Amsterdam, August 25–29*, edited by J. J. M. van Dijk, R. G. H. van Kaam, and J. Wemmers, 1–12. Monsey, NY: Criminal Justice Press.

Vidal-Ortiz, Salvador, María Amelia Viteri Burbano, and José Fernando Serrano Amaya. 2014. "Resignificaciones, Prácticas y Políticas Queer en América Latina: Otra Agenda de Cambio Social." *Nómadas* 41: 185–201.

Violi, Patrizia. 2015. "Femminicidio: Chi ha paura della Differenza?" *Gender/Sexuality/Italy* 2: 142–143.

von Lurzer, Carolina, and Carolina Spataro. 2016. "Cincuenta sombras de la cultura masiva: Desafíos para la crítica cultural feminista." *Nueva Sociedad* 265: 117–131.

Von Schnitzler, Antina. 2014. "Performing Dignity: Human Rights, Citizenship, and the Techno-politics of Law in South Africa." *American Ethnologist* 41(2): 336–350.

Wainwright, Paul, and Ann Gallagher. 2009. "On Different Types of Dignity in Nursing Care: A Critique of Nordenfelt." *Nursing Philosophy* 9: 46–54.

Warner, Marina. 1976. *Alone of All Her Sex: The Myth and the Cult of the Virgin Mary*. London: Weidenfeld and Nicolson.

Warner, Michael. 2002. *Publics and Counterpublics*. New York: Zone Books.

Weber, Cynthia. 2014. "Encountering Violence: Terrorism and Horrorism in War and Citizenship." *International Political Sociology* 8(3): 237–255.

Whitehead, Neil L., ed. 2004. *Violence*. Santa Fe, NM: School of American Research.

Williams, Raymond. 1977. *Marxism and Literature*. Oxford: Oxford University Press.

Wilson, Perry. 2006. "From Margin to Centre: Recent Trends in Modern Italian Women's and Gender History." *Modern Italy* 11(3): 327–337.

———. 2009. *Women in Twentieth-Century Italy*. Basingstoke, UK: Palgrave Macmillan.

Wolf, Naomi. 1993. *Fire with Fire. The New Female Power and How It Will Change the 21st Century*. London: Chatto and Windus.

Ziarek, Ewa P. 2001. *An Ethics of Dissensus: Postmodernity, Feminism, and the Politics of Radical Democracy*. Stanford, CA: Stanford University Press.

———. 2012. *Feminist Aesthetics and the Politics of Modernism*. New York: Columbia University Press.

Zigon, Jarrett. 2007. "Moral Breakdown and the Ethical Demand: A Theoretical Framework for an Anthropology of Moralities." *Anthropological Theory* 7(2): 131–150.

———. 2008. *Morality: An Anthropological Perspective*. Oxford: Berg.

Zinn, Dorothy. 1996. "Adriatic Brethren or Black Sheep? Migration to Italy and the Albanian Crisis." In *European Urban and Regional Studies* 3: 241–249.

———. 2015. "An Introduction to Ernesto de Martino's Relevance for the Study of Folklore." *Journal of American Folklore* 128(507): 3–17.

Žižek, Slavoj. 1989. *The Sublime Object of Ideology*. London: Verso.

Websites (Last Accessed March 21, 2019)

Accademia della Crusca, http://www.accademiadellacrusca.it/

Agedo Lecce, http://agedolecce.blogspot.it

Al di là del Buco, http://abbattoimuri.wordpress.com

Amnesty International Volunteers, http://amnesty-volunteer.org

Associazione Lea, http://associazionelea.org

Bari, https://bari.repubblica.it/

Bari Today, http://www.baritoday.it/

Bollettino di Guerra, http://bollettino-di-guerra.noblogs.org

Casa Internazionale delle Donna, http://www.casainternazionaledelledonne.org/index.php/

Change.org, http://www.change.org/

Ci riprovo, http://ritentasaraipiufortunato.blogspot.com

Città di Galatina, Regione Puglia, http://www.comune.galatina.le.it/item/disanimate-il-corpo-delle-donne-nella-pubblicita-sessista-e-nei-media

Cittadinanze, https://www.cittadinanze.it

Consigliera di Parità Puglia, http://www.consparitapuglia.it/newsite/consigliera

Coordinamento Teologhe Italiane, http://www.teologhe.org

Il Corpo delle Donne, http://www.ilcorpodelledonne.net/

Corriere della Serà, Milano, http://milano.corriere.it/milano/notizie/cronaca/

Corriere della Serà, Politica, http://www.corriere.it/politica/

Corriere della Serà, Roma, http://roma.corriere.it/roma/notizie/cronaca/

D, http://d.repubblica.it/

Il Dialogo, http://www.ildialogo.org/donna/INFOSTAFFETTAUDI.pdf

D.*i*.Re, http://www.direcontrolaviolenza.it

Diversamente Occupate, http://diversamenteoccupate.blogspot.it/

Enel, https://corporate.enel.it/

L'Espresso, http://espresso.repubblica.it/

Il Fatto Quotidiano, https://www.ilfattoquotidiano.it/

Femicidio, http://femicidiocasadonne.wordpress.com

Femminicidio, Feminicide, Feminicidio, http://femminicidio.blogspot.com/

Femminile Plurale http://femminileplurale.wordpress.com/

Femminismo a Sud, http://femminismo-a-sud.noblogs.org
Femminismo Proletario Rivoluzionario, http://femminismorivoluzionario.blogspot.com
Femministe Nove (F9), http://femministenove.wordpress.com/
Ferite a Morte, http://www.feriteamorte.it/
Firenze, http://firenze.repubblica.it/
Fuori Genere, http://fuorigenere.wordpress.com/
Gazzetta Ufficiale, http://www.gazzettaufficiale.it/
Generazione, https://comunicazionedigenere.wordpress.com/
Giovani Prolife, http://www.giovaniprolife.org/
Gitanistan, http://www.gitanistan.com
Giulia Giornaliste, http://giulia.globalist.it/
Giuristi Democratici per la CEDAW, http://gdcedaw.blogspot.com
Guida al Diritto, http://www.diritto24.ilsole24ore.com/guidaAlDiritto/
Huffington Post (Italy), http://www.huffingtonpost.it/
Le Idee di Repubblica, http://www.repubblica.it/la-repubblica-delle-idee/
Instituto Nazionale de Statistica, http://www.istat.it/
IPRES, http://www.ipres.it
I.Stat, http://dati.istat.it
Laboratorio Donnae, http://laboratoriodonnae.wordpress.com
Libera Università delle Donne, http://www.universitadelledonne.it/
Libero Quotidiano, http://www.liberoquotidiano.it/
Libreria delle Donne di Milano, http://www.libreriadelledonne.it
Like @ Rolling Stone, https://mauropresini.wordpress.com/
Lipperatura di Loredana Lipperini, http://loredanalipperini.blog.kataweb.it/
maipiùclandestine #campagna194, http://maipiuclandestine.noblogs.org/
Il Manifesto, http://ilmanifesto.it/mai-piu-clandestine-a-roma-le-donne-manifestano-per-la
    -legge-194/
Melty Buzz, http://www.melty.it/
Il Messagero, Roma, http://www.ilmessaggero.it/roma/
MicroMega, http://temi.repubblica.it/micromega-online/
Movimento per la Vita, http://www.mpv.org/
Musicados Editore, http://musicaos.org/
NapoliToday, http://www.napolitoday.it/
Non Una di Meno, https://nonunadimeno.wordpress.com
Notizie ProVita, http://www.notizieprovita.it/
La Notte della Taranta, http://lanottedellataranta.it
Orlando Associazione di Donnae, http://orlando.women.it/en/
Papaboys, http://www.papaboys.org/
Partito Democratico Lussemburgo, http://www.partitodemocratico.lu/
Pasionaria, http://pasionaria.it/
Press Dinamo, https://www.dinamopress.it/
La Puglia, delle Pari Opportunità, http://www.pariopportunita.regione.puglia.it/
Rai, http://www.rai.tv/
Rassegna Sindacale, http://rassegna.it/
Regione Puglia, http://www.regione.puglia.it/
La Repubblica, Politica, http://www.repubblica.it/politica/
La Repubblica, RepTV, http://video.repubblica.it/
La Repubblica, Roma, http://roma.repubblica.it/cronaca/

Roma, http://www.ilroma.net/
Senato della Repubblica, https://www.senato.it/
Sentinelle in Piedi, http://sentinelleinpiedi.it
Il Sole 24 Ore, http://www.ilsole24ore.com/
La Stampa, http://www.lastampa.it/
s.t. foto libreria galleria, https://www.stsenzatitolo.com/st/
Spazio Sociale, http://www.spaziosociale.it/
Tempi, http://www.tempi.it/
TGCom24, http://www.tgcom24.mediaset.it/
30 Years CEDAW, http://cedaw30.wordpress.com/
Treccani, http://www.treccani.it/
La 27esima Ora, http://27esimaora.corriere.it
UDI Nazionale, http://www.udinazionale.org/
UNESCO, http://www.unesco.it
UNESCO World Heritage List, http://whc.unesco.org/en/list/
Vice (Italy), http://www.vice.com/it/
A Voice for Men, http://it.avoiceformen.com/
Winning Women Institute, http://www.winningwomeninstitute.org/
Wired (Italy), http://www.wired.it/
World Economic Forum, Global Gender Gap Index, http://reports.weforum.org/global
    -gender-gap-report-2014/rankings/
XXD, http://www.danieladanna.it/xxdonne/

INDEX

confliggere (conflicting), 58–59, 68, 135
conversion, 63, 172
crying or weeping, 18, 37, 82–83, 115–125, 127, 135–137

Dave, Naisargi, 2, 18, 88, 110n18, 146n2, 164n17, 172, 182n22
De Gregorio, Concita, 91–92
De Luna, Giovanni, 46n18, 95, 101
De Martino, Ernesto, 5–6, 117–119, 147n27
desire, 44, 61–63, 88
"die-in" protests, 84, 110n11. *See also under* performance
difference, feminism, 2, 9, 43, 48, 52, 64, 66, 69. See also *Pensiero della Differenza Sessuale*
dignity, 18, 34–35, 53, 55, 58–59, 65, 77, 85, 91–93, 115, 116, 118–122, 129, 146n16; as aesthetic performance, 133–139, 156, 166, 172; and doing-as-if, 179–180; as emotion, 135, 179–180, 180–184; and pride/honor, 92, 115, 118, 120, 121, 184
Disanimate, 153–156, 163n12, 176
disparità (disparity, practice of), 54, 69, 74n48, 167, 182
dissensus, 8–9,18, 43–44, 68, 88, 121, 126, 138, 148, 150, 155–156, 161–162, 179, 183, 186; and disagreement, 9, 68
divorce, 28, 52, 54, 72n9, 84, 103
DNA Donna, 7, 19, 49, 100–102, 115–116, 122–129, 137, 153–154, 157
DWF (DonnaWomanFemme), 33, 64

economic gender gap, 29
emancipation, 52, 143. *See also* liberation
ENEL Sole, 77–82
equality, 28, 43, 98, 99
erotico diffuso, 13
ethics, 136, 146n24, 169, 182, 184; anthropology of, 18, 165, 171–179, 181n11, 181n13, 182n15; of representation, 116, 171; of sacrifice 92, 107–108

Facebook, 14–16, 34, 47n34 59, 71, 82–83, 100, 139, 180n2, 181n5; and politics, 38–40, 72n10, 156, 165–168. *See also under* persona
familismo, 91

fare-come-se (doing-as-if), 18, 44, 132, 165–182, 169–171, 184
Fassin, Didier, 46n18, 102, 113n48; and Rechtman, 30, 46n18, 102, 143, 112n39
femminicidio, 1–4, 9, 21n11, 27–29, 31–32, 35–38, 40, 41, 76–114, 126–128, 133, 139, 145n8, 149–151, 162, 179, 183, 185; American contexts, 1; as emergency, 2, 15; femicidio in South struggle against, 81, 97, 139; and marketing, 97
femminismo (Italian feminism), 60; *femminismo molecolare*, 60, 61; *femminismo moralista*, 108; Second Wave, 52
Femministe Nove (F9), 13, 64, 69–71, 85, 104–108, 141
Ferite a Morte, 1, 19n5, 126, 141
50e50 Ovunque si decide, UDI national campaign, 72n15, 87, 110n14, 170
Forza Italia (FI), 89
Foucault, Michel, 66, 146–147n24, 148, 172, 176, 181n14

gazes, 40, 49, 51, 55, 72n16, 95, 121, 139, 161, 170, 175, 177, 180n2, 181n4
genealogies, 32, 52, 63, 69, 70, 72n16, 73n34, 74n36
Giordano, Cristiana, 46n18, 72n12, 131
Global Gender Gap, 27, 56. *See also* economic gender gap
grammar, 95, 100, 131, 156, 160
Grecìa salentina, 7, 10, 23n32, 117, 118, 122

Halperin, David, 172, 181n14
Hartman, Saidiya, 32
Herzfeld, Michael 27, 119, 122, 132, 137–139, 145n3, 146n12, 171
history, 4, 42–43, 51, 52, 54, 62, 164n17; of the Catholic Church, 106, 113n48 (*see also* Catholic Church or Catholicism); of Italian feminism, 14, 44, 44n1, 48, 50, 57, 175; Italian political, 2, 89, 91, 92; local, 12, 21n13, 119; personal, 25, 34, 133; religious, 113n46; social, 2, 102; of term "dignity," 179
honor: and gender,121, 138; and honorability, 92; and human rights, 18, 115, 133–139;

162, 179, 183–185; of anti-violence campaigns, 8; continuum of, 32, 95, 179, 183; sexual, 28, 40; structural, 177; SVAW (Stop Violence against Women), Amnesty International, 79; symbolic, 24, 31; and trauma, 46n18, 127, 143,144, 145n8; violated bodies 85, 88. *See also under* representation

visibility/invisibility, 17, 20n20, 49–75, 132, 166, 167, 176, 180–181n4

visuality, or ways of seeing: schooling in, 72–73n16, 78, 80, 83, 98, 161, 168

"We Are Witnesses Not Victims" motto, 2, 115, 127–128, 143

witnesses, 2, 18, 43–44, 81, 110n18, 115–147, 168, 176, 179, 180n4, 183, 185; as martyrs, 104–108, 113n48; producing, 43,148–164; women as, 172

women's question, 2, 16, 31, 53, 56, 76, 84, 86, 89, 91–93, 107, 115, 183

women's shelters, 15, 54, 102–103, 109–110n10, 157–159

Ziarek, Ewa P., 144

GIOVANNA PARMIGIANI is a Senior Fellow at the Center for the Study of World Religions at Harvard University.

www.ingramcontent.com/pod-product-compliance
Lightning Source LLC
Chambersburg PA
CBHW071020280326
41935CB00011B/1427